LAW FOR SOCIAL WORK PRACTICE

Law for
Social Work Practice
Working with Vulnerable Adults

Robert Johns and Andrew Sedgwick

MACMILLAN

First published 1999 by
MACMILLAN PRESS LTD
Houndmills, Basingstoke, Hampshire RG21 6XS
and London
Companies and representatives
throughout the world

ISBN 0–333–69378–7 paperback

A catalogue record for this book is available
from the British Library.

This book is printed on paper suitable for recycling and
made from fully managed and sustained forest sources.

10 9   8   7   6 5   4   3   2 1
08 07 06 05 04 03 02 01 00 99

Editing and origination by
Aardvark Editorial, Mendham, Suffolk

Printed in Malaysia.

Contents

Preface

Social care is provided for people and the law makes certain rules about it. Sometimes the law identifies which people are to receive care and which people are to provide it. Sometimes the law is silent about this. Nevertheless, the law must apply to the kinds of social care needs and circumstances that occur day by day.

Yet those who are engaged in social care work, especially the care of vulnerable adults, often regard the law as being not really relevant to their work. The law is seen as theoretical, as distant, even as a nuisance. The complaint is frequently that the law is too complex: it is not clear what can or should be done or how one piece of legislation relates to another in the practice context. This is understandable, since social care is after all offered by professional and non-professional carers who are not lawyers.

This book is therefore dedicated to those who care for vulnerable adults who need a book that is firmly rooted in social care practice. For this is not a legal text book as such. Instead, its aim is to provide a map through the relatively uncharted territory of the law relating to the social care of vulnerable adults. It does this by starting with the types of real-life situation confronting carers and exploring how the law relates to them.

We believe that this is an approach which will commend itself to practitioners. We believe that there is a need for texts that explain and explore the interconnections between law and social care. We also believe that vulnerable adults need carers and professional helpers who are more knowledgeable about the law generally. Knowledge is power, and in encouraging carers to become more knowledgeable about the legal context of their practice, this book is in effect about empowerment.

As teachers of social workers on professional training courses, we have noted for some time that students find applying the law to social work practice quite problematic. Students may understand what the law says; they may understand what social work principles and values are; they may skilfully assess and interpret the needs of vulnerable people; but they are thrown when trying to put these all together. When confronted with a real-life situation or even a simulation exercise, there is a tendency to choose *either* social work principles *or* the law. Even quite experienced practitioners have on several occasions informed us that what was being said about the law was all very well and good, but what they did in their social services department was quite different. In one or two cases we have a lurking anxiety that they may have inadvertently been telling the truth.

It quickly became obvious that the difficulty students encountered was reflected in the approaches taken in textbooks. Many of these were good at presenting systematic overviews of the law, chapters being neatly subdivided by subject matter. For legal texts this was fine, but carers who work with vulnerable adults obviously start with people and then proceed to assessing their needs by relating them to the law. So why not a book that did this?

Thus this text takes a relatively novel approach. The main chapters start with a brief introduction, followed by some fictional but realistic case material, usually a case study. The case material is then analysed. The ensuing discussion sets out an analysis of the case, highlighting relevant issues for social care workers, including reference to social work principles and values. There is also a discussion of the social policy context in which the current care arrangements were made. In our view this fills a gap in the current literature since practitioners need to be aware of the broader context within which they practise and within which the law was formulated.

The reason for adopting this case study approach is twofold. First, it accurately reflects the reality of everyday practice. Second, social care is by its nature diffuse, and it is sometimes difficult to identify boundaries of roles. Carers and social workers can unwittingly stray into unfamiliar territory or, worse still, move into areas that are more properly the prerogative of another profession. In some situations this can be dangerous, so clarity of role and purpose is essential. For this reason we have endeavoured to direct the reader to the relevant legislation with some indication of why it is pertinent to the particular case.

Any references to law are, of necessity, references to the law of England and Wales as it stands at the time of writing. Where the law is quoted directly, readers will note that legislation uses the male personal pronoun – this is a legal convention, not ours; in the rest of the book we have endeavoured to use inclusive language at all times. Readers will be aware that the law changes from time to time, and the book should not be taken as a definitive statement of the law. Legal reference books, suitably updated, or advice from specialist legal practitioners, would be more authoritative, although strenuous efforts have obviously been made to make the book as accurate and as useful as possible.

It should also be noted that while the general principles of practice and the role of the law in social care practice are relevant to practitioners and carers in Scotland and Northern Ireland, there are significant differences in the law itself. In Scotland the law relating to managing property on behalf of vulnerable adults, for example, is substantially different. Court processes and procedures are also different, so readers may need to refer to more specialised legal texts for further clarification.

The case examples are of course fictional, but are all based on typical real situations. The situations presented are diverse, and there has been an attempt to cover as broad a spectrum as is possible. Background information has been confined to what is directly relevant, so, for example, references to specific racial or cultural groups is only included where there is a specific point relevant to this that we wish to make. We have tried to keep to contemporary conventions with the use of terms such as 'service users' and 'carers', although it is acknowledged that some practitioners consider carers as service users for very obvious and logical reasons. Similarly, 'community care services' is taken to include residential care, although again some commentaries draw a clear distinction between the two. We have also recognised that it is not possible to separate out values from social work practice and the law, so some discussion is given over to this in each case study. This book acknowledges that law, social policy, social work values and everyday practice are intertwined.

The focus throughout the book is on the social care of vulnerable adults, and for this reason a number of topics are explored more fully than in other texts. At the same time it is only possible to touch on some topics, and some omissions will be noticed. One such is welfare rights. It is not practicable to include this, principally because of the complexity of social security and benefit regulations. This is not because we underestimate its importance; instead it is our view that welfare rights issues are already adequately dealt with elsewhere, especially in a number of excellent guides that are now available, so it is preferable to concentrate on the issues that tend to be overlooked.

For this reason the choice of topics may seem a random mixture, but there is overall coherence to them. The book is primarily about social or personal care. This is taken to include protecting people who are potentially being abused or exploited. The empowerment of vulnerable adults is a recurrent theme, although there are areas of social work or social care that border on this but are excluded: assisting vulnerable adults who are themselves accused of committing an offence, for example. This topic would have brought in quite different issues requiring familiarity with police and court procedures, together with an awareness of legal approaches to issues of criminal responsibility, which were considered to be beyond the scope of this book.

So what topics does the book actually address? In Chapter 1 we examine some general principles and broad legislation that apply across the board, that is, to all vulnerable adults. Discrimination and rights of redress are a particular feature here. In Chapter 2 the focus is on assessment for community care services. Chapter 3 concentrates on the provision of services and ensuring that these meet people's diverse needs. Chapter 4 asks what happens when people cannot manage their own affairs, and what happens when they move from hospital to the community. In Chapter 5 we explore the general issue of how vulnerable adults might live together and examine special provision for their needs. Chapter 6 deals with the abuse of vulnerable adults, specifically with local authority responsibilities for responding to allegations of abuse of whatever sort. Chapter 7 examines procedures for protecting people from themselves when they are especially vulnerable. Chapter 8 raises the issue of what happens when vulnerable adults are the victims of crime.

Each of these chapters includes a general conclusion that summarises the main themes of each chapter and in some cases includes reference to the strengths and weakness of current provision. These analyses are brought together in Chapter 9, which asks how the law could be reformed in order to provide a better system for responding to the needs of vulnerable adults. Why is the system so piecemeal and haphazard? What can be done about it?

While conceding that even all the chapters taken together can never be truly comprehensive, the book nevertheless aims to scan the broad spectrum of social care with adults and introduce readers to the many different ways in which, within the legal framework, the needs of vulnerable adults can be met. If readers find the book a useful tool in meeting this objective, we will have achieved our ambition.

Legislation, Regulations and Circulars

Legal Cases

Anns *v.* Merton London Borough Council [1978] AC 728

L. *v.* Bournewood Community and Mental Health NHS Trust, *Times*, 8 December 1997

Patel *v.* Patel [1988] 2 FLR 179; (1988) 18 Fam Law 213

R. *v.* Avon County Council, ex parte Mark Hazell [1994] 2 FCR 259; [1994] 2 FCR 1006, QBD

R. *v.* Civil Service Appeal Board, ex parte Cunningham [1991] 4 All ER 310; [1992] ICA 816

R. *v.* Cleveland County Council, ex parte Cleveland Care Homes Association and Others 17 BMLA 122, 12 November 1993 (QBD)

R. *v.* Durham County Council, ex parte Curtis [1995] 1 All ER 72 CA; [1995] 1 All ER 89 QBD; [1993] 91 LGR 479

R. *v.* Gloucestershire County Council, ex parte Barry and Others 30 BMLR 20 (QBD), 94 LRG 593, 16 June 1995

R. *v.* Gloucestershire County Council, ex parte Mahfood *Times* Law Report, 21 June 1995 (QBD)

R. *v.* Hereford and Worcester County Council, ex parte Chandler [1991] CO/1759/91 discussed by Clements in *Legal Action*, September 1992: 15–16

R. *v.* Islington London Borough Council, ex parte Rixon *Times*, 17 April 1996 (QBD)

R. *v.* Kingston-upon-Thames, ex parte T [1994] 1 FLR 798

R. *v.* Kite and Others [1996] 2 Cr App R (S) 295, Court of Appeal, 8 February 1996

R. *v.* Lancashire County Council, ex parte Royal Association for Disability and Rehabilitation and Gilpin, Court of Appeal, 27 June 1966

R. *v.* London Borough of Ealing, ex parte Leaman *Times,* 10 February 1984 (QBD) (Crown Office List) CO/562/83

R. *v.* P&O European Ferries (Dover) Limited [1990] 93 Cr App Rep 72

1
Social Care Law in Practice

Purpose and aims

This book is about vulnerable adults. It is about the kinds of issue that confront people who care for them or who advise them. It is about real-life situations and how these relate to the law regarding social care. It is about relating law *to* practice.

The main focus, therefore, is social care law as it affects people who are considered 'vulnerable'. In a legal context, it is about the needs of vulnerable adults and how those needs are met (or not). The book is designed to assist *all* those who care for vulnerable adults or who advise them. While its focus is law and practice linked to social care, the book should not be thought of as just being for social workers. It is also very relevant to carers, volunteers and indeed anyone who is concerned about the needs of vulnerable adults.

The book has a number of specific aims:

- to provide information about the law as it relates to typical cases relating to social care
- to enhance the reader's knowledge of the law
- to explore alternative options for action in the context of what is legally feasible
- to present case analyses that clearly distinguish the relevant key elements of a case
- to clarify a number of key legal and practice issues
- to empower those who work with vulnerable adults by providing the key information that they need; empowerment is sometimes

1

seen as an attitude substituting for real knowledge whereas in fact knowledge is power
● to encourage a more enlightened approach to work with vulnerable adults generally
● to set out specific ways in which the needs of vulnerable adults could be better met.

This book is also intended as a guide for the general reader who would like to know more than is usually available about social care practice, the law and policy in relation to social care. It includes guides to services that care agencies have to provide, as well as concerning the needs of vulnerable adults who are unable to express their own needs and may on some occasion need protection from exploitation or harm.

Who are vulnerable adults?

Before proceeding to look at the law generally, we need to ask 'Why talk about *vulnerable* adults?' The main reason is because this is generally the preferred phrase to cover a wide group of people and is also a phrase accepted by policy-makers and legal bodies. Certainly, the phrase 'vulnerable adults' is preferable to a categorisation of adults according to disability and also tries to move away from the notion that everyone who, for example, has a physical disability needs social care or protection. The Law Commission (1993a), for example, has drafted proposals based on identifying vulnerable adults in the community, taking vulnerability to indicate people who are for various reasons unable to take care of themselves or protect themselves from others. The Commission draws a distinction between people who are vulnerable and those who are incapacitated, that is, those who are unable to understand information related to a particular issue (Law Commission, 1993a). This issue is explored further in later chapters.

The Commission's contribution to the debate was welcome not least because it filled a gap that policy-makers seemed remarkably unwilling to fill. In essence, the gap is that there is no systematic or coherent approach to the needs of vulnerable adults. In fact, there is *no law relating to vulnerable adults* as such, in contrast to law relating to children. Instead there is a welter of law connected to codes of guidance and practice, all of which should inform and influence social care practice, and practitioners need to be aware of the range of legislation that

2

could impinge on the lives of vulnerable adults. Yet despite the quantity of law and practice guidance, there are some distinctly noticeable omissions, and the whole system is like a patchwork quilt with holes:

> Community care law is a hotchpotch of conflicting statutes, which have been enacted over a period of fifty years; each statute reflects the different philosophical attitudes of its time. Community care law is in much the same state as the law relating to children in the 1980s.

> (Clements, 1996: 10)

It follows from this that one major task of this book is to introduce the reader to the variety of ways in which law and practice attempt to address the needs of vulnerable adults. There will inevitably be a number of ways in which the legal framework is inadequate, and these will be indicated towards the end of each chapter where the wider social policy issues are discussed. Chapter 9 brings these all together by examining the whole framework for assisting vulnerable adults.

Another task will be to help those who have responsibilities for providing care to understand how vulnerable adults can be empowered, how they can be protected if necessary, and how on some occasions decisions can be made for them.

Applying the law to practice

Susan wants to know what help the social services department can give her mother, who has just been registered as partially sighted.

The manager of an independent home has a resident with a hearing and speech impediment who wants to go home.

Raymond has been in hospital for 9 months recovering from a very serious road accident. He needs accommodation and practical support for the rest of his life.

John and Sylvia live in a centre for people with learning and physical disabilities. They have decided they want to get married.

Betty Smith believes her neighbour is being physically abused by her carer.

Twelvetrees management have to respond to an allegation of sexual abuse of a vulnerable adult.

Beechwood House are suspicious that one of their residents is being exploited by a relative.

cont'd

> **A GP** is concerned about someone who appears to be very confused and unable to look after herself.
>
> **Pauline and Anne**, who live in a group home, are the victims of a crime committed in broad daylight.

These are the kinds of case that workers in the social care field actually deal with. They are realistic and sometimes quite complex. They are the actual case studies that will be addressed in the following chapters.

This book adopts a case analysis approach. This means that the case scenario or scenarios that introduce each chapter are the basis of an examination of practice and application of the law. They are intended to be illustrative and reasonably typical of the kinds of problem that vulnerable adults and their carers have to face. There then follows an analysis that starts with that person's needs and attempts to relate them to the legislative framework. This framework consists not just of statute (written down) law, but also of official regulations and guidance, which may include codes of practice. In all chapters there will be an emphasis on interpretation and commentary since the book is fundamentally about law and social work in action. It is the application of law and legal principles in the social welfare field that concerns us, and this case analysis approach lends itself to a broader understanding of these issues since it starts with people, which is where social care practice starts anyway.

The case studies form the basis on which the discussions are developed. Working through the social care response to the cases helps us to understand the law more clearly. Sometimes the law is very clear and there are specific, definite actions that social workers ought to take. More often the waters are muddied. The law is not as clear cut as we may have thought, and the position is occasionally quite confusing. For it is part of the purpose of this book to try to address real-life situations and not to oversimplify complexities. This book aims to clarify issues that arise in practice. Occasionally, there are simply gaps in the legislation when it comes to be applied to real-life cases. This book highlights and explains those inadequacies, indicating reasons for them where these relate to policy issues. Above all, the book examines social care practice in the context created by the current legal framework.

It follows that the book is not, and never can be, a comprehensive summary of the law in this area. There are a number of texts that cover law relating to people with disabilities (Ashton and Ward, 1992; Cooper and Vernon, 1996) and the law relating to older people (Griffiths and Roberts, 1995; McDonald and Taylor, 1995), and now some that specifically address community care law (Clements, 1996; Mandelstam and Schwehr, 1996).

This book does not aim to 'solve' the case study since this presupposes that a 'solution' is possible, although ideas will often be put forward that attempt to meet people's needs; in this sense, the book starts at the point at which most carers and social work practitioners start. Instead, the case study is used as a means of highlighting various issues that arise for vulnerable adults and their care: who is responsible for what is a key theme as well as how the law relates (or does not) to the illustrative scenario. This, we believe, is the book's real value. It is our hope that this approach will commend itself to readers who are confronted by people in need, and have to start with people and their difficulties rather than with a body of theory or legal knowledge that they attempt to apply abstractly.

The law as it applies to vulnerable adults generally

As far as the case studies themselves are concerned, we need to say that there are some general points applying to all of them:

1. A mixture of laws applies to each case: in some the role of the local authority in service provision comes to the fore; in others the focus needs to be on criminal law or law concerning private property. It is important, therefore, to be clear about the distinction between public and private law, between what is mandatory and permissive, between common law, statute law and official guidance.
2. There is no fixed definition of vulnerability, a point to which we will return in Chapter 9. It is therefore not sufficient to establish that someone is vulnerable; it is also important legally to establish to which identified group they belong before rights and entitlements can be established. Only then can we consider how the local authorities and other service providers might be obliged to act and how they ought to act.
3. Laws that cut across all groups, applying to a whole range of service providers and advisors, exist. Chief among these are laws dealing with certain kinds of discrimination.

4. Finally, certain laws and procedures provide for rights of redress against public bodies when someone feels aggrieved, for example when they have not been offered the level of service that they consider they need. This is an increasingly important aspect of community care law, as we shall see later.

In the rest of this chapter we shall be examining each of these briefly in turn. Bear in mind, therefore, that what follows applies to all the cases covered in all subsequent chapters in the book. Where especially relevant, there will be reference back to these issues. However, some of what follows is important in setting the overall context rather than being relevant to specific circumstances in individual cases.

In discussion of the cases in later chapters, there will also be references to common law, statute law, regulations, circulars and codes of guidance, and various other provisions. It is important to be clear at the outset what the differences are between all of these, since some are more obligatory than others and there is often confusion about them.

Statute law and common law

We are, all of us, duty bound to observe the law, which can take the form of written-down law, which is statute law, or law that has evolved over many years to form a series of unwritten laws, which is common law.

Statute law is usually more familiar, taking the form of a specific Act of Parliament. One Act that will be mentioned many times in this book is the National Health Service and Community Care Act 1990, an example of statute law.

Common law is more difficult simply because it is not written down but it is a common law principle; for example, every person over 18 years of age is deemed competent to manage his or her affairs unless it can be demonstrated otherwise. In any dispute between the two, statute law takes precedence.

The differences between the two can be demonstrated by Table 1.1.

Table 1.1   Statute law and common law

Statute Law	Common Law
Written-down laws: deal with specific topics (for example, local authority social services) or specific groups of people, such as the 'chronically sick and disabled' and can also be more generally applied (for example, the Race Relations Act 1976)	General unwritten rules that are commonly understood to be the law of the land: for example, the limits of the role of local authorities and the rights of courts to intervene in what local authorities do Can fill the gaps between statutes
Interpreted by reference to what the law actually says and how judges interpret what Parliament intended	Interpreted by judges' reference to long-established unwritten rules and what has happened before
Judges cannot change what statute law says, but Parliament can	Judges can change common law, but statute law always overrides common law, so authority ultimately lies with Parliament

Statutory instruments, circulars and codes of guidance

An Act of Parliament may state what must be done but it does not always say how it is to be done. Sometimes there are schedules or rules, which set out how an Act is to be implemented. A schedule appears at the end of an Act of Parliament and sets out certain specific points: instructions about how the Act is to be implemented, or to whom it is specifically to refer, for example. The advantage of a schedule is that it can be changed by Parliament without changing the Act itself. The difference is therefore procedural; in practice, a schedule is as binding as the Act of Parliament itself.

Similarly, rules and regulations are also legally binding. These rules and regulations tend to be imposed by a Secretary of State who has been given authority to do so by a specific Act of Parliament. In Chapter 8 there is an example of an Act (the Criminal Injuries Compensation Act 1995) that simply says that the Home Secretary can set out the rules governing awards of compensation to the victims of crime. Another example would be the Court of Protection Rules 1994 that relate to a specific Act, in this case the Mental Health Act 1983. The advantage of having rules separate from the Act is that they can be changed without having to revise the whole Act, as has happened in this particular case (rules devised in 1984 being super-seded by the 1994 rules). Sometimes the term 'regulations' is used, as in the National Health Service (General Medical Services) Regula-tions; an alternative is directions, as in the National Assistance Act 1948 (choice of accommodation) Directions 1992. The terms 'rules', 'regulations' and 'directions' may be regarded for our purposes as being interchangeable. They are all compulsory and in effect 'law of the land'. They are the means (instruments) of implementing statutes (Acts of Parliament) and must therefore be obeyed in the same way as the Act itself.

Implementation of an Act of Parliament can also be achieved through:

- circulars from the relevant department that set out how local author-ities should implement the legislation, perhaps linking this to finan-cial grants from central government to local authorities; these do not have the full force of law
- codes of guidance or codes of practice that provide what are considered to be models of good practice.

There is some confusion among practitioners in the social care field over the status of the circulars and codes. This is not surprising as local authorities are sometimes told by courts not to follow guidance 'slavishly' but are at other times held to be in error by not conforming to central government guidelines. Social work practitioners will be aware that the Department of Health issues a considerable number of circulars and codes of practice, and there will be several examples of these in later chapters. Because of the provisions of the Local Authority Social Services Act 1970, these are more that just advisory. Section 7(1) of the 1970 Act states that local authorities shall 'act under the general guidance of the Secretary of State'. This has consis-tently been taken to mean that local authorities should not depart from the 'statutory' guidance, that is, guidance issued under section 7(1) of the 1970 Act, without good reason:

> If this statutory guidance is to be departed from it must be with good reason, articulated in the course of some identifiable decision-making process, even if not in the care plan itself. In the absence of any such considered decision, the deviation from statutory guidance is in my judgement a breach of law.
>
> (judgement in *ex parte Rixon*, quoted in Clements, 1996: 17)

In other contexts, where reference has not been made to the Local Authority Social Services Act 1970, local authorities have been required by the courts to interpret the codes of guidance flexibly, and there is consequently considerable uncertainty over their exact legal standing; further discussion of this can be found in Mandelstam and Schwehr (1995: 71–2) and Clements (1996: 14–18).

Principles behind application of public law

Underlying all social care practice are a number of legal principles that carry with them a number of assumptions about who qualifies for services and about the role of local authorities in providing services.

The first principle is that the group to which the vulnerable adult belongs must be identified. It will be noted that several Acts refer to specific groups: the Chronically Sick and Disabled Persons Act 1970, for example. Others may do so not in name but in practice. For example, the National Health Service and Community Care Act 1990 in practice accords more rights to people with disabilities than to other categories of people in need.

On the positive side, if Parliament says that services should be provided, the relevant Act will apply across the board. In addition, as far as social services are concerned, each local authority has to appoint a Director of Social Services and carry out duties set out in the various Acts (section 2 of the Local Authority Social Services Act 1970). The duties cannot be delegated to another department, although if the law allows, services may be provided by other agencies, including those in the independent sector.

A further point related to this is that there are some functions that a local authority must carry out and some that it may carry out if it wishes. There is a very sharp distinction between mandatory and permissive powers, and when under budgetary restraints, local authorities will clearly focus on what they have to do by law.

Possibly more confusing is the issue of 'ultra vires'. This can be explained quite simply. All local authority actions have to relate to an Act of Parliament. This Act of Parliament sets out the powers. If a local authority does something that is outside what the Act of Parliament says, it is acting beyond powers: ultra vires. A local authority can only do what an Act of Parliament says; there is no scope for independent action. For example, a local authority cannot compel someone to enter residential care: there is no power for the local authority to do this, the only extreme power possible to achieve this end lying with medical officials (see the later discussion of section 47 of the National Assistance Act 1948). Sanctions for acting beyond powers are severe: councillors who authorise 'unlawful expenditure' on services that the local authority is not entitled to provide have to meet the cost of the unlawful provision themselves. Ultra vires is not strictly a means of redress but more a means of preventing public bodies encroaching too much into people's private lives and rights to make their own decisions.

Discrimination and the law

Issues of discrimination are important in all aspects of social care since care is so often provided for groups who are subject to discrimination or oppression. While some of the case studies that follow raise specific issues related to discrimination, and these are addressed when relevant, it is also important to bear in mind that some laws apply to all service providers and all people to whom they provide a service. For this reason this chapter includes a summary of anti-discrimination law.

Much of the law against discrimination in Britain is fairly limited in its scope, and in relation to race and gender much of it is concentrated on employment law. However, there are some specific provisions regarding service provision and some more general principles set out in the legislation.

Three areas of potential discrimination are recognised in law:

● gender or, as the law terms it, sex discrimination
● racial discrimination
● discrimination against people with disabilities.

There is no legislation relating to discrimination on the grounds of sexual preference, quite the reverse in fact, since the Local Government Act 1988 states that a local authority shall not:

(a) intentionally promote homosexuality or publish material with the intention of promoting homosexuality.

(section 28)

This is highly controversial, and although no prosecution has taken place, the threat of it is sufficient to impede social work practice with some groups. For example, social workers may feel inhibited about discussing issues of sexuality with young people with learning disabil ities, and have indeed in some instances been instructed by their local authority employers not to do so.

Gender discrimination

The Sex Discrimination Act covers employment, housing, education, and the provision of goods and services. It excludes sex discrimination by the state (especially taxation, social security and nationality laws) and in private, but does cover the actions of local authorities. Most relevant here would be the legislative framework in relation to provi- sion of services.

The Sex Discrimination Act 1975 covers five types of discrimination:

- direct sex discrimination
- indirect sex discrimination
- direct discrimination against the married
- indirect discrimination against the married
- victimisation.

There is a considerable amount of case law on direct discrimination but none of this refers directly to the provision of social services. A full account of this may be found in O'Donovan and Szyszczak (1988).

With regard to indirect discrimination, the Sex Discrimination Act 1975 says:

> a person indirectly discriminates against a woman (in the contexts of employment, education and the provision of goods, facilities, services and premises) if he applies to her a requirement or condition which he applies or would apply equally to a man but (i) which is such that the proportion of women who can comply with it is considerably smaller than the proportion of men who can comply with it, and (ii) which he cannot show to be justifiable irrespective of the sex of the person to whom it is applied, and (iii) which is to her detriment because she cannot comply with it.
>
> (section 1(1)(b))

Again there is a considerable volume of case law on this, but local authorities have been involved primarily in cases concerning educa- tion rather than social services.

The Sex Discrimination Act is implemented through establishment of discrimination as a statutory 'tort', or legal wrong. In effect this means that those who can prove they are the victims of discrimination

11

have the right to have damages as compensation awarded by the county court (industrial tribunal in the case of employment discrimination).

The Act is also put into effect by the creation of specific powers and duties to the Equal Opportunities Commission, whose role is to:

- assist individuals in bringing complaints
- act against discriminatory advertising
- seek injunction to restrict persistent discrimination
- issue non-discrimination notices and enforce them
- issue codes of practice.

Racial discrimination

The legislation in relation to race broadly reflects the same approach as gender discrimination legislation, that is, individuals can pursue their own cases for compensation tort and there is a statutory body, in this case the Commission for Racial Equality, that can issue orders to compel compliance and can help or advise people considering pursuing cases.

As with sex discrimination legislation, the law recognises both direct and indirect discrimination. Direct discrimination means:

> when one person treats another less favourably than he treats or would treat someone else on racial grounds.
>
> (section 1(1)(a), Race Relations Act 1976)

Indirect discrimination means:

> where conditions or requirements are imposed which apply equally to everyone but which will be harder for certain racial groups to comply with and cannot be justified on other than racial grounds.
>
> (section 1(1)(b), Race Relations Act 1976)

Racial grounds means any of the following: colour, race, nationality (including citizenship) or ethnic or national origins. Note that religion as such is excluded from the list of grounds.

Section 71 of the Race Relations Act 1976 emphasises that the Act applies to statutory authorities as well as private individuals. It imposes on all local authorities the duty to make appropriate arrangements with a view to securing that their various functions are carried out with due regard of the need:

to eliminate unlawful discrimination, and

to promote equality of opportunity and good relations between persons of different racial groups

(section 71, Race Relations Act 1976)

This has to be read in conjunction with section 20, which introduced specific duties to ensure that services are non-discriminatory, that is:

it is unlawful for anyone who is concerned with the provision of goods, facilities or services to the public, or a section of the public, to discriminate; this includes discrimination by refusal or deliberate omission or 'as regards their quality or the manner in which or the terms on which' they are provided

(section 20, Race Relations Act 1976)

Under section 40 of the Race Relations Act 1976, it is unlawful to discriminate in the way in which access to benefits, facilities or services is offered and facilitated.

What all this means in effect is that a local authority must be careful not to discriminate, and by implication provides a basis of ensuring that service providers, with whom the local authority may have contracts, also do not discriminate. While the legislation has been criticised for putting the onus on the 'victim' of discrimination to prove that he or she has been discriminated against, it is nevertheless important to remember that the legislation applies across a wide spectrum of activities. It is probably best to think of anti-discrimination legislation as contextual legislation that sets the context within which social care is provided. At the same time it is readily acknowledged that there are significant limitations of this legal approach and some scepticism about whether the law is of any value in promoting anti-oppressive practice (Dalrymple and Burke, 1995).

Disability Discrimination Act

Legislation concerning disability discrimination is very new in Britain and will initially be applied in the field of employment. However, eventually, when the Disability Discrimination Act 1995 is fully implemented, it will also cover obtaining goods and services, education and access to public transport. Implementation is to be phased in over a lengthy period.

13

The Act introduces a general prohibition on discrimination against disability in employment. Discrimination is taken to mean treating one person less favourably than another because of their disability, unless there is good reason to do so. Employers will be expected to facilitate reasonable changes to enable disabled people to do their jobs.

As far as the provision of goods and services is concerned, the Act will, when implemented, make it illegal to refuse to provide services solely on the grounds of disability, or to provide services in such a way that disabled people find it impossible or unreasonably difficult to access them. Given that much of social service legislation is specifically about providing services for people with disabilities, sometimes to the exclusion of the non-disabled, it is difficult to see how these provisions might be relevant in this context.

Educational establishments will eventually be required to provide information on access and information about facilities for disabled people. Minimum standards will be set for public transport vehicles in order to ensure accessibility.

As with gender and race discrimination, rights of redress are obtained through damages to be sought in the civil courts: either industrial tribunals or county courts.

Rights of redress generally

Specific rights of redress are provided for in laws concerning discrimination, but also relevant are general rights of redress available against public bodies and others when things go wrong. The general principle is that courts will intervene if there is evidence of unjust treatment or unreasonable interpretation of statute law. However, there is a general expectation that other avenues of redress will be attempted first.

It is possible to outline the general process relating to obtaining rights of redress by means of a diagram (Figure 1.1).

Complaints procedures

The first obvious step in seeking redress is to complain to the person who is supposed to be providing the service, and this is usually the most effective way to get something changed relatively quickly. All local authorities have complaints procedures, which in the case of community care services need to conform to requirements of rules made under the National Health Service and Community Care Act

1990 (this is explained in more detail in Chapter 2). Most complaints procedures involve three stages:

1. informal procedures, which usually start with complaints made to the person providing (or more usually failing to provide) the service
2. formal complaints set down internal procedures operated by public sector agencies and also by the independent sector, especially where independent service providers have a contract with a local authority
3. appeals to independent complaints panels, which in the case of local authorities comprise elected members (councillors).

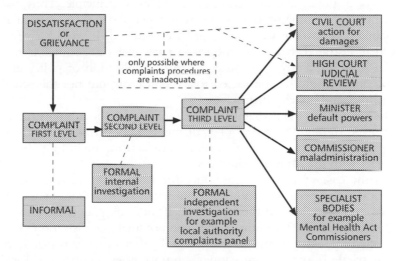

Figure 1.1   Redress procedures

It is only when these remedies have been attempted that it is possible to pursue other procedures, such as judicial review or applications to the ombudsman (*R.* v. *Kingston-upon-Thames, ex parte T* [1994]).

Maladministration and injustice

In the case of public bodies, complaints of maladministration may be referred to one of the ombudsman services:

- the Parliamentary Commissioner for Administration, who deals with complaints about maladministration by government departments
- the Commissioner for Local Administration, who deals with local authorities
- the Health Service Commissioner, who responds to complaints concerning the health service.

These commissioners may only investigate injustice caused by maladministration. Complainants have to demonstrate that they have suffered injustice through the misapplication of procedures or a lack of care over their application or whatever. Specifically excluded are matters of policy and allocation of resources in principle. Thus, for example, a complaint that services for people with a particular disability are inadequate would not be considered. It would have to be demonstrated that, in relation to a particular case, someone had been treated unfairly. Inconsistency in the application of policy and procedures would be considered for adjudication, but not the actual principles and policies themselves.

Complaints to the Parliamentary Commissioner for Administration are made through Members of Parliament. This permits the MP to attempt other means of obtaining satisfaction, including direct contact with the Minister concerned.

In the case of the Commissioner for Local Administration, an advocate may make the complaint on behalf of someone, or individuals may complain on their own behalf, but complaints have to be registered within 12 months of the action of 'maladministration'. It is expected that such complaints follow only after other remedies have been tried. If the Commissioner's report goes against the local authority, the local authority has the power to pay compensation, but the Commissioner's decision is not legally binding on the local authority. It is the threat of publicity (the Commissioner's reports usually being published in the press) that is the most effective part of this form of redress.

Civil action for damages

If an individual has suffered damage or loss as a consequence of someone else's actions, he or she may wish to sue for damages in the civil court, and this is possible whoever is the service provider or indeed whatever the contract. (For example, this might apply to someone who is the victim of crime – see Chapter 8.) This is rarely used as a means of obtaining redress, since other means are more effective, and the purpose of the legal action is in any case to obtain financial compensation for a wrong that is provable on the balance of probabilities in a court.

Judicial review

In relation to public bodies, the courts might be invited to order them to act or not to act in certain ways. However, it is important to emphasise that judicial review concerns the process by which the local authority arrived at its decision rather than the actual decision itself. It follows that if the legal action succeeds, it will not result in the court making the local authority's decision for it, but directions will be given about how that decision ought to be made. An example of this in connection with community care law arose in the case of Gloucestershire County Council, which has established the principle that services may not be withdrawn without a reassessment of need (see Chapter 2 for further discussion of this).

Judicial review also differs from some of the other means of redress discussed here in that it is a legal process involving the courts, and as such there will be funding implications for the applicant. Legal aid is not generally available for this sort of legal action, and many cases are consequently sponsored by voluntary organisations or pressure groups acting on behalf of vulnerable adults.

It is possible to group together the sorts of issue that would be relevant to a judicial review:

- A local authority has acted illegally, beyond its powers (ultra vires; see above), or without due regard for the law. For example, in R. v. *London Borough of Ealing, ex parte Leaman* [1984], the court ruled that the local authority was wrong to refuse to consider holiday application since the local authority had 'excised' part of the law by introducing blanket exclusions.
- A local authority has acted unreasonably. For example, in R. v. *Cleveland County Council, ex parte Cleveland Care Homes Association and Others* [1993], the local authority did not consult private care home owners about terms of contracts that the authority was likely to draw up.
- A local authority has breached natural justice by doing something that is manifestly unfair. For example, in R. v. *Durham County*

Council, ex parte Curtis [1993], the local authority was in error by failing to consult with the residents of a home before considering its closure.

Other means of redress

There are a number of other means of redress, ranging from inviting the Secretary of State to use default powers (section 50 of the National Health Service and Community Care Act 1990) to complaints to the Family Health Services Authority or the European Court of Justice. These are comparatively much rarer even than judicial review so are not considered here in detail. Legal texts (for example Ashton and Ward, 1992: 153–69; McDonald and Taylor, 1995: 95–140; Mandelstam and Schwehr, 1995: Chs 23 and 24) will provide more detail on these. Any specific rights linked to one particular Act of Parliament are covered under the relevant chapter; for example, the specified complaints procedure under the National Health Service and Community Care Act 1990 is summarised in Chapter 2, while Chapter 7 will include reference to the Mental Health Act Commission.

Conclusion

The distinctive characteristics of the law in relation to vulnerable adults are:

- the lack of clarity about the definition of 'vulnerability'
- the need to draw on a variety of sources in order to understand
  – the responsibilities and duties of local authorities
  – the rights and entitlements of vulnerable adults and their carers
- the intertwining nature of laws, often enacted in contrasting political climates, which have to be accommodated in order to illuminate a particular scenario.

While sometimes drawing attention to the contrast between the apparent complexity of the law in this area and the (superficial) straightforwardness of legislation relating to, for example, children and young people, the chapter makes a number of points that are equally applicable to all areas of social work practice and bear further emphasis:

- the need for practice to be firmly embedded in an understanding of the law, which is not to say that social workers should be lawyers but that they should always realise the constraints placed on them by the law and the opportunities that legislation also creates
- the tension between what care providers can do and want to do, and between the needs and rights of carers and users
- the need to think creatively about the use of the law in social work practice.

Too often we look only to the Children Act 1989 for professional solutions to child care dilemmas, or to criminal justice legislation for issues to do with offenders. The accounts of legislation relating to discrimination (see above), and to the routes by which people might seek redress against bad practice or inadequate service delivery, should alert us to the fact there are laws intersecting with everything in which we engage. It would be foolhardy to ignore the law until such time as there is a genuine grievance or cause for complaint.

We also need to reflect on the lack of a systematic approach to vulnerable adults, a theme that recurs throughout the book. For practitioners in this field the overwhelming question is 'How do the pieces of the jigsaw fit together?'

Further reading

Dalrymple, J. and Burke, B. (1995) *Anti-oppressive Practice: Social Care and the Law*, Open University, Buckingham.

2 Assessing Needs and Providing Services

Introduction

In this chapter we explore the ways in which someone who thinks they need social care services might set about having those needs met. The focus will be on someone who does not really know much about those services or indeed how to gain access to them. This issue is particularly relevant to people who have acquired a disability and have been 'referred' to the welfare agencies that ought to be able to advise them.

There are a number of important issues explored here. First, at what point does someone come to acquire a 'need', and how is this to be assessed? Second, how does this need fit with local authority social services departments' priorities and their mechanisms for assessing need? Specifically, what happens when local authority priorities do not accord with those of the person who might require services: are there rights of redress? Finally, what about carers in all of this? For a long time, welfare agencies have been criticised for overlooking the needs of carers and indeed for making assumptions about who should be providing care in families and to what extent.

Inevitably, much of this chapter will be concerned with the role of local authority social services departments, since these departments play a pivotal role in the provision of services to adults who need care in the community. The first part of the chapter introduces the relevant legal issues that relate primarily to the National Health Service and Community Care Act 1990. However, the chapter will also touch on disability as an issue for service providers, as well as for potential 'customers', with some indications of the deficiencies of the whole approach to disability and the needs of disabled people, explored further in Chapter 3. The social policy context and consideration of wider issues will form the focus of the final part of the chapter.

In order to clarify a number of issues related to professional practice, the case selected is relatively straightforward and will be presented in two stages. The initial focus will be on what happens at the pre-assessment stage. How is an initial request for services responded to? What screening processes operate, and how can these be justified? This is followed by a fuller consideration of the case, when a full assessment is to be carried out with a view to drawing up a care plan.

Needless to say, what follows should not be taken as a full, complete and comprehensive account of the law as it relates to people with disabilities and services for other adults in 'need'. There are more specialised legal texts that cover disability and the law (for example Cooper and Vernon, 1996), the needs of people with specific disabilities (Ashton and Ward, 1992; McDonald and Taylor, 1995) and the community care assessment process itself (Mandelstam and Schwehr, 1995; Clements, 1996) in far greater legal detail than is possible here. There are also a number of texts that discuss the social work role in community care in general terms (for example Payne, 1995) as well as guidance on social work practice in statutory agencies, contained in various government publications (Department of Health, 1990a, 1991, 1994). Instead what is offered here is an exploration of how the law applies in context and of the issues for professional workers to consider in practice.

Susan Walters telephones the social services department on behalf of her mother, Jean. She tells the social worker on duty that her mother went to see her GP yesterday on a routine visit, since she has diabetes, and was told that her eyesight was deteriorating to the extent that she will shortly qualify for registration as partially sighted. The GP advised Mrs Walters to enquire about services available to her as she is becoming increasingly 'cut off' from the world.

Further discussion revealed that Jean Walters lives with Susan and that, although there are worries and anxieties about the long-term future, there is no urgent need for help. What is required at this stage is information and advice about how to gain access to services that might be available. Susan thinks that it would help if her mother could talk to someone about this.

cont'd

21

The social worker explains that in her department there is at the moment a 3-month waiting list for assessments carried out under the National Health Service and Community Care Act 1990. In the meantime Jean could by all means call at the social services department office where she could be given information about the range of services offered in Monkton for people with disabilities.

Assessing immediate needs

Responding to immediate physical needs is clearly the prerogative of the GP, and GPs also have the responsibility for referring patients for more specialist treatment when the need arises. In this case registration as partially sighted is being considered; such registration is carried out by a consultant ophthalmologist who completes a form referred to as a BD8. Lovelock and Powell (1995) present a discussion of visual impairment in the context of community care legislation. Registration as partially sighted will automatically qualify Mrs Walters for entry on the local authority register of disabled people, and this brings with it a number of rights to services that are explored in more detail later in the chapter. However, for the moment, it should be noted that registration is not compulsory, nor is it a prerequisite before someone can gain access to services. Jean Walters does *not* have to be registered partially sighted before the assessment process may begin.

Views may differ on whether the social work response is adequate, given that Jean Walters may be experiencing distress that has barely been explored in the initial telephone conversation, but for the moment let us consider whether the response was legally acceptable from the body responsible for providing services.

The social worker correctly referred to two aspects of the service provision process that are important:

● the duty to provide information about services
● the duty to assess need.

The duty to provide information arises in this case from the Chronically Sick and Disabled Persons Act 1970 rather than the National Health Service and Community Care Act 1990. This is because while the 1990 Act requires local authorities to publicise their community care plans (section 46(1)), it is the Chronically Sick and Disabled

22

Persons Act 1970 that requires local authorities to provide information about actual services to disabled people:

> Each local authority
>
> (a) shall... prepare and publish a plan for the provision of community care services in their area
>
> and shall modify this plan from time to time.
>
> (section 46(1), National Health Service and Community Care Act 1990)

> 1(1) It shall be the duty of every local authority having functions under section 29 of the National Assistance Act 1948 to inform themselves of the number of persons to whom that section applies within their area and of the need for the making by the authority of arrangements under that section for such persons.
>
> 1(2) Every such local authority –
>
> (a) shall cause to be published from time to time at such times and in such manner as they consider appropriate general information as to the services provided under arrangements made by the authority under the said section 29 which are for the time being available in their area; and
>
> (b) shall ensure that any such person as aforesaid who uses any of those services is informed of any other of those services which in the opinion of the authority is relevant to his needs...
>
> (section 1, Chronically Sick and Disabled Persons Act 1970)

The duty to assess need, however, does arise from the National Health Service and Community Care Act 1990:

> Where it appears to a local authority that any person for whom they may provide or arrange for the provision of community care services may be in need of any such services, the authority
>
> (a) shall carry out an assessment of the need for those services
>
> (b) having regard to the results of that assessment shall then decide whether his needs call for the provision by them of any such services.
>
> (section 47(1))

The intersection of separate pieces of legislation is important. All must be interpreted within the context of local authorities' general duties, including the need to provide services within a non-discriminatory or anti-discriminatory framework, as discussed in Chapter 1.

Chapter 1 also highlighted the distinction between common law, statute law, regulations, codes of guidance and circulars. This issue is relevant here since responding to requests for information about services needs to be dealt with by reference to both statute law and regulations, taking into account what is stated in government circulars, Social Service Inspectorate reports and various codes of guidance. A list of relevant reports and codes of practice will be found at the end of the book.

For our purposes, it needs to be noted that the National Health Service and Community Care Act 1990 does not itself say in what form or in what way that assessment should be carried out. Nor does it say within what time span. For guidance on this, practitioners need to look at policy and practice guidelines. Particularly relevant here are those which focus on the application of community care policies in practice (Department of Health, 1990a, 1990b, 1991, 1994). Figure 2.1 sets this out more clearly and in more detail.

In this case the local authority has declared that it is not able to provide an assessment for about 3 months. Leaving aside the question of whether it is good practice to keep people waiting this long, the delay points to an interesting omission in the law and guidance in that nowhere are any time limits stipulated. Instead the question that ultimately presents itself is 'To what extent can a local authority delay providing an assessment without the risk of being accused of doing so deliberately in order to avoid fulfilling its statutory duty to provide services?' To date this question cannot be definitively answered by reference to case law, but as will be seen later in this chapter, judicial review of local authority decisions is possible. It would not be acceptable to the courts for local authorities to delay providing assessments for extended periods since this might be held to be tantamount to a refusal to carry out statutory duties. An alternative remedy might be to complain to the local government ombudsman, since delay might well be considered to be 'maladministration'. In fact, the ombudsman has adjudicated on this precise issue on several occasions, taking the view that compensation should be awarded when potential service users experience very lengthy delays (Mandelstam and Schwehr, 1995: 124–130; Clements, 1996: 38).

Is the local authority entitled to exercise discretion over whether someone actually needs an assessment? In other words, is a screening process legally acceptable? Clearly, it is important to exercise some control over this or potentially anyone who is an adult could request an assessment virtually 'on demand'. Here there is a little more clarity, since certain groups are entitled to an assessment, specifically people who are registerable as 'disabled' in accordance with the National Assistance Act 1948 (as amended; see below), whereas others will

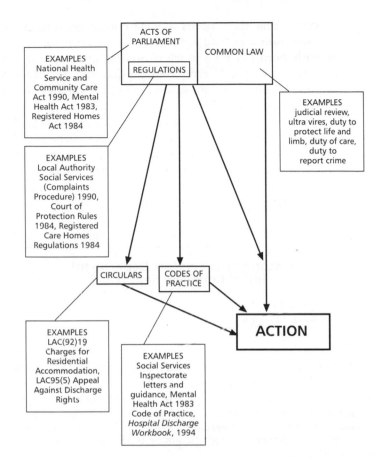

Figure 2.1   Sources of legal authority for action

by implication only receive an assessment if it appears *to the authority* that one is needed. (This point is amplified later in this chapter in the discussion of who is entitled to an assessment.) It is not open to potential service users to determine their own need for an assessment; they might have to persuade the local authority unless they belong to a group that is entitled to an assessment.

Finally, what about Susan, who is asking for an assessment on behalf of her mother? The social worker may have overlooked that Susan is the main carer; as such is entitled to participate in the assessment process and indeed to have an assessment of her own needs carried out alongside those of her mother. It would be good practice to reassure carers that their needs will be considered rather than simply subsumed into a general assessment of the need for services. This has recently been put on a much clearer statutory footing with the implementation of the Carers (Recognition and Services) Act 1995, which provides for a specific assessment of the carer's needs. (A more detailed discussion of what the law actually says will be found later in this chapter.) It is worth noting at this stage, however, that carers do not have a right to an assessment totally independently of the assessment of the person who needs services. The two assessments, or components of the assessment, must run in tandem.

In the meantime Jean Walters follows up the suggestion made and calls at the social services department office.

Monkton Social Services Department
Initial Interview Report

Jean Walters, age 75
22, Station Road, Monkton

Request

Mrs Walters called into the social services department office to ask for information about services she might be entitled to.

She explained that she had recently been to see her GP and Dr Redding had advised her to contact the social services. Has to visit GP regularly as she has diabetes. Problems with eyesight; GP says she may soon qualify for registration as partially sighted. Daughter telephoned social services department 2 days ago.

Mrs Walters was widowed 6 months ago. Her husband, up until his death, had been very fit, but died suddenly from a heart attack. Mrs Walters said she was finding it difficult to cope after his death. Relied on him for a lot of practical help; did not realise how dependent she was until he died. Her daughter, who is single, gave up her housing association flat last month to move in with her.

Has arthritis in hands and is sometimes not able to complete household chores. Feels lonely and isolated.

Picked up leaflet in GP's surgery that lists range of services offered but not sure what services she needs: thinks she would benefit from help in the home and companionship.

Action

Information obtained concerning relatives and general circumstances.

Monkton Social Services Department
Initial Interview Report *(cont'd)*

Information given about range of services offered by voluntary and independent organisations.

Explained that if she could not afford the services offered, she would have to wait for an assessment of needs as she was not in a priority group for this.

Needs assessment requested.

Family support

Relatives: daughter Susan is main carer; son and another daughter both live out of the area with their respective families. Jean's own sister lives in the same town but is 10 years older and virtually housebound. Only occasional contact with neighbours, who are generally families with adults who are working.

Finance

State retirement pension, small widow's pension from her husband's former employers. Owns her home; lived there for many years, brought up her own family there.

Issues for professional workers

There will inevitably be a variety of reactions to the challenges that Jean Walters has to face. There are a number of reasons why she may be somewhat fearful of the future, and one could speculate on why the family came to the conclusion that Susan ought to move in to live with her mother. Thoughts provoked by the situation described here will centre on:

- the disability or rather disabilities: the feelings evoked by the knowledge of increasing disability and increasing dependence on others; the practical needs raised by the advent of a disability
- bereavement and feelings of loss, centred on the loss of not only a close relative, but also an important faculty, namely the ability to see properly
- what is implied about family relationships: there may, for example, have been a presumption that it was Susan's duty to provide companionship, help and support for her mother

27

- social attitudes towards disability and ageing, and the gender assumptions that underpin all of this.

It would be a mistake to focus too much on a narrow interpretation of local authority duties here, and professional care workers do have responsibilities to consider disability within a wider context. At the same time it would also be a mistake to assume that the needs of disabled people are no more and no less than practical needs, 'needs for daily living' as they are sometimes referred to. Empowerment is clearly important, since one of the underlying rationales for current community care policies is the belief that 'People are, and always will be the expert on themselves' (Smale and Tuson, 1993: 13). In this case it may be necessary to assist Jean in articulating her views; it will certainly be important to acknowledge Susan's needs as the main carer.

Loss of sight is a frightening prospect, and it is important to acknowledge and respond to the emotional impact that this might have. In the current context where service provision is emphasised, it is easy to overlook the personal effects that any disability might have on an individual. There is nothing in legislation or guidance that denies the appropriateness of personal counselling and support; instead it is the accountability aspect and the organisational context that now appear to gear services for people with disabilities towards practical help. While practical help is important, it should not be employed to the detriment of personal individual supportive help. The question here might be whether this is necessary and, if so, who is going to provide it. If the local authority confines itself to a brokering role and does not offer counselling support services, counselling or support may have to be provided or 'purchased' from another welfare agency.

This all underlines the importance at an early stage of thinking about how an assessment might be planned. Note here that we are not thinking about what services Jean and her daughter might need since if we did so we would run the risk of fitting the needs into the framework of available (and affordable?) services. What we are considering is what preliminary decisions need to be made, how an assessment can be organised that both respects individuals' rights and fits with the priorities of the agency charged with carrying out the assessment. While these considerations would actually apply to any agency confronted with a request for assistance, the next section focuses on the specific issues that staff employed by social services departments need to consider since they are the principal assessors when it comes to ascertaining the needs of people with disabilities.

Role of social services departments

The first and important point to make is that there is nothing wrong with people assessing and determining their own needs and making arrangements to have those needs met. If the family can afford to meet their needs in ways which *they* think are appropriate, that is of course entirely a matter for them. The parallel here is with shopping for clothes or some other basic necessity. Every individual has freedom of choice with regard to clothes, can choose where to shop, what sort of clothes to buy, how much to spend, but this freedom is utterly dependent on one essential ability: the ability to pay or to 'afford' the clothes. When we are unable to afford the clothes of the quality or style we would like, we are obliged to make compromises and fit what we would like into what we can afford. In a very real sense we have to discriminate between what we *want* and what we *need*.

Similarly, using this free market principle, potential customers of community care could decide that they needed major adaptations to their houses in order to make lives easier for themselves and to minimise the practical effects of a disability. However, such adaptations might prove very expensive and therefore beyond the budget of the individual. An alternative, cheaper, solution might have to be found, raising questions about what is actually needed rather than is just desired. If the conclusion is that there are no alternatives that actually meet the need, decisions will have to be made at a policy level on whether the need is so great that it can be met by subsidy from public agencies. This is effectively what part of the National Health Service and Community Care Act 1990 is all about: at what point is a need an objective need that it is reasonable to expect local authorities to meet when families cannot do so themselves?

Hence the first question that confronts the local authority social services department is whether the need is substantial enough to justify the expenditure of public money on meeting that need; if not, the family are compelled to meet whatever needs they identify using whatever resources they have at their disposal. If the local authority accepts that there is a need, this is assessed by reference to one person's need assessed *objectively*. In other words, the identified need has to be set off against other people's needs and against the call that may be made on local authority provision to meet their needs. This may at first sight seem unpalatable, implying that there is competition for resources, but this is the reality. As a consequence it is important to recognise the key role that the local authority plays in adjudicating on needs and priorities when it comes to determining to what extent needs are to be met.

This all sounds rather theoretical but it does demonstrate why assessment has to be the first stage in the whole process of providing services. The whole area of assessment, procedures by which assessments are carried out and principles that underlie sound assessments is therefore of the utmost importance.

In this particular case some preliminary assessment has already been carried out. Significantly, a screening process has been implemented that may have been designed to avoid the necessity of carrying out assessments where there is no conceivable prospect of a person qualifying for local authority-funded services. A number of issues are highlighted by this process:

1. Is screening itself really a fair process?
2. How sensitive and responsive are the processes by which people are initially assessed (or pre-assessed)?
3. How clear is it to the people involved what is actually happening?
4. Screening, or pre-assessment – assessment with a view to seeing whether a full assessment is needed – is actually a very powerful process and is often overlooked. It is important for several reasons:

   ● Some people may not get as far as the social services department's door, since they may not be aware that they should be knocking on it in the first place.
   ● Some people may be deterred from asking for help because of apprehension, fear, stigmatisation or a host of other reasons connected with their anxiety over declaring to a stranger that they cannot cope or are in need.
   ● Some people may feel demeaned by asking for help, may feel they are a burden if they do so, may be overinfluenced by a prevailing ideology insisting that people should 'look after themselves'.
   ● Some people may have been diverted away from social services departments by other agencies, sometimes appropriately, at other times not.
   ● Some people may have been diverted by front-line staff in the social services departments themselves. The importance of the approach and responsiveness displayed by reception staff has only comparatively recently been recognised and may be of

particular concern to black or Asian potential service users (Cameron *et al.*, 1996).

- Some people may be deterred by the lack of information available, particularly if this is only available in English and/or is written in formal language.
- Some people may be deterred by difficulties of access to the building or may simply be put off by the setting in which the preliminary interviews take place.
- Some people may have been diverted by misinformation.
- Some people may have been diverted by convoluted pathways whereby trying to find the people responsible for an assessment is difficult and bureaucratic.
- There is a lack of definition in the presenting request (very confused, very general), unintentional misrepresentation (requests for direct financial help that would appear to be the prerogative of the Department of Social Security), overassertiveness/aggressive requests ('You have got to provide me with... or else...') or requests that are not assertive enough ('I am sure you probably won't be able to help but...', 'I am sorry to bother you but...').

Having identified the importance of the screening process as an important practice issue, care workers need also to consider how sensitive and responsive the assessment process itself should be in relation to those who 'succeed' in passing through this initial screening.

Planning an assessment is important since all the indications are that what potential service users appreciate most in assessors is their ability to be open, honest and clear about what they are doing, and to be responsive to the points that are being made to them (Payne, 1995: 95, 104).

Specifically, in this case, it would be useful if the assessor:

- had some knowledge of the various disabilities that Jean Walters has, without of course pretending to be a medical expert
- were conversant with procedures and were prepared to explain these
- were skilled at interpreting what people were saying in the context of empowering people to present their own case
- were clear about the purpose of the assessment
- engaged both Jean and Susan in the process, making it clear that the carer's needs were being taken into account
- gave consideration to the setting in which the assessment was to take place and its timing

- had given some thought to the various stages of assessment and what needed to be included in it (Payne, 1995: 100–1)
- were absolutely determined to be fair and rigorous rather than make assumptions about the family or the impact of the disability, but was fully prepared to engage with the family and see the issue through their eyes – the difficulty of this is acknowledged, being likened by Coulshed (1991: 139) to jumping on to a moving bus
- finally, were prepared to consider the appropriateness of a multi-disciplinary assessment (Payne, 1995: 102–6) about which more will be said in Chapter 4.

Relating social work practice to the law

Imagining that this is a summary of Mrs Walter's visit to the social services department, what does this demonstrate so far about the way in which law interacts with social work practice and the manner in which community care assessments are carried out?

As this is such an important topic, the focus in this part of the chapter will be exclusively on the local authority's responsibilities. In later chapters there will be reference to the roles of other agencies.

Specifically, a number of questions may be put:

1. What *must* the local authority do?
2. What else could the local authority do?
3. Who *should* carry out its responsibilities in this case?

These questions will be addressed together when examining local authority duties.

Finally, what could Mrs Walters do if she were dissatisfied with the local authority's response? What rights of redress does she, and her daughter, have? Rights of redress were discussed generally in Chapter 1, so we are looking here specifically at possible redress where assessment or the provision of services is an issue.

Local authorities must provide information about services

Mrs Walters was correctly advised by her GP that the local authority was responsible for providing information about services for people like her. The local authority has a duty to provide information about services, and Mrs Walters is entitled to information about them since she is a person to whom the various Acts concerning welfare services might apply. In addition, the local authority has a duty to ascertain the extent to which people are *likely* to need their services, and to this end there is a statutory obligation to find out what the potential need for services might be.

These local authority duties arise from both the Chronically Sick and Disabled Persons Act 1970 and the National Health Service and Community Care Act 1990. The relevant extracts were quoted earlier in the chapter when discussing assessing immediate needs. In short, the social services department has a duty to publish information about the support services it provides and also about those provided by local voluntary or private organisations.

Local authorities must assess needs

The issue of how local authorities actually carry out their duty to assess gives rise to a number of supplementary questions, which are woven through the following discussion of how local authorities carry out their functions:

1. Who is entitled to an assessment?
2. How are needs to be assessed?
3. Who might be offered services as the result of a needs assessment?
4. What services might be offered as the result of a needs assessment?
5. Who provides the services?
6. Is the local authority obliged to offer services if it determines that someone 'needs' them?

Finally, how and in what circumstances are needs reassessed?

Who is entitled to an assessment?

Anyone may request an assessment if they think that they have some kind of entitlement to community care services. However, as we saw earlier, it is for the *local authority* to determine at the initial stage whether the person might potentially qualify for services.

However, if a person is a legally defined 'disabled person', he or she has the right to have needs assessed and acquires additional rights (section 4 of the Disabled Persons (Services, Consultation and Representation) Act 1986):

If at any time during the assessment of the needs of any person under subsection (1)(a) above it appears to a local authority that he is a disabled person, the authority

(a) shall proceed to make such a decision as to the services he requires as is mentioned in section 4 of the Disabled Persons (Services, Consultation and Representation) Act 1986 without his requesting them to do so under that section; and
(b) shall inform him that they will be doing so and of his rights under that Act.

(section 2, National Health Service and Community Care Act 1990)

Broadly speaking, the Disabled Persons (Services, Consultation and Representation) Act 1986 confers rights to an assessment with regard to services provided by local authorities under section 2 of the Chronically Sick and Disabled Persons Act 1970 (these are listed on p. 39 below). It is possible for an advocate to request the assessment on behalf of a disabled person by virtue of section 4 of the Disabled Persons (Services, Consultation and Representation) Act 1986.

The Act also makes it clear that carers have rights to request this assessment, a point confirmed and extended by the Carers (Recognition and Services) Act 1995:

Where

(a) a local authority carry out an assessment under section 47(1)(a) of the National Health Service and Community Care Act 1990 of the needs of a person for community care services, and
(b) an individual provides or intends to provide a substantial amount of care on a regular basis for the relevant person

the carer may request the local authority, before they make their decision as to whether the needs of the relevant person call for the provision of any services, to carry out an assessment of his ability to provide and to continue to provide care for the relevant person; and if he makes such a request, the local authority shall carry out such an assessment and shall take into account the results of that assessment in making that decisions.

(section 1)

In addition, section 2 of the Carers (Recognition and Services) Act 1995 makes it clear that where a person's needs are being assessed under the:

- Chronically Sick and Disabled Persons Act 1970
- National Health Service and Community Care Act 1990

34

- Children Act 1989 (Part III of which refers to disabled children as being children in need)

the carer is also entitled to an assessment if:

- they are providing private care
- they are providing regular and substantial care (regular and substantial to be interpreted in accordance with policy guidance).

For the purpose of legislation, a carer includes a young carer caring for an adult, and someone caring for a disabled child.

Note, however, that assessment here is of the carer's needs running alongside the assessment of the person being cared for. Legally, the two assessments are in tandem; the Carers (Recognition and Services) Act 1995 does not provide carers with the right to assessment independently of the person for whom they are caring.

How are needs to be assessed?

First, needs are to be assessed by local authorities themselves rather than being delegated entirely to third parties, although third parties can assist with parts of the process. Circular LAC(93)2 gives further guidance on the use of third parties, and section 47(3) of the National Health Service and Community Care Act 1990 lays on health authorities the duty to co-operate in providing an assessment. The central role of local authorities in carrying out an assessment was strongly and forcefully advocated in the Griffiths Report (Griffiths, 1988).

Assessments should be carried out as a first and separate activity before social services departments decide how those needs should be met. In other words, assessments must be 'needs led'. In addition:

> The assessment process should be as simple, speedy and informal as possible.
>
> (Department of Health, 1991: para. 3.3)

The social services department must give reasons if it decides not to carry out an assessment (interpretation of case law: *R. v. Civil Service Appeal Board, ex parte Cunningham* [1991]):

> The individual service user and normally, with his or her agreement, any carers should be involved throughout the assessment and care management process. They should feel that the process is aimed at meeting their wishes. Where a user is unable to participate actively it is even

more important that he or she should be helped to understand what is
involved and the intended outcome.

(Department of Health, 1990b: para. 3.15)

Local authorities will need to have in place... published information
accessible to all potential services users and carers... setting out the
types of community care services available, the criteria for provision of
services, the assessment procedures to agree needs and ways of
addressing them and the standards by which the care management
system (including assessment) will be measured (the purpose of which
is to) enable users and carers to exercise genuine choice...

(Department of Health, quoted in Mandelstam and Schwehr, 1995: 336–7)

Who is to be assessed?: registering someone as disabled

The description of Jean Walters indicates a number of reasons why
she might qualify for consideration as a person 'in need'. These
reasons centre on her disabilities: her visual impairment, the diabetes,
her arthritis. These could all potentially be examples of disabilities.
The definition of disability is as under the National Assistance Act
1948:

persons who are blind, deaf or dumb, (or who suffer from mental
disorder of any description) and other persons who are substantially
and permanently handicapped by illness, injury, or congenital deformity
or such other disabilities as may be prescribed by the Minister.

(section 29(1))

Various circulars extended the definition to include mental disorder
and also clarified that people who are partially sighted or hard of
hearing should also be included. It is also worth noting that there are
specific registration procedures for blind and partially sighted people,
involving assessment by an ophthalmologist. (McDonald and Taylor,
1995: 13)

If applicants for services are defined as 'disabled', they have clear
rights to assessment under the Disabled Persons (Services, Consultation and Representation) Act 1986 and National Health Service and
Community Care Act 1990. Social workers often refer to a 'comprehensive' assessment, meaning one which takes all factors into account
and considers the full range of an individual's needs, but this is not
the only kind and it has been suggested that not everyone is entitled
to a *comprehensive* assessment (Clements, 1996: 42). Note that registration as disabled with the social services department is not a pre-

36

requisite for entitlement to an assessment; it is sufficient that the applicant be registerable, although local authorities are required to keep a register of disabled people (LAC(93)10: paras 2 and 3). In determining who is disabled, social services departments have been advised to give a wide interpretation and always take full account of individual circumstances (LAC(93)10: Appendix 4, para. 8).

This definition may now seem to those engaged in social care to be somewhat out of date since it includes phrases such as 'congenital deformities' that are no longer considered appropriate. However, the definition has regrettably not been updated. It is important to note the permanency criteria, that is, that the disability cannot simply be temporary, breaking a leg for example, because although this is serious for the individual concerned, it does not give rise to a long-term need, which appears to be the priority in the legislation. Moreover, the degree of the disability is a significant factor since the statutory definition insists on inclusion of the word 'substantial'. Although this is for local authorities to interpret, it would clearly preclude comparatively minor disabilities, for example being very short-sighted, but registration as partially sighted would generally be regarded as a definite disability. It is also important to acknowledge that disabilities do not always occur singly, and that although each disability may not of itself be substantial enough to qualify for registration, taken together they would point to a very real limitation on a person's lifestyle and could therefore be considered to be a 'registerable' disability.

Why is the issue of registration so important anyway? The answer to this is that being identified as having a specific disability provides the key that unlocks the community care door. Local authorities cannot *just* provide services to whomsoever they choose; all local authority duties have to be set in legislation, they have to relate to a specific law saying that the local authority *must* or *may* provide a particular service.

If a local authority provides a service for which there is no legal authority, it risks being declared ultra vires by the courts, the consequences of this being severe for local authority members (councillors) who could be surcharged, that is, made to pay the costs of providing the 'illegal' service out of their own pockets. This legal principle that local authorities can only act where legislation says they can is very well established, reaching back to the very earliest days of local government in Britain. It is deemed to be one of the principal methods whereby the power of the state is kept in check so that individuals do not find their rights trammelled by public authorities and can potentially challenge an authority guilty of intruding into their private lives.

Who might be offered services as the result of a needs assessment?

Having said this, it is possible for law to be framed in such a way as to give local authorities fairly wide discretion in terms of what they might do and the people they might help. This is particularly true in relation to older people. Legislation has for a long time recognised that the ageing process itself may give rise to specific needs for welfare, and, interestingly, in social welfare legislation there are no prescribed age limits for the provision of such care.

An example of this in practice would be section 45 of the Health Services and Public Health Act 1968, which provides for a local authority to 'promote the welfare of old people'. The term 'old people' is not statutorily defined. Similarly, the Chronically Sick and Disabled Persons Act 1970 lays on the local authority a duty to make adequate provision for the needs in their area for home help in households where such help is required 'owing to the presence of... a person who is... aged...' (section 2 of the Chronically Sick and Disabled Persons Act 1970). So in this case some local authorities might agree to assist Jean Walters simply on the grounds that she is aged 75.

Turning the argument the other way round, however, it is important to note that disability is not age related. This may or may not accord with the practice in several local authority social services departments that nominate teams to be providers for older people and people with disabilities. The juxtaposition of these two groups may not always be beneficial. Specifically here one could point to the needs of younger disabled people, of relevance being the demarcation between child-hood and adulthood. Generally, disabled 'children' under 18 years of age would qualify for services provided by local authorities under Part III of the Children Act 1989 (disability automatically identifying these children as being 'in need') whereas adults would qualify for registration under the National Assistance Act and therefore be entitled to local authority services from the age of 18 upwards.

What services might be offered as the result of a needs assessment?

A local authority may provide residential accommodation for persons who, by reason of age, are:

> aged 18 or over who by reason of age, illness, disability or any other circumstances are in need of care and attention which is not otherwise available to them.
>
> (section 21(1)(a), National Assistance Act 1948)

This is subject to directions by the Secretary of State (LAC(93)10). Local authorities are also empowered to make arrangements with private and voluntary homes (section 26(1) of the National Assistance Act 1948).

A local authority may provide domiciliary or day care services for people who are disabled (see above for a precise definition). Such domiciliary services are provided in accordance with the Secretary of State's directions (LAC(93)10) relating to section 29 of the National Assistance Act 1948 or else in accordance with section 2 of the Chronically Sick and Disabled Persons Act 1970. Current National Assistance Act 1948 services include (LAC(93)10: Appendix 2):

- social work advice and support
- social rehabilitation – including day care centres that provide this
- maintaining registers
- occupational, social, cultural and recreational facilities – again including day care centres
- workshop services

(all the above being compulsory)

- holidays
- free or subsidised travel
- assistance in finding accommodation
- subsidy of warden costs
- information

(the latter being permissive).

The list contained in the Chronically Sick and Disabled Persons Act 1970 section 2 can be broadly categorised as follows:

1. practical assistance
2. radio, television and library facilities
3. recreational facilities
4. travel assistance in connection with these services
5. works of adaptation
6. holidays
7. meals at home or elsewhere
8. telephones.

Note that this does not refer solely to arrangements made directly by the local authority. For example, one local authority was in error when it refused to consider giving financial help to someone who had made their own arrangements for a holiday. The policy of the local authority, which only permitted assistance with holidays the authority had itself arranged, was held to be unlawful (R. v. *London Borough of Ealing, ex parte Leaman* [1984]).

The Chronically Sick and Disabled Persons Act 1970 also provides for local authorities to issue badges of a 'prescribed form' for motor vehicles driven by or used for the carriage of disabled persons and thereby ignore certain parking restrictions (section 21(1) of the Chronically Sick and Disabled Persons Act 1970).

Note that all of these domiciliary and day care services can be provided only for people with disabilities. For other groups of vulnerable adults, especially older people, we have to look to other legislation, principally the Health Services and Public Health Act 1968 duty to promote welfare. Again, the extent of service provision is subject to directions from the Secretary of State, although in this case the directions go back to 1971 (Department of Health and Social Security circular 19/71). They are:

1. to provide meals and recreation in the home and elsewhere
2. to inform the elderly of services available to them and to identify elderly people in need of services
3. to provide facilities or assistance in travelling to and from the home for the purpose of participating in services provided by the local authority or similar services
4. to assist in finding suitable households for boarding elderly persons
5. to provide visiting and advisory services and social work support
6. to provide practical assistance in the home, including assistance in the carrying out of works of adaptation or the provision of any additional facilities designed to secure greater safety, comfort or convenience
7. to contribute to the cost of employing a warden on welfare functions in warden-assisted housing schemes
8. to provide warden services for occupiers of private housing.

The same Act lays on local authorities the duty to provide a home help service and a permissive power to offer laundry facilities (section 13 of the Health Services and Public Health Act 1968).

Who provides the services?

Although it is a duty to provide information about services, to assess needs and to determine whether assessed needs call for the provision of services, there are no specific services that the local authority actually *has* to provide *itself*. Where there are duties, these are to 'secure the provision of services' or to 'make arrangements'.

The law does not actually say a great deal about the way in which services are to be provided. For this, reference needs to be made to codes of practice and circulars. However, the National Health Service and Community Care Act 1990 does carry substantial implications for the organisation and delivery of services. It includes facilitating provisions for the contracting-out of services and for creating 'internal markets'. Sections 42(2), 42(7) and 46(1)(d) taken together allow local authorities to discharge their duties under section 21 of the National Assistance Act 1948 and elsewhere by making arrangements with voluntary organisations and/or private individuals or organisations, providing they are registered and in some cases approved.

Is the local authority obliged to offer services if it determines that someone 'needs' them?

Applicants for services should be informed of the result of the assessment. This need not be a written statement unless (a) a continuing service is to be provided, or (b) a written statement is specifically requested (Department of Health, 1991: para. 3.27). Applicants also have the right to see information held on file by the social services department and are entitled to a copy of that information (section 2 of the Access to Personal Files (Social Services) Regulations 1989).

If the carer's needs are being assessed alongside those of the applicant for services, the results of the assessment must be included when the local authority makes decisions about services that may be provided (section 1 of the Carers (Recognition and Services) Act 1995).

Having assessed the applicant's needs, the local authority is under a duty to take that assessment into account in determining how to meet those needs and whether to provide services. In the case of a registerable disabled person, the authority is under a duty to make arrangements to provide any of the services set out in section 2 of the Chronically Sick and Disabled Persons Act 1970. While lack of financial resources cannot absolve the social services department from this legal duty, once the need has been assessed and declared (section 47 (1)(b) of the National Health Service and Community Care Act

1990), resources are a factor that the local authority is entitled to take into account when determining the *extent* to which the local authority meets those needs (House of Lords judgement in Gloucestershire case, 20 March 1997).

This judgement effectively overturned previous decisions which held that local authorities were obliged to provide services once they had made a declaration of need for those services (as, for example, in *R. v. Hereford and Worcester County Council, ex parte Chandler* [1991], in which the social services department agreed that the disabled person needed a full-time helper but then said that it did not have the money to provide this assistance). The issue of a local authority withdrawing or curtailing services as a result of budgetary cuts has caused considerable controversy, and a review of the law may result from decisions in cases concerning Gloucestershire, Sefton and Lancashire. These are discussed further in Chapter 9.

How do local authorities ensure that they act in a non-discriminatory way?

The law generally in relation to discrimination has been dealt with in Chapter 1, so the focus here will be angled more on the degree to which local authorities take on board the needs of all sectors of the community when it comes to assessing and providing services.

Very little has in fact been written on this topic, but some analysis has been carried out examining the assessment process as implemented with black and Asian service users (Cameron *et al.*, 1996). This research, based on interviews with 71 people and service providers, focused on the needs of old Asian and black people in Wolverhampton. The overwhelming conclusion from the research was that local authorities encounter difficulties in providing services for all groups in society. The research is summarised in more detail in Chapter 3.

As explained in Chapter 1, in order to substantiate claims for discrimination in Britain, the 'victim' has to prove that discrimination took place and that hardship resulted from it. Calling public bodies to account for possible discrimination is therefore difficult, and this applies to gender as well as to racial discrimination. However, the requirement of the Disability Discrimination Act 1995 in relation to access to services and other rights may in the long term have greater effect, although to what extent is difficult to say since the relevant sections of the Disability Discrimination Act are relatively new.

Remedies for people dissatisfied with local authority assessments or provision of services

Dissatisfaction should initially be expressed to the person who made the assessment, and from there on the complaints procedures could be instigated.

It is helpful to distinguish complaints at two levels:

1. specific rights in relation to the National Health Service and Community Care Act 1990
2. general rights of redress for applicants for local authority services.

A concise account of these general rights was contained in Chapter 1. The specific rights under the National Health Service and Community Care Act 1990 derive from section 50, which states that authorities may be required to establish complaints procedures, which are publicised. The Secretary of State may hold inquiries as a consequence and has default powers, that is, he or she can directly take over the local authority service, provide this through a central government agency and charge the local authority for doing so. The complaint can be laid by a qualifying individual or someone acting on their behalf. A qualifying individual is someone for whom:

(a) the authority have a power or duty to provide, or to secure the provision of, a service for him and
(b) his need or possible need for such a service has (by whatever means) comes to the attention of the authority

    (section 50, National Health Service and Community Care Act 1990)

In fact, local authorities have been required to operate specific complaints procedures for matters arising after 1 April 1991. Such complaints procedures must take a specific form, separate from a local authority's disciplinary or grievance procedures and in accordance with the Complaints Procedure Directions of 1990. This consists of three stages: an informal stage, a formal ('registered') stage and finally a review panel who can make recommendations to the Director of Social Services. Although these recommendations are not binding, they are subject to individual review, and it would therefore be imprudent to ignore them without very good reason. McDonald and Taylor (1995: 97) cite the case of *R. v. Avon County Council, ex parte Mark Hazell* [1994] which confirms this approach.

The Commissioner for Local Administration has made a number of adjudications in cases concerning assessment procedures, especially in connection with delays. For example, a delay of 6 months in assessing a disabled person's needs was considered to amount to maladministration (Clements, 1996: 38).

Can services be withdrawn? Can needs be re-assessed?

Once the local authority has determined that someone is in need of services, and undertakes to provide those services, can the authority subsequently withdraw them if budgets are tightened? Moreover, can they take their own resources into account when determining the extent to which to meet their obligations? These issues have been the subject of a number of disputes in the courts (*R. v. Gloucestershire County Council, ex parte Barry and Others* [1995]; *R. v. Gloucestershire County Council, ex parte Mahfood* [1995]). In the Barry case, the local authority had provided twice-weekly home care but withdrew this in 1994, along with the service to 1,000 other people, when it faced a £2.5 million shortfall in its income. The High Court decided that the local authority did have the right to withdraw the service but only after it had reassessed need. Thus it was in error in simply withdrawing a service without enquiring into the recipient's needs. However, had it reassessed the need in the light of its own changed circumstances, it would then have been entitled to withdraw or curtail services, notwithstanding the fact that the service user's needs might remain unchanged.

This raises the spectre of assessment of need varying not only in different parts of the country, but also at different times according to the financial situation of the local authority that assesses them. One strong message arising from these cases, however, is that local authorities must reassess need before altering service provision, although they could presumably do so with the agreement of the service user. If local authorities are confronted with a substantial reduction in their own income, they presumably have no choice but to undertake a wholesale and systematic review of the needs of everyone who receives a service for whom they have accepted some financial responsibility.

Social policy context

Neither social work practice nor the law governing it exists in a vacuum. There is both a political and historical context to it, and for a number of reasons, community care is a politically controversial area. Current debates tend to centre on the adequacy or otherwise of resources allocated to community care, but little attention is paid to the changes in thinking and ideology that underpin it.

The notion of community care is, of course, not new. By default, communities have always had to 'care', and in the UK and many other European countries it is only since the nineteenth century that segregating certain groups from the rest of society has been a seriously pursued policy.

Taking a global view, it is noticeable how the West has, in the nineteenth and twentieth centuries, has become preoccupied with segregating specified groups from the rest of society and providing institutions to care for them. In some cases the institution played a protective or custodial role, protective that is of the wider society, since the identified groups were often perceived as a threat. The Poor Law Amendment Act of 1834 demonstrates this approach to the poor, who were identified as paupers and confined to the workhouse as a penalty for their poverty. Workhouses provided a visible deterrent against poverty, which at that time was viewed as a kind of social disease caused by indolence, fecklessness and a refusal to take proper care of oneself. While the harshest aspects of this policy were gradually mollified over the years, the fundamental ideology that it represents – failing to look after oneself or to be looked after by one's family merited a degree of social disapproval – has proved remarkably resilient. It formally persisted as part of social care policy until 1948, when workhouses were finally abolished by the National Assistance Act 1948, along with the legal duty of adult children to care for their ageing parents. Interestingly, this legal duty of adult children to meet the costs of their parents is still enshrined in legislation in France, Germany and Italy (Hantrais, 1995: 140).

It is important to distinguish two quite separate strands of influence that lie behind the current community care policies:

- The political shifts of the past 20 years or so have moved Britain, along with several other European countries, to reappraise the whole notion of the welfare state and to rearrange service provision in order to reflect a 'mixed economy' of welfare (Hantrais, 1995: Ch. 7).
- Social work thinking has encouraged and supported the shift away from institutional care, arguing for the integration of people with disabilities into the community and seeking to support people living within their own communities for as long as possible.

The political changes in Britain have not simply been a matter of party politics, as many suppose; the emphasis on reducing public expenditure can be traced back to negotiations with the International Monetary Fund in 1977 during the period of a Labour government. However, it would certainly be true to say that the need to reduce public expenditure has dramatically affected the provision of long-stay hospital beds and the provision of residential care. Government policies since 1979 have encouraged moves away from state care towards a system based on a mixed economy, that is, where local authorities compete with the private (for profit) and independent (non-profit-making) sectors on an equal footing. Services within whichever sector can therefore be provided by a variety of people or organisations, with the operation of free market forces regulating the supply of and demand for services. In simple terms this means that if someone believes they have a need for a community care service, they will want to purchase this for themselves (or their relative), and competition between service providers will result in a variety of services at the lowest cost, thereby offering a real choice for community care 'consumers'.

The demographic context that gave rise to increasing anxiety about an increasing older population is well documented. Hantrais (1995: 130) quotes European Union (EU) figures that suggest a rise between 1960 and 1990 of 50 per cent in the number of people aged over 60 living in EU member countries. The government White Paper on community care (Department of Health, 1989: 62) cited Office of Population Censuses and Survey figures suggesting that:

- the number of people aged 65+ was projected to rise from 8.4 million in 1985 to 9.0 million in 2001
- the number of people aged 85+ was projected to rise from 695,000 in 1986 to 1,146,000 in 2001
- of the 65+ age group, it was estimated that 750,000 were severely disabled, and this figure was expected to rise to 900,000 by 2001.

This significant demographic forecast has caused some consternation that there will be intergenerational conflict between young and old on the basis of hostility to the perceived increased dependence of older people, although some believe that the danger of this has been overstated (Phillipson and Walker, 1986).

At the same time, social work thinking has tended increasingly to look on residential care as a last resort, doubts being cast on its effectiveness. These doubts have centred not on the organisation of the care but on the very notion of residential care itself. Specifically, the effects of institutionalisation have been noted (Goffman, 1961), in particular with regard to what this says about 'difference' (Wolfensberger, 1975).

Some sympathy for a move away from large institutions was therefore already in existence when government came to consider specific measures to 'reform' community care in line with their political beliefs. However, the major influence on the precise form of these changes was undoubtedly North American, deriving from developments that took place in the 1970s arising from concerns about the fragmentation of services and their costs. Phillips and Penhale (1996), drawing on the work of Moxley, identify the salient features of the American developments as being tailor-made services designed to meet individual need, the mobilisation of resources to provide an integrated, co-ordinated response, and the provision for continuity of care. The focus was on outcomes, with a heavy emphasis on financial and budgetary aspects. Further American research demonstrated that two key elements were necessary for community care to be successful: an extensive dependence on informal care, and an integrated system of services. Care managers also needed to have control over the resources allocated to them (Phillips and Penhale, 1996: 2). In Britain, some key projects in which workers were given control over resources were established and were later cited as good practice models. Thanet in Kent provided one pioneering example in the early 1970s, although this and similar projects have been criticised as blueprints by Means and Smith (1994). They pointed out that such projects tended to be selective (some groups being excluded) and that workers within the projects had unusually low caseloads.

The American concept of care management was translated into UK practice despite significant differences between the USA and Britain. The most important of these differences was undoubtedly the preponderance of the public sector in Britain, which ran alongside the principle of free or heavily subsidised public care and the allied role of professional dispensers of care within the state system. This issue had to be addressed in the Griffiths Report (Griffiths, 1988), which concluded that professionals and local authorities in particular should continue to have an important role in allocating resources where individuals could not afford their own care. In allocating such resources, local authorities would be the arbiters of need, assessing needs with a view to determining what services should be provided and paid for by the state. This model of community care as a way of deploying resources commended itself to Griffiths, since there appeared to be considerable potential for transferring service provision, as opposed to commissioning, to the independent sector. Griffiths noted that, at the time the report was written (1988), local authority social services departments employed 232,000 staff, of whom:

- 88,200 were employed in residential care
- 27,200 were employed in day care establishments
- 59,500 were home helps.

At that time, social services departments directly offered:

- 133,800 places in residential homes
- 108,700 places in day centres
- 46.4 million meals on wheels (Department of Health, 1989: 17).

Thus local authority social services departments were big businesses and presented potential for privatisation. Nevertheless, not all of the local authority's functions were to be moved over into the independent sector. The report did not recommend the abolition of local authority social services departments, as some had feared, but instead proposed that social services departments should be central to the service commissioning part of community care. The principle behind the Griffiths Report, and therefore behind the community care legislation, was that local authority social services departments should become brokers rather than service providers, although they would still retain the legal power and authority to provide services themselves directly.

The policy is now enshrined in the National Health Service and Community Care Act 1990 Part III, but since this is a facilitating Act, so much depends on the codes of practice and guidelines that run alongside it. The Act makes it clear that local authority social services departments can provide residential care for adults, but on equal terms with the private and voluntary sectors. There should be no presumption that local authority care is better, and local authorities 'will be expected to take all reasonable steps to secure diversity of provision' (Department of Health, 1989: 22). The emphasis throughout is on:

- a wider range of choice of services
- more flexibility and innovation in the services offered
- competition between providers of services

with the local authority playing a back-up, developing and monitoring role.

In practice, this means that local authorities have six key responsibilities:

1. carrying out an appropriate assessment of an individual's needs
2. designing packages of services, including the appointment of care managers
3. securing the delivery of services through a purchasing and contracting role
4. establishing complaints procedures
5. monitoring the quality and cost-effectiveness of services
6. making financial arrangements.

It clearly follows from all of this that departments have to separate the assessment process from service provision, and inspection of services has to be at arm's length. The degree of separateness still remains a matter of some controversy and debate, some suggestions being put forward that inspection units ought to be moved to local authority trading standards departments and that local authorities ought to become solely commissioning agents.

In other spheres of social policy, particularly health care, the move towards this model of community care has seen:

- the closure of many of the Victorian psychiatric hospitals and an increasing number of people with mental health problems living in the community
- the running down of large hospitals for the 'mentally handicapped' or people with learning disabilities, much smaller-scale homes or units being established in the community to care for people discharged from them
- a move away from residential homes for older people that offer a large number of 'beds' using shared facilities, towards smaller units, including sheltered housing in preference to residential care.

Conclusion

If the emphasis in the previous chapter on the need to locate social work intervention in the law has created the impression that knowledge of that legislation will eventually provide us with all the answers, this account of the 1990 National Health Service and Community Care Act soon challenges that expectation. For here we learn the following:

- There are specific legal responsibilities laid on local authorities, and they need to be aware of them and responsive to them if they are to avoid litigation.
- Laws are nothing if they are not communicated to people. Many people are unaware of the welfare legislation that impinges on them, and this raises a question for practitioners about their own role in disseminating information.
- There are also operational constraints on services, and these compel authorities to interpret the law, seeking compromises in order to match what may be unpredictable and ever-growing demands to finite and often dwindling resources.
- The compromise sought above in turn raises moral and ethical questions that are constantly being debated by practitioners.

On this last point, it may be worth saying that no amount of study of the law or legal exactitude is going to resolve these conflicts for the practitioner who may be left wondering whether, if local eligibility criteria are so strict, and delays in service provision so lengthy, people are actually receiving any service at all. Can local policy effectively withdraw a service by making it so notional as to be non-existent?

Further reading

Clements, L. (1996) *Community Care and the Law*, Legal Action Group, London.

Mandelstam, M. and Schwehr, B. (1966) *Community Care Practice and the Law*, Jessica Kingsley, London.

Payne, M. (1995) *Social Work and Community Care*, Macmillan, Basingstoke.

3 Advocacy: Speaking on Someone's Behalf

Introduction

The previous chapter introduced us to the concept of 'assessment'. It took up the issue of the changing nature of need over time and of the opportunity to revisit or challenge decisions. If it made assumptions about service users and providers, it was that they worked in a spirit of co-operation and open communication. Before we move on to the legal and ethical issues of intervention when people are unable to act on their own behalf, however, we need to develop further our understanding of the relationship between assessor and assessed. The themes to be developed here will cover:

- the importance of the quality of communication at the assessment stage
- the need for advocacy at the time of assessment and during delivery of the service
- the clarification of the financial arrangements for residential and community care services
- the scope for service providers to respond to people's cultural needs in their residential and community care resources.

Am I through to one of the care managers in the social services department?

Yes.

This is Fiona Gatsby, officer in charge of Elmbank House. I need to speak to you about one of my residents.

cont'd

51

I am sorry, I don't know Elmbank House. Is it a residential home?

Yes, it is an independent registered home for eight older people with substantial physical disabilities. Our residents either pay the full cost themselves or are subsidised by the local authority, namely yourselves. The resident I need to talk to you about is self-financing. She is very proud of the fact that she can pay her own way – she's been drawing on money she received from an insurance policy when her husband died. Now that this is coming to an end, we need to arrange for an assessment to be completed by your department. There are a couple of slight complications, however.

Oh, what are they?

Well, Monica has a hearing difficulty, and communication with her is, to be frank, a major problem. She has a tendency to say she has understood when she hasn't. My staff are very good at making allowances for her, but there have been a few misunderstandings.

And the second complication?

Well, it's a bit embarrassing from our point of view, but she says she wants to go home. However, I think this is because she misunderstands the situation regarding the accommodation fees. She thinks I am trying to turf her out of the home, which is nonsense of course. I certainly hope she is not serious about going home. She is far too frail to care for herself, and so much support would be needed that its cost would be far in excess of our modest charges. Besides which, one of her relatives, one of her sons I think, has moved into her house as it is nearer his work.

And there's another thing. We always treat our residents as individuals – well you have to really don't you? Monica is saying she wants go home now as she is the only black resident left here. She is talking about returning to Trinidad. I think this may because her family do not come to see her nearly so often as they did when she first moved here 2 years ago. She does own a house, so I suppose she could actually do that if she wanted, but she does need a great deal of help and the family are all against the idea.

Issues for professional workers

Communication with someone with a hearing impairment

The telephone comments from the home suggest that they have a limited view of the implications of hearing loss on the quality of life of someone in residential care. To dismiss these as 'slight complications' is at best naïve, at worst insensitive and in any case poor professional practice.

This resident has clearly been in care for some time, and there is now a situation where either her needs have changed or it is just beginning to be understood how incompletely they have been met. What must be done at this point is to ensure that the assessment gives due weight to the factors that hinder her full enjoyment of the services on offer. This means taking into account the communication difficulties – both in the manner in which the assessment is conducted and as a factor that has to be responded to within that assessment.

With hearing loss we need to know the nature of the difficulty. Is it pre-lingual or post-lingual deafness? With the former, in which people have never had the benefit of hearing to help them form their own spoken language, it might be expected that their preferred form of communication will be British Sign Language. If this is indeed their language of first choice, good professional practice dictates that they be interviewed in this way. Written communication is not an acceptable substitute in these circumstances, although for someone who is post-lingually deaf, depending on the point in their lives at which the deafness occurred, it may be a possibility.

There may also be problems of conceptualisation and terminology if the communication is between someone dependent on signing and someone who uses the spoken word. This discussion in particular is already fraught with misunderstanding. The sense of having to 'pay one's own way' is historically located – it will be a priority for some and less significant for others depending on their age and history of their contact with state provision. If Ms Gatsby is talking about 'turfing her out', who knows what the service user may be thinking. She may imagine a radical change to the carpet in her room or sods being rolled back so the gravediggers can commence! Assessment is already a delicate process, and we need to find a way of acknowledging these problems without exacerbating the situation. The assessment will preferably be carried out by staff who are themselves proficient in the chosen language of the potential service user or in conjunction with a colleague who has that expertise. If this is not possible, an alternative solution might be to use an interpreter.

To interpret means 'to bring out the meaning of'. We must go beyond a literal translation of everything the interviewee or social worker says, which means clarifying the pattern of communication beforehand. The process should be that the social worker will ask a question and the interpreter will initially say what that might mean in the language and culture of the recipient. This may lead to a change in the wording of the question. The reformulated question will then be relayed to the interviewee and the response, literally translated back to the social worker. The interpreter will subsequently tell the social worker what the cultural context was for the reply they received.

Communication is at best slow and cumbersome, and is not to be embarked upon without clarification of the ground rules. Otherwise zealous assistants will start to add their own thoughts and questions, and leave the user wondering who is really doing the assessment. Multiple meetings may be necessary to achieve what could be accomplished in one meeting with other potential service users. Working with community care law in this context, there is the added complication that there is not a consolidated Act, so even the most insightful and articulate can find it difficult to understand what they might be entitled to. The law creates a situation in which users (and carers) need time to clarify their thoughts yet fails to provide the money that could buy that precious commodity for them. Whatever problem there is for the hearing person, we can see that it will be amplified for someone with communication difficulties.

Lest we forget, short cuts here will not produce real savings. Selecting translators from acquaintance, be they family or friends, because they know enough about the language to be able to help out, is not a solution. 'Translating' rather than 'interpreting' is already a step backwards – it just changes one language for another without saying anything about context. 'Acquaintances' may be acquainted with the situation, but they also have their own agenda that may or may not be the same as that of the person for whom they are interpreting.

All this and more applies to Monica.

Race

Overlaying the above discussion are also the communication issues confronting black and Asian people seeking social service support. Research on ethnicity and community care management in Wolverhampton (Cameron et al., 1996) alerts us to a range of communication issues:

- Asian and black people generally do not appear concerned about the issue of community care; instead the emphasis is on self-sufficiency and independence. This can lead to variations in the point at which people start to discuss care needs 'officially'.
- The use of the word 'carer' as a service-created category, rather than meaning someone within the family, is more commonly used by white than black people. It implies an immediate familiarity with

the nature of the discussions around need and the provision of assistance. For those not attuned to the thinking of social service departments, there is then the additional hurdle of 'I don't know what I don't know' to be dealt with before engaging in discussion of which service on what day.

- The difference in the perception of roles by users/carers and social workers may lead to the reinforcement of stereotyped views of the other, which in turn hinder the assessment process.
- Black and Asian service users sometimes have an underlying fear that services will be reduced if people challenge or complain, and this can lead to an in-built hesitancy in discussions about the suitability of the service.
- The knowledge that, in many residential establishments or group care settings, the prospective user will be the only black or Asian person can lead them to decline a service that professional staff conducting the assessment see as suitable for their needs.

Relating social work practice to the law

The legal basis for effective communication

The question that now interests us is the extent to which some of the messages above about communication and good practice are embodied in the law.

Recent legislation on mental health has not shied away from bedding good practice in the legal responsibilities of social workers. If it becomes necessary to assess Monica under the 1983 Mental Health Act, there is a legal obligation to interview her 'in a suitable manner' (section 13 of the Mental Health Act 1983), that is, a manner suitable for her. To maximise communication, we would have to find an interpreter. Life-saving situations aside, assessment interviews would have to be delayed until the appropriate arrangements were set in place. With community care law, this is not so. It is implied in the *Care Management and Assessment: Practitioners' Guide* (Department of Health, 1991), but this does not have the force of law. The Guide alerts us to three factors in the assessment process:

- the need to negotiate the scope of the assessment
- the need to choose an appropriate setting in which the assessment can take place

- the need to give consideration to the involvement of the user in the assessment process.

The need to negotiate the scope of the assessment

What does it mean to talk about the 'scope of the assessment' in Monica's case? Does it mean that we focus on the housing/residential issue and the associated financial ramifications, or do we have to include questions about the psychological impact of living in an environment that might not only present her with communication difficulties, but also cut her off from wider cultural experiences that have formed a part of her earlier life? The legal message is confused. Although the Guide acknowledges that there are different levels of need, and therefore of complexity of assessment, it also confusingly suggests that everyone might be entitled to a 'comprehensive' assessment. This in turn contradicts section 4 of the Disabled Person (Services, Consultation and Representation) Act 1986, which plainly states that:

> When requested to do so by:
> (a) a disabled person.
> (b) his authorised representative, or
> (c) any person who provides care for him in the circumstances mentioned in section 8,
>
> a local authority shall decide whether the needs of the disabled person call for the provision by the authority of any services in accordance with section 2(1) of the 1970 Act (provision of welfare services).

This would seem to suggest that assessments are related to the need for the range of services available under section 2 of the Chronically Sick and Disabled Persons Act 1970, in which case we would refer in vain to that legislation to require us to provide services that specifically addressed the cultural dimension of the case.

The need to choose an appropriate setting in which the assessment can take place

The Guide concerns itself with the importance of meeting people in a setting in which they are comfortable, and also in which it is anticipated that they might reside. Thus if the intention is to support them in the community, some of the assessment must be carried out in the place in which they intend to reside.

In the case of the person with a hearing difficulty, 'setting' has other ramifications. If Monica is post-lingually deaf, the stage at which the hearing loss developed may be critical; the degree to which hearing has been lost and the amount of residual hearing she retains become major factors in her assessment, not just in determining what the pattern of communication is going to be, but also in the assessment of need and the appropriate response to it.

If Monica supplements partial hearing with lip reading, the interview has to be arranged to account for that. Extraneous noises, for example the clatter of cutlery being arranged in the dining room next door, should be blocked out as much as possible. Distractions for the lip reader – the sipping of tea so kindly provided by Ms Gatsby that obscures lip movements, the tropical fish tank bubbling behind the interviewer, inadvertently drawing Monica's eye away – make the task in hand more difficult and should be avoided.

This message about the need to attend to communication difficulties was contained in section 3 of the Disabled Persons (Services, Consultation and Representation Act) 1986:

(6) Where:

  (a) the disabled person or his authorised representative is unable to communicate, or (as the case may be) be communicated with, orally or in writing (or in each of those ways) by reason of any mental or physical incapacity...

  the local authority shall provide such services as, in their opinion, are necessary to ensure any such incapacity does not –

  (i) prevent the authority from discharging their functions under this section in relation to the disabled person, or
  (ii) prevent the making of representations under this section by or on behalf of that person.

The section clarified some issues about the assessment process. Unfortunately, it was not formally implemented in 1986. Subsequently, it was argued that it became unnecessary with the passing of the 1990 legislation.

...o give consideration to the involvement of the ...e assessment process

...ll tell whether former Prime Minister John Major's minor conu. .)ution to the evolution of the welfare state, the Citizens' Charter, is of lasting significance. Whatever political quandary that specific idea was seen as being the solution to, the notion that the law is both a charter of state responsibility to provide services and a means by which citizens can call into account authorities failing to live up to their responsibilities is a discernible trend in welfare legislation in the 1980s and 90s. Public service provision may have been reduced or replaced by the private sector in the past 20 years, and this may be good or bad depending on one's point of view, but the formal recognition of the right of users to have their views taken into account when decisions are being made is a clear gain during that period.

The trend can be illustrated by the code of practice accompanying the Mental Health Act 1983. It reads as a statement of the kind of service that prospective patients can expect of social service and health departments. With regard to assessment, the code states:

> In judging whether compulsory admission is appropriate, those concerned should consider not only the statutory criteria but also:
> - the patient's wishes and view of his own needs:
> - the risk of making assumptions based on a person's sex, social and cultural background or ethnic origin;
> - the possibility of misunderstandings which may be caused by other medical/health conditions including deafness...
>
> (Mental Health Act 1983 Code of Practice, 1991: para. 2.6)

Similarly, in the child care field the 1989 Children Act tells us that when courts are making decisions in regard to children they must take into account:

> (a) the *ascertainable* wishes and feelings of the child concerned (considered in the light of his age and understanding).
>
> (section 1(3), Children Act 1989)

The account of the circumstances in which Monica might be assessed under community care law is of course written as if she were articulate, confident and able to express her preferences. Making oneself heard is not seen as problematic in quite the way it is with someone with a mental disorder or with someone who may not be fully mature. However, this may be to take too much for granted. We should not underestimate the enormity of the task we are asking Monica to take on, and as well as doing everything possible to facilitate communication, we should look at other means of involving her in the process.

Appointing an advocate

'Authorised representative'

This possibility was first envisaged by the Disabled Persons (Services, Consultation and Representation) Act 1986. Ambitious in its scope, it envisaged in section 1 'authorised representatives' being appointed either by the disabled person or on their behalf. The rights of a person so authorised were highlighted in section 2:

> 2 (1) A local authority shall permit the authorised representative of a disabled person, if so requested by the disabled person –
>
> (a) to act as the representative of the disabled person in connection with the provision by the authority of any services for him in the exercise of any of their functions under the welfare enactments, or
>
> (b) to accompany the disabled person (otherwise than as his representative) to any meeting or interview held by or on behalf of the authority in connection with the provision by them of any such services.
>
> (2) For the purpose of assisting the authorised representative of a disabled person to do any of the things mentioned in (1)(a) and (b) a local authority shall, if so requested by the disabled person –
>
> (a) supply to the authorised representative any information, and
>
> (b) make available for his inspection any documents that the disabled person would be entitled to require the authority to supply to him.

Thus the representative could be involved in case conferences, have access to files about the person and be able to put forward that person's own views on what was in his or her best interests. The nature of the advocacy was clear. On some occasions, the advocate might sit alongside the person and provide moral support, but on others, where someone was unsure of themselves or too incapacitated to be able to take part, the advocate would act independently on their behalf.

For someone with mental health problems of a nature that brought them under guardianship (section 7 of the Mental Health Act 1983), the combination of these powers could have created a powerful, supportive advocate outside the social services who had the interests of the service user at heart and the opportunity to make a real impact on the quality of care they were offered. Guardianship, as we shall see elsewhere, has never developed in this way and nor has the authorised representative notion.

Had authorised representatives become a reality, we can anticipate that access to information would have been a contentious issue. The Access to Personal Files Act 1987 stipulated the circumstances in which service users could see the information held on them by social service departments. The Regulations accompanying the Act obliged social service departments:

(a) to inform any individual whether the accessible personal information held by them includes personal information of which that individual is the subject, and

(b) to give that individual access to any personal information of which he is the subject.

(Regulation 2, Access to Personal Files (Social Services) Regulations 1989)

This did not give users *carte blanche* to commandeer the Filofax or rifle through the filing cabinet. The procedure for accessing information is highly structured (notice has to be given and a fee paid), and the definition of 'personal information' has a number of exclusionary clauses particularly concerning information relating to other individuals and information supplied by health practitioners.

The right is to access to a selection of information rather than to everything, and it does not cover third-party access. Referring to the Disabled Persons (Services, Consultation and Representation) Act 1986, we note there that advocates' access information was to have been limited to:

any documents that the disabled person would be entitled to require the authority to supply to him.

(section 2(2)(b))

Thus the restrictions imposed on users would have been the same for anyone representing them.

The ambitions of the 1986 legislation might ultimately have been responsible for its downfall. The critical section 1, 'Appointment of authorised representatives of disabled persons', and section 2, 'Rights of authorised representatives of disabled persons', were never implemented, a curious omission when section 3 of the self-same Act became the forerunner for section 47 of National Health Service and Community Care Act 1990.

The *Care Management and Assessment: Practitioners' Guide* (Department of Health, 1991) tries to retrieve the situation by continuing to support the concept of advocacy and by suggesting that advocates be given access to information in order to express their views on the needs of the person in the most powerful way possible, but in the light of the above, we have to be circumspect about the degree to which this is possible.

Independent advocacy service

The *Care Management and Assessment: Managers' Guide* (DoH 1990a) encourages local authorities to develop advocacy services. These may be internal, with the appointment of consumer relations staff or users' rights officers, or external, where the authority funds existing voluntary agencies to carry out the role.

One area has responded with an Older People's Advocacy Project. This trains volunteers to become advocates and then speak for those who feel unable to make their own representations. The approach has the advantage of creating a pool of accumulated experience at working with statutory agencies that the lone carer cum advocate may never achieve. It can be empowering where users are emboldened by someone they see as sharing some of the characteristics and challenges they themselves face; it can reduce the sense of isolation that many feel when they think they are the only people ever to have been in their position.

Carer as advocate

The reality is that carers often take a leading role in negotiating on behalf of service users. Concern and necessity can create carers who are more familiar with the benefit and community care service maze than are the professional staff with whom they come into contact. There is a powerful argument for saying that they should be seen as the natural candidates for 'advocate', but should they?

Since 1986 there has been formal recognition of the part that carers may play in community care. The Disabled Persons (Services, Consultation and Representation) Act 1986 talked of the need to:

> have regard to the ability of that other person to continue to provide such care.
>
> (section 8)

The Carers (Recognition and Services) Act 1995 now builds on that. This Act has a more confined definition of 'carer', excluding volunteers and voluntary organisation employees, but attaches more significance to the outcome. The Act says that social services must carry out an assessment of their ability to care rather than just *'have regard'* to it.

It should be emphasised that carers are not being tested in their abilities or directed to take on additional responsibilities. The intention is to assess the contribution they make to the overall care of the user and the place that that assistance might have in the package of care granted to them. This assessment is an entitlement of the carer and is specifically linked to the wider assessment of the service user. Carers can request that it be done, assuming of course that they know they have this right in the first place.

In the context of our discussion on the selection of an advocate, the Practice Guide to the Act identifies a range of possible conflicts between users and carers that mitigate against the appointment of the latter to this role. Tension can occur in the following circumstances:

- The user refuses an assessment under section 47 of the National Health Service and Community Care Act 1990. This would have the effect of depriving carers of an assessment of their contribution and the entitlement to support that may spring from it. Carers can only be assessed where the user is undergoing an assessment him or herself.
- The assessment of the needs of one conflicts with the needs of the other. The consequent necessity of undertaking the two assessments independently and of maintaining confidentiality cuts across the openness and sharing of information that might be expected between advocate and user.
- Language is a problem (on the part of either person). As we have seen above, familiarity can ease communication, but it does not follow that the easiest channel of communication for the assessor will necessarily reveal all. Indeed it may be skewed to the interests of the party who is articulate. Carers can be all too powerful in

controlling information about users and therefore not properly representing their views.

● The user's needs are such that professional care becomes necessary and carers have to relinquish their charge. Relief may be one response, but the change of role may equally create an unwelcome void, and the selfish needs of the carer might influence his or her judgement.

With these thoughts in mind, we might well conclude that advocacy should be sought elsewhere.

Self-advocacy and empowerment

Monica could turn to a community care rights project for support. Rights projects in other fields – welfare rights, employment rights, housing rights – are more fully developed, but some areas may offer this kind of assistance.

The type of support will depend on the nature of the project. It may on the one hand take self-referrals and offer people whatever time is necessary to establish their community care entitlements; it may on the other hand be a consultancy service for other agencies in the community care field, with limited opportunities for direct casework.

In Oxford, where this kind of service has been pioneered, many service users found it helpful in clarifying their rights. The strength of the project was its ability to locate entitlements precisely in the morass of legislation, codes and regulations that users are expected to make sense of and to provide a style of assistance that users liked. The approach was characterised by:

● a willingness to allow the user to define the terms of the relationship
● clarity of communication so that the user always knew who had agreed to do what and when
● concentration on the presenting community care issue as the user saw it
● minimal record-keeping combined with a complete openness of files
● a reluctance to refer on.

This was judged to be in marked contrast to the style of staff in the statutory agencies, where the assessment agenda seemed to be set by them and users had to adapt their wishes around that.

With this kind of support, combined with attention to the communication issues we have already dealt with, Monica might be able to deal with the problems now confronting her at Elmbank House. In an ideal world, the rights worker will give her not only the information she needs, but also the confidence and the skill to take up future issues herself. If that does not prove possible, at least it will provide a model for a working relationship between Monica and those who are involved in her care with which she feels comfortable.

Other sources of support and protection

Support can be bought. Monica is uncertain about a range of things, one of which is her financial position. Care staff might have concerns about whether or not her resources, particularly her house, are being used to secure the best form of care for her. In this case we might have to think about sources of professional advice. Appointing a legal attorney is one possibility to be looked at; in slightly different circumstances, in which it was thought that she might have a mental health problem, reference to the Court of Protection might be something else to explore. Both of these strategies are dealt with in more detail in Chapter 4.

The broader issues

Financing future care

In a free market Monica, or Monica under the influence of her relatives, can choose to live in a residential environment if she has the ability to pay. This can be a matter of personal choice for those with money and does not depend on any assessment of needs. We must assume that until Ms Gatsby's telephone call to social services, this was the situation, and there was sufficient money in her bank account to meet the weekly charges.

When she exhausts her funds the situation changes, not just with regard to the question of payment, but also in terms of whether this is indeed the most suitable environment for her needs. At this point the social service department must answer a series of questions.

Should Monica be in residential care?

When the money runs out the residential option is no longer a matter of personal choice. If the local authority is going to be involved in the provision of financial support, it must first establish that Monica needs it.

In Chapter 2 we saw how an assessment is made under section 47 of the National Health Service and Community Care Act 1990. We now need to develop a more complete understanding of Monica's relationship to the assessment process because section 47 is ambiguous. It does not tell us precisely whether Monica is entitled to an assessment as of right or whether the local authority is obliged to assess whatever her expressed wishes are.

For community care assessments there is an underlying assumption of co-operation. It is assumed that local authorities will involve themselves appropriately and that potential users will respond to their enquiries. However, if we look at section 47 of the National Health Service and Community Care Act 1990 from the professional's perspective, the wording:

where it appears to a local authority

suggests that the authority has to make a prior decision about whether it is going to respond to the request for the assessment at all. Assessment as such is therefore not an all-embracing entitlement: it is something that prospective users may get if, on face value, it appears that they may be in need. There is a selection process concerning assessment even before we get to the official system of the prioritisation of cases.

The question of compulsion also hangs in the air. It is not clear whether local authorities have to assess or whether individuals have to submit to their assessment. There are hints but not directions. Clements (1996: 35) has no doubt, stating unequivocally that:

> Section 47(1) obliges social services to carry out an assessment of an individual's needs for community care services even where the individual has made no request for an assessment (and indeed, even where the individual is not co-operating in the assessment process).

This interpretation is based on a particular reading of section 47(1). '*Where it appears to a local authority*' sets the obligation to intervene in any case brought to its attention; '*any person for whom they may provide... community care services*' defines the group over whom they are to exercise this power of assessment; '*be in need of any such services*' deals with any lack of co-operation because it is their being in need, rather than the request for assistance, that justifies the intervention. Without disputing this view, we may ask whether or not local authorities act in this way. Many cannot already respond to requests for attention within the time limits they set themselves without actively going out and seeking additional, possibly disagreeable, residents.

Again in this field, we notice the stark contrast with the clarity of the Mental Health Act 1983 or the Children Act 1989. In the mental health field, local authorities must respond to requests to undertake assessments (section 13) and have the backing of the law if people try to obstruct them in their duties (section 129). For child care workers, section 47 of the Children Act 1989 propels them to investigate cases in which there might be issues of harm being suffered by young victims. Community care law is by no means so clear cut.

This is, however, to stray from our concern with this service user. Let us assume that assessment goes ahead and that Monica's level of need is such that she requires the care that only a residential environment can give. What next for the local authority?

Can the local authority respond purely to needs without reference to ability to pay?

It has long been recognised under the 1948 National Assistance Act that local authorities have to charge for residential accommodation. The level at which they charge is:

the full cost to the authority of providing that accommodation.

> (section 22, National Assistance Act 1948, as amended by the National Health Service and Community Care Act 1990)

This wording effectively prevents a local authority from subsidising its own accommodation and opens up the private and independent residential sectors.

If Monica is assessed as needing residential care, the local authority will have to buy a place for her that is suitable for her needs. In an open market, we can well imagine that the authority will go for the cheapest place that satisfies her requirements and, if that is not available, may support her elsewhere on the understanding that she may be required to move when the situation changes. Monica's attention will have to be drawn to the National Assistance Act 1948 (choice of accommodation) Directions 1992 Number 5, which protects her freedom to choose, stating:

66

If the individual concerned expresses a preference for particular accommodation ('preferred accommodation') within the UK, the authority must arrange for care in that accommodation, provided

- the accommodation is suitable in relation to the individual's assessed needs
- to do so would not cost the authority more than it would usually expect to pay for accommodation for someone with the individual's assessed needs
- the accommodation is available
- the person in charge of the accommodation is willing to provide accommodation subject to the authority's usual terms and conditions.

Once again this emphasises how important it is that the agenda for the assessment is a relevant one. The local authority could take a very circumscribed view of 'need' and couch the assessment in terms of the need of that person for community care services, which are in turn identified as being those services which an authority can provide under section 2 of the Chronically Sick and Disabled Persons Act 1970. Alternatively, it can lean to the generality of the word 'need' and include such things as social, cultural, emotional and religious needs, which might all be addressed by different community services. Given the concerns that Monica has expressed about the quality of care she is receiving at present, it is important to secure the wider interpretation for her.

Monica may now face the prospect of having to move in the light of her assessment. The local authority's responsibility is to provide a service that meets her needs, and it may judge that the sauna and restaurant services at Elmwood are superfluous (and an expensive addition). To resist the pressure to move (yes, we know Ms Gatsby says she does not like it there, but one thing at a time in community care rights), she should take one of the following courses of action:

- Either challenge the assessment: she might feel that it did not take full account of the particular way in which Elmbank House met her needs and the damaging effects that a move would have. To challenge the assessment she would have to go through the complaints procedure set up in the 1970 Local Authority Social Services Act as amended by section 50 of the National Health Service and Community Care Act 1990 and discussed in Chapter 2.
- Or offer to meet the difference in cost between Elmbank and the cheaper establishment that the local authority identified as meeting her needs. She can make top-up arrangements herself or ask relatives and friends to chip in with the readies.

However, this deals only with a small part of the financial issue. To complete our advice to her we need to know how the local authority is going to deal with her financial resources, and to do this they will need to know whether she has 'nothing', 'something' or 'lots'.

For the person with 'nothing'

If Monica has exhausted her funds, she need not worry for the moment. She presumably has some income even if it is only in the form of state benefits. The local authority will assess this, allow her to retain a small amount as a personal allowance and put the rest towards the cost of her residential care. The local authority will then take responsibility for making up the difference. In the event of Monica subsequently failing to pay the fees as agreed, the local authority will be liable for the accumulated arrears.

Where there is 'something'

The rider to 'something' is 'how much?' At the time of writing, bank account holdings of less that £10,000 are ignored. If, however, savings are above the 'disregard' limit yet below £16,000, it will be assumed that each £250 or part of £250 of that amount earns a 'tariff income'. This is then added to the earlier assessed income and the contribution to the fees increased accordingly. If Monica had savings above that figure, she would of course be required to meet the full fee for her care until she fell within the margins outlined above.

Ms Gatsby originally said that Monica was coming to the end of her money. If that is to be taken literally, she has clearly been given poor financial advice. What should have happened is that as soon as her savings dipped below the set level (currently £16,000), she should have looked to the local authority for a needs assessment and then a means test of her ability to pay for the services she was felt to be in need of. Even if her means-tested contributions gradually chipped away at that sum, she would be assured that the residue (currently the final £10,000) remained intact, available for topping-up if she so chose, thereby securing a place in accommodation that the local authority might not deem necessary for her needs, or for spending in the way in which the rest of us might, on CDs, take-aways and birthday surprises for grandchildren.

For the person with 'lots'

Few carry £10,000, let alone £16,000, in loose change; many hold their reserves in bricks and mortar. When service users own houses and then have to move into residential care, we are talking about 'lots', and the tricky question then arises of whether they have to sell in order to finance their own care. The short answer is that, after a deduction of 10 per cent for disposal costs, the value of a house is taken into account as capital. However, if Monica had a partner who continued to occupy the house, its value would be disregarded, as it would if she had a relative living there aged 60 or over, under 16 and dependent on her, or incapacitated.

If Monica does not have a partner or such a relative, the scene unfolds differently. We have heard that the son has moved in. Suppose that this had occurred some time in the past, that he had long shared with his mother and had indeed gradually bought a stake in the property, with the view to giving her some additional money in her old age and to securing his own place to live. The two would then have joint beneficial ownership of the house. The value of Monica's share (and the amount the local authority would take into account in its means test) would be based on the value of her interest in the house rather than on the value of the house itself. The value of her interest is in turn determined by the possibility of there being a market for that interest. If half of the property were put up for sale, her son retaining his residence there, we can imagine that the number of takers would be few and far between and the amount they would be prepared to pay would be limited. It is this amount (less 10 per cent disposal costs) that would be seen as part of Monica's capital and treated as above for 'tariff income'.

The difficulty really arises if the son, or any other relative for that matter, made a more calculated occupation of the house. If he took up residence because the local authority started to ask questions about her ability to pay their fees, if he insisted that his mother had sold him the property for a nominal sum or that she had spent all of the proceeds just before going into care, the questions around the sale and use of the funds would become more problematic. In these circumstances, where the resident had disposed of capital to avoid charges, the authority could decide to treat her as if she had that capital and assess her charges accordingly. Had the transfer taken place within the 6 months prior to her admission, they might seek to reclaim the fees from any third party who had benefited. If the transfer had been made somewhat earlier, the local authority would be on less sure grounds. A transfer of the house from her name to that of someone else 3 years previously, or a less than generous esti-mate of its worth so that Mum did not end up with £120,000 in her account just before she moved into the residential home, would place the onus on the local authority to demonstrate that the decision had indeed been made in order to avoid subsequent fees. Under the Insol-vency Act 1986 the authority could try to reverse the situation by a court order restoring the situation to that which it had been before the transaction, but the passage of time clearly makes it more difficult to establish the intent to avoid the fee payments.

Income, cash holdings and capital are therefore critical in deciding who pays for what, but the availability of any of these items does not affect the level of service the user receives from the local authority. That depends purely on need.

Users anticipating their future care needs have a difficult calcula-tion to make with regard to disposing of their property, which is the most probable source of funds for their care. Monica could have sold up when she first went to Elmwood, invested the money and not yet reached the point at which she was having to ask the local authority to assess her in order that she might stay. Realising her assets in this way, she might have reduced her anxiety about the upkeep of her property and have had the pleasure of distributing some of the estate to her relatives. Had her needs changed and she required more expensive care, or had the fees at Elmwood risen dramatically, she might have precipitated a situation in which the local authority had to intervene and assess, and then ask questions about whether or not the sale and subsequent generosity were a ploy to avoid paying the bill for her care.

There are no easy answers to this dilemma, and as we become a society of ageing home owners, it will be a problem with which increasing numbers of people have to deal.

All of this places care workers in a very difficult position. Are they to respect the fact that service users have the same ambitions as anyone else and are entitled to pass their hard-won wealth on to their children? Should they recognise that, with cuts in public expen-diture, the service that the local authority can afford may not be the best available and therefore encourage users to delve into their own resources to supplement the quality of their care? Does their loyalty lie with someone whom they feel they should empower by laying out before them the financial consequences of their actions, or lie with the employer, knowing that savings in the care budget may ensure that services for others equally needy are not cut and colleagues' jobs not placed under threat?

And if, after all, Monica needed support in the community rather than residential care?

If circumstances prove to be different and the residential option is not suitable for Monica's needs, the conclusion on finance would have been different.

In contrast to the instruction to charge for residential services at full cost, community care service charges do not have to be recouped in the same way. The power derives from section 17 of the Health and Social Services and Social Security Adjudications Act 1983:

> (1) Subject to subsection (3) below an authority providing a service to which this section applies may recover such charge (if any) for it as they consider reasonable.

The authority is able to use its discretion to determine how much to charge and for which services to charge. This changes the terms of the discussion. It raises the need for users, carers, advocates and service staff to constantly test out the boundaries of local authority discretion. Many of those in receipt of community care services are in financial hardship, and even minimal charges can have dramatic effects on the quality of their lives.

Community care services and the cultural needs of people they serve

The debate here is multifaceted. We want to know whether or not services have to be responsive to the cultural needs of their users, whether any specific offence of discrimination has been committed against Monica, and the extent to which a service might legally address its deficiencies by recruiting staff to cater for the needs of specific groups.

Has the establishment contravened the law in the provision of its services?

Local authorities are now encouraged to support the private residential care market, but as they have moved from being providers to purchasers, they have retained the overall responsibility for maintaining standards.

Elmbank will be covered by the Registered Homes Act 1984. If it has fewer than four residents, the controls on them under this legislation will be less rigorous than for larger premises (Registered Homes Amendment Act 1991). Nevertheless, the authority will have some check on the standard of care, although when we look at the scope of section 1, we see that it is not very ambitious. The requirement is for the registration of an establishment:

> which provide(s) or is intended to provide, whether for reward or not, residential accommodation with board and personal care...
>
> (section 1, Registered Homes Act 1984)

Unfortunately, the Act does not specify the scope of the term 'personal care', which is critical. Circular LAC(77)13 has described this as including:

> help with washing, bathing, dressing; assistance with toilet needs; the administration of medicines and, when a resident falls sick, the kind of attention someone would receive in his/her own home from a caring relative.

This indicates a narrowness of vision, suggesting that discussions about standards will focus primarily on the physical needs of the service user.

There is a code of practice for residential care, commissioned by the government from the Centre for Policy on Ageing, which should indicate to local authorities issues to address in inspection, but one would search in vain for specific mention of a requirement that they respond to Monica's cultural needs (and here we might refer to both black culture and the culture of the non-hearing world). As we have seen elsewhere, codes are not legally binding. In an ideal world they could become the vehicle for pushing the diligent inspecting officer to set more demanding standards with respect to the quality of life offered in a home, but this is an outside chance.

For the moment we must conclude that, despite the validity of Monica's complaint, Elmwood has not committed an offence under the Registered Homes Act in the provision of services to her. This lack of attention to cultural diversity in residential care and community care services is widely documented. In Wolverhampton, Cameron *et al.* (1996: 119) have pointed out that, as far as community care provision generally is concerned:

● multiracial policies are noted as being largely undeveloped
● where policies address multiracial issues, they tend to focus on cultural diversity needs, 'seeing "need" as stemming from culture'

- services for particular groups tend to be seen as additions to 'main-stream' services:

> Where there have been initiatives in providing 'ethnically sensitive' services, these have often been 'bolted on' to existing provision, where users are seen as having 'special' needs. Services thereby often simply replace old stereotypes with new ones. (Cameron *et al.*, 1996: 119)

- ethnicity is considered to be overused as an explanatory factor, thus ignoring the immense diversity within ethnic minority groups
- racism is reflected in the general organisation of services.

None of this is to excuse the staff at Elmwood. The fact that other services are equally insensitive is no justification, but what is interesting is the failure to locate any of these issues in legislation.

Has Monica been discriminated against?

On closer examination it may be that when Monica voices her sense of isolation at Elmbank, she feels that the home has discriminated against her. If this is the case, we need to see whether there is any form of redress for her.

Under section 71 of the Race Relations Act 1976 there is a duty on local authorities:

> Without prejudice to their obligation to comply with any or other provision of this Act, it shall be the duty of every local authority to make appropriate arrangements with a view to securing that their various functions are carried out with due regard to the need –
> (a) to eliminate unlawful racial discrimination; and
> (b) to promote equality of opportunity, and good relations, between persons of different racial groups.

For our purposes, it is a moot point whether or not this duty extends to those outside agencies the local authority has used in order to fulfil its legal obligations to provide care for this person. We could just as easily set the discussion in a local authority home. For there to be a case of discrimination we would then have to satisfy four requirements:

1. That the case did involve 'race' as defined by the 1976 Act. This includes colour, race, nationality, although not citizenship, ethnic or national origin, and religion.

2. That there was actual discrimination. The issue is not one of intention but of consequence. If the practices of the home had the effect of discriminating against Monica, it is no defence that that was not the intention.

3. That it was either direct discrimination, in which one person was treated less favourably than others in the same position and that the reason for the difference in treatment was their race, or indirect discrimination, in which an unjustifiable requirement was imposed on people that superficially had nothing to do with race but which in practice meant that people of that race were treated differently. In its crudest form, if Elmbank had a policy stating that black applicants to the home would not be accepted, it would be guilty of the former; if single rooms on the ground floor could only be allocated to people who could show evidence of their families having lived in the area for three generations, it might be guilty of the latter.

4. That the discrimination was unlawful. The areas in which discrimination might be unlawful are employment, education, housing and premises, and the provision of goods and services. The provision of residential and community care services will fall into the final category. This requirement has two consequences. It can help those who have been discriminated against in the areas above, and it can also create the possibility that lawful discrimination becomes a tool enabling service providers to produce facilities responding to the needs of particular groups.

What positive steps could the home take?

Are there things the home could do of a positive nature that would help it to provide a service responsive to the needs of residents from different racial groups? Taking up the discussion in item 4 above, Elmwood staff could use the 1976 Race Relations Act to provide services that are more responsive to the needs of their local communities.

The employment regulations of the Act allow for the appointment of staff from particular racial groups if there are genuine occupational needs for that. Thus in a facility that provides personal services to promote the welfare of, for example, Asian women, it is acceptable to advertise for a female, Asian social worker. Elmwood will of course have to look to its community to decide what needs should be reflected, but there is the potential there to create something more satisfactory for both present and future residents.

If it is not the lack of black staff but their invisibility that is the issue in the establishment, it is possible to take positive action through training. If Elmwood managers complain that they would appoint black staff to positions of responsibility if only they would apply, they should look to their training strategy. Where the proportion of black staff in the senior ranks does not reflect their proportion in the workplace, or the more general workforce from which people are drawn, additional training can be offered to enable them to get into a position where they might apply for those posts in future.

Conclusion

For Monica the messages above may not be very encouraging. On a personal level it may be that we can only intervene after something pretty awful has happened to her, or that things may get better in the distant future. At too many points in the account of her assessment we are faced with advice, guidelines and recommendations but few clear statements of entitlements.

In the face of this lack of clarity, one response would be that we should be prepared to take more agencies at their word, that when they promise users standards of service in their charters and glossy brochures, we should insist they deliver them. The danger in the confusion of community care law is that service providers and service users take up entrenched positions in which one grimly hands out minimal services, as if they were paying for them out of their own pockets rather than the public purse, and the other feels they are entitled to everything without reference to the need to prioritise and budget. In reality, of course, nothing could be further from the truth. Most care workers do have the interests of users at heart, and users are in turn appreciative of those who help if only they are kept informed of what is going on.

If, perhaps for the sake of clarity, we started with oversimplifications – that social workers who knew where they stood legally could then 'solve problems' and that all citizens are equal before the law – we now find that the reality is not so clear cut.

The application of the law requires an intermediary. Someone has to communicate messages of entitlement, service access or responsibility to the public. Where that person is the social worker we can expect an awareness of potential discriminatory practices and a commitment to challenge these. But social workers, unlike lawyers, do not have the same clarity with respect to the primary focus for their attention – they may be all too aware of the web of conflicting family expectations within which they have to operate and feel, just as they work in the interests of that person, that they should identify another, an advocate, who might in turn challenge the work they are doing and believe in.

Introducing us to some hard factual material about the payment for residential services, the chapter has also alerted us to the potential for discrimination in the delivery of services. As we start to read the criteria for disregarding resources in the calculation of liability for the cost of residential care, we can hardly prevent ourselves from wondering about our own futures and protecting our 'estates' for the benefit of our loved ones. This is an understandable reaction but one which begs the question 'What about those who do not know about the rules and do not have time to plan in advance?'

Further reading

Cameron, E., Badger, F. and Evers, H. (1996) Ethnicity and community care management. In Philips, J. and Penhale, B. (eds) *Reviewing Care Management For Older People*, Ch. 10, Jessica Kingsley, London.

Cooper, J. and Vernon, S. (1996) *Disability and the Law*, Jessica Kingsley, London.

Smale, G. and Tuson, G. (1993) *Empowerment, Assessment, Care Management and the Skilled Social Worker*, HMSO, London.

4

Advocacy: Acting on Someone's Behalf

Introduction

In the previous chapter the discussion centred on advocacy, speaking on someone else's behalf. In this chapter the focus is on doing more than speaking up for someone; we are thinking here about situations when someone is (temporarily or permanently) incapable of looking after their own interests. The reasons for the incapacity could be physical or related to a mental illness or disability, or it could simply be that someone does not have the knowledge or ability to understand what they need to do. These situations primarily arise in relation to handling money, especially large sums of money, but this scenario does not arise quite as rarely as one might suppose.

The chapter starts with an example of where these issues might arise. The example relates to a hospital discharging a patient into the community. This serves an additional purpose, namely that of highlighting the collaborative arrangements that need to be made when those who cannot speak for themselves are moved from a medical to social care setting. It also raises another issue, one concerning property rights.

Arrangements for looking after other people's property is an important topic as it is quite often overlooked. There is a temptation to opt out and assume that relatives, or some well-meaning person, are going to take on the responsibility for financial affairs. However, this would be a short-sighted view and one that does not fully respect people's rights. There are specific reasons for this:

- First of all, the statutory social care agencies have particular duties and responsibilities in relation to people's property as well as in relation to their physical and social care.

- Second, people often become very anxious about what happens to their property, particularly as property is often taken to include pets. Practitioners with experience of working with adults who need social care will doubtless understand how much pets can mean to people. It would be a mistake to underestimate their psychological and emotional significance. It is also only too easy to assume that property generally is of less significance than personal care, and as a value statement that is of course true, but worry about what is happening at home or about what happens when they die is a matter that causes many people considerable distress. It is therefore important that due recognition is given to this and some steps made to safeguard people's property or to advise them on where to go for help and assistance.

- Third, relatives (or others) do not always have the full knowledge to take appropriate steps. Relatives sometimes assume they have powers to act on someone's behalf, but this may in fact not be legally correct. Assumptions might be made about what is in someone's best interests or, worse still, decisions made without them being informed. At its most extreme there is the possibility of intentional financial abuse, a form of abuse that may be much more common than is generally realised. While little has been written about this, there is obviously a potential for the unscrupulous to take advantage of someone's loss of faculties and thereby effectively defraud them of considerable sums of money. Even in relatively straightforward cases, some attention and thought ought to be given to this aspect.

The second part of the chapter therefore provides a summary of the legal aspects most relevant to social care practice in the case explored here. A number of issues are highlighted, ranging from hospital discharges to Power of Attorney, appointeeship and the role of the Court of Protection. The discussion will also include references to the duties of the different agencies involved and the legal context in which they operate. In this area it is important to understand where potential difficulties lie and when there is a need for specialist legal help. It should be remembered that this book does not aim to answer all questions. Instead it aims to make readers aware of potential needs and circumstances in which those needs might arise. It is also not an authoritative statement of the law but, wherever possible, references are provided so that further information can be obtained.

Finally, since there is a need to think more widely about these issues, some consideration is given at the end of the chapter to the very broad social policy context within which social care practice and the law operate. Some weaknesses of the current system are high-lighted, which will be addressed in Chapter 9 when the Law Commission's proposals are analysed.

The case described below therefore highlights several key issues for:

- the people or agencies involved in providing care
- people who cannot manage their own affairs
- people who may be partially able to manage their own affairs
- policy relating to the property rights of vulnerable people in the community
- the legal processes whereby people have their property rights safe-guarded.

Hospital discharge summary

Patient: Raymond Clewer
Age: 23
Date of admission: 11 October
Date of discharge: 23 August

Reason for admission

Admitted following a serious road traffic accident in which he suffered severe brain injury and multiple fractures.

Raymond was driving a car that skidded at high speed in wet weather conditions and hit a wall. Both his parents, who were passengers in the car, were killed.

Progress in hospital

While in hospital, Raymond received extensive treatment, including surgery to rectify damage to his skull. His power of speech is now returning, but the capacity for reasoning is still limited and physical mobility remains a problem. Needs wheelchair assistance but may eventually be able to walk with the aid of crutches, although the chances of this are remote. Will need further physiotherapy, but the primary need will be for help with adjustment to limitations in capacity to make decisions and deal with his own affairs.

Discharge plans

To be discharged to Four Acres, a residential home that caters for people with physical disabilities. The decision to move Raymond to this home was taken after a full assessment of his needs, and the full costs of this are to be met by the local authority pending arrangements to sort out the complexities of the finances in this case.

Hospital discharge summary *(cont'd)*

Prognosis

While there is a possibility of very slight improvement, this is only very slight, and it is unlikely that there will be a significant change in his medical condition. It is likely that Raymond will be dependent on care staff for a great deal of support, both physical and emotional. It is therefore envisaged that he will stay in Four Acres on a long-term basis.

Immediate needs after discharge

Physical and emotional needs will be addressed by care staff at Four Acres in accordance with the assessment and review system that operates in the home.

There are a number of immediate practical financial needs that need to be addressed:

1. As there are no immediate relatives, some arrangement needs to be made for sorting out financial matters and taking long-term responsibility for Raymond's affairs. There are no brothers and sisters; his nearest relative is an uncle who has visited regularly while he has been in hospital.
2. Specifically, Raymond is due to inherit a substantial sum of money through his parents' wills. He will also inherit their house, but it is unlikely that he will be able to live there.
3. He will also receive a substantial payment from the car insurance company, which is intended to cover him for loss of earnings. This payment will be somewhere in the order of £750,000.

Arrangements also need to be made on a longer-term basis for the costs of residential accommodation to be met. It is assumed that Raymond will have sufficient income to cover this through the bequest and payment from the insurance company, but this needs to be checked.

Raymond does not fully understand his situation and needs help with this.

What are the immediate needs?

In addition to the needs identified by the hospital, there are a number of other needs worth identifying.

Physical

The hospital has understandably concentrated its efforts on Raymond's physical care, and its plans appear to be quite sound, although some liaison will obviously be necessary to ensure continuity of care in Four Acres.

Raymond will continue to have significant medical needs, and to this end health authority and GP responsibilities need to be set along-side those of the care services. Relevant here will be the statutory duty of the NHS (section 1 of the National Health Services Act 1977), along with the GP's responsibilities under the NHS (General Medical Services) Regulations Act 1992. There may be questions of whether Raymond should be discharged at all, in which case those who know him would need to be aware of appeal against discharge rights set out in circular LAC(95)5.

Accommodation

More problematic will be the issue of whether care in the community should be primarily nursing care or social care with medical support. To clarify this, we need to look at section 47(3) of the National Health Service and Community Care Act 1990 and section 28(A) of the National Health Services Act 1977, together with various circu-lars and codes of guidance, the most important of which may be the *Hospital Discharge Workbook* (Department of Health, 1994a).

Once satisfied that adequate care arrangements have been made, the focus will need to be on the practical consequences of these arrangements, particularly the financial aspect. Who is going to take responsibility for sorting out Raymond's affairs? How does he stand in relation to safeguarding his insurance lump-sum payment and any benefits he may be receiving from the Department of Social Security? Where does the local authority fit into this in terms of community care assessment and their responsibilities towards people's property?

Emotional

The events that occurred in October were clearly devastating so it would be wrong to confine discussion of his care simply to practical and financial matters. However, the two are not separate, and this points to the importance of having social workers involved in cases such as this. No-one wants to take over Raymond's life completely since such an approach would be oppressive and contrary to all social work notions of empowerment. At the same time it is not appropriate to leave Raymond on his own. He needs support both to ensure continuity of care and to help him plan for the long-term future. These plans must both cover the adjustments he needs to make in his life and ensure that he has as much say as is possible in managing his own affairs. Given that his capacity to control his life may change, there may be a need to provide opportunities for regular review and reassessment.

Financial planning

This is important here since it is unlikely that Raymond will have a future source of income, and therefore the substantial payments he is about to receive will have to compensate for an income for the rest of his life. Drawing up plans to make best use of these clearly needs professional advice, but before this can be undertaken, the extent to which Raymond is going to be involved in these discussions needs to be clarified. If his disability prevents him from having any under-standing, what should happen then? Conversely, if his understanding is greater, what role should carers and advisors take?

Assessment of capacity to understand

Clearly then, before definitive plans can be made, there needs to be some assessment of Raymond's ability to understand what is happening. From a legal point of view this is crucial since on this hangs decisions of who should take responsibility for managing his financial affairs. If he has the capacity to delegate responsibility, an ordinary Power of Attorney or an arrangement for someone to act as an agent may be appropriate. Otherwise, there might be a need for appointeeship in relation to social security payments, a trust to control his income and secure protection for it, or even possibly the jurisdiction of the Court of Protection.

It may well be that the hospital's doctors can assist further with advising the extent of Raymond's capacity to understand. This is particularly important if he is to be placed under the jurisdiction of the Court of Protection since the court will want evidence of this. For a fuller discussion of this and the legal options, see below.

What are the roles of those involved in this case?

Hospital

While it is obvious that the hospital has a duty to provide medical care (sections 1 and 3 of the National Health Service Act 1977), more contentious is the issue of the extent of their responsibility for patients once they are discharged. The long-standing convention is that once a hospital consultant decides to discharge a patient, he or she then becomes the responsibility of GPs in the community, the provision of supplementary support being co-ordinated through the GP if it is medical support, or through the social services departments in the case of social care.

However, there may be a dispute over whether the hospital should discharge Raymond at all. In this case reference will need to be made to LAC(95)5, which sets out discharge procedures and allows certain rights of appeal (Clements, 1996: 175–92).

A number of circulars and guides have pointed to the importance of proper planning of the patient's continuing care (LAC(95)5; LAC(95)17; Department of Health, 1994b). In addition, the health service ombudsman has upheld a number of complaints concerning lack of consultation and planning in relation to hospital discharges (Mandelstam and Schwehr, 1995: 244–8).

In this particular case it would also be advisable to obtain the local authority's view concerning placement at Four Acres, since if the health authorities placed Raymond there without the prior agreement of the social services departments, the local authority would be under no obligation to meet the cost of his placement.

There is, of course, nothing to stop families providing their own care or arranging this through private or voluntary organisations.

Community health services

The NHS (General Medical Services) Regulations 1992, which is a Statutory Instrument (No. 635) and therefore has the force of law, sets out conditions under which GPs provide these medical services.

Surprisingly, there is no obligation on health service staff to participate in community care assessments, although they can be *invited* to assist under National Health Service and Community Care Act 1990, section 47(3). However, health authorities do have obligations to provide services under the National Health Service Act 1977, and

GPs have contractual obligations to provide certain levels of service in accordance with the National Health Service (General Medical Services) Regulations 1992.

Social services department

While it might seem obvious that the social services department should be consulted before Raymond is discharged, this is not actually compulsory by law but simply a matter of good practice. Moreover, discharge from hospital does not *of itself* give someone the right to an assessment under the National Health Service and Community Care Act 1990. More relevant here is the question of who pays for the residential care. The health authority, since it cannot oblige the local authority to pay for residential care unless it has told the local authority of its plans, would be prudent to include the social worker in preparations and planning for the proposed move. Nor can the decision to move to Four Acres be imposed on the local authority. Strictly speaking, the local authority should assess Raymond's needs in accordance with their procedures under section 47 of the National Health Service and Community Care Act 1990 and then set about securing the services that meet those assessed needs. If their conclusion is that Four Acres is the best way of meeting his needs, they are clearly then under an obligation to provide that service in accordance with the law and regulations. Specifically in this case, this means that they will take into account the extent to which Raymond can pay towards his accommodation and the extent to which they are prepared to 'subsidise' him.

There is no mention in the case study of whether Raymond possesses any other property, such as a house or flat, or indeed any other substantial possessions. This might be worth mentioning since the local authority has duties under section 48 of the National Assistance Act 1948 to safeguard the property of people in hospital or residential care. Specifically, the local authority has a duty to take 'reasonable steps' to prevent or mitigate loss or damage to moveable property. Further details on both these aspects are provided below.

Four Acres

The home's role in this case would presumably be to provide continuing care for Raymond, but there are one or two points worth making about homes that people enter when they may be incapable of managing their affairs:

- The responsibility for managing someone's affairs rests either with that person, with someone nominated by them or, in exceptional cases, with the Court of Protection. Homes should not assume responsibility for managing the residents' affairs, yet in a number of cases they have clearly done so; for other examples of similar issues, see Means (1996).
- Although the local authority may not actually be providing the care itself, it may have to be directly involved in administering the person's affairs. Some local authority finance departments undertake this role, which clearly has to fall into line with the legal provision made for administering people's affairs (see below).
- The fact that someone is incapable of managing their affairs does not exempt them from the responsibility for financial contributions towards their care. However, if the local authority is providing the services under the National Health Service and Community Care Act 1990, it is for the local authority to collect the fees payable.

Professional advisors

Either solicitors or accountants could have a role in this case since the investment of very large sums of money should be undertaken with care. The temptation is to believe that the sum will easily provide an income for life, whereas in fact the capital can quickly be eroded and financial acumen is required in order to ensure that the best returns are obtained. A legal advisor would be able to assist with setting up a trust, and this is often the most effective way of making arrangements for those who either cannot run their affairs at all or cannot be entrusted with running their own affairs responsibly. For a fuller discussion of this, see below

Care workers or social workers involved in a case like this may well have to obtain legal advice through their employers since payment for services is a major factor here, but there is also a need to ensure that Raymond has enough money to meet all his future needs.

Which law is relevant here?

Local authority duties

Duty to assess and duty to provide services

The discharge plans clearly indicate a prima facie need for accommodation and possibly also for additional services. Raymond would undoubtedly be considered to be 'disabled', and therefore all the legislation relating the assessment of disabled people in need comes into play. These provisions were covered in Chapter 2. Particularly relevant here would be:

- services provided under the Chronically Sick and Disabled Persons Act 1970
- services provided under the National Assistance Act 1948
- services provided under the Health Services and Public Health Act 1968.

The duty to assess Raymond's needs in order to determine which services he needs derives, predictably, from the National Health Service and Community Care Act 1990. However, to underline this, there is a general duty laid on the local authority to co-operate with the health services (section 22(1) of the National Health Service Act 1977) as well as a power to provide after-care for people who have been ill (section 2 of the Chronically Sick and Disabled Persons Act 1970).

Duty to charge for services

This is an important issue since, while NHS facilities are generally provided free of charge, local authority social services department-arranged services are not. This affects Raymond, who is moving from an NHS resource to services potentially financed by the local authority. His financial assets may therefore be taken into account by the local authority. The local authority does have the right to levy a charge, either directly or indirectly, for services that they provide, but this charge must be 'reasonably practicable' for the applicant to pay, that is, it is means tested (sections 44 and 45 of the National Health Service and Community Care Act 1990; section 17(3) of the Health and Social Services and Social Security Adjudication Act 1983).

Department of Health circular LAC(92)27 offers specific guidance concerning charges when these are made for residential care:

If the residential care costs more than the social services department would normally pay, the social services department must still arrange this and pay the full cost unless they can show that there is equally suitable accommodation available at a lower price. If this is the case, then the applicant will have to find some way of paying the extra amount of money if they wish to remain in a particular home.

Note that the applicant for care has this right to choose under the National Assistance Act 1948 (choice of accommodation) Directions 1992.

It is also worth noting that there is authority under the National Health Service and Community Care Act 1990 (sections 44 and 45) to top up payments to voluntary and private service providers.

In deciding what kind of help to provide, the social services department should be guided by the following principles:

services should 'as far as possible, preserve or restore normal living' which means providing

- support for the user in his or her own home including day and domiciliary care, respite care, the provision of disability equipment and adaptations to accommodation as necessary
- a move to more suitable accommodation, which might be sheltered or very sheltered housing, together with the provision of social services support
- a move to another private household, that is, to live with relatives or friends or as part of an adult fostering scheme
- residential care
- nursing home care
- long-stay care in hospital;

generally speaking, social services departments should try to do the things at the top of this list rather than those at the bottom.

(Department of Health, 1991: para. 3.24)

Furthermore, it is possible for local authorities to make direct payments to some people who need care (Community Care (Direct Payments) Act 1996). Thus in this case it might be thought that, instead of arranging or providing services, the local authority could assess the extent of the need for services and then make the payments necessary to deal with that level of need directly to Raymond. However, this would only be true in this case if Raymond's needs could be met primarily through domiciliary or day care services. This is because certain limitations and provisos are placed on direct payments (LASSL(96)11); broadly speaking these are as follows:

- The local authority does not have to make direct payments, but it may do so if it wishes.
- The service user has to agree.
- The service user has to be a disabled person under 65, although the government has declared its intention to extend the system to all adults in 1998.
- Services cannot be part of a package following compulsory detention.
- Direct payments cannot normally be used to secure a service from the recipient's spouse, partner or close relative.
- Payments, being limited to a maximum of 4 weeks respite care per year, cannot therefore be made for permanent residential care.

In no other circumstances are direct payments allowed (section 29(6)(a) of the National Assistance Act 1948). A possible way round this would be for a trust fund to be set up and for the local authority to pay money into this (see below).

Duty to protect property

In the case study, Raymond is the owner of property, including a house, which it may be the local authority's duty to protect. The local authority duty to protect property is probably best viewed as a reserve power for use where no-one can be found to take care of someone's property. It is primarily used where someone is admitted to hospital or care, and includes pet animals as well as obvious moveable and permanent property such as housing. The powers derive from the National Assistance Act 1948:

Where a person

(a) is admitted as a patient to any hospital, or
(b) is admitted to accommodation provided under Part III of this Act, or
(c) is removed to any other place under an order made under subsection (3) of [section 47 of the National Assistance Act 1948]

and it appears to the council that there is danger of loss of, or damage to, any movable property of his by reason of his temporary or permanent inability to protect or deal with the property, and that no other suitable arrangements have been or are being made for the purpose of this subsection, it shall be the duty of the council to take reasonable steps to prevent or mitigate the loss or damage.

(section 48)

Many local authorities employ specialist staff who are familiar with the means of protecting property and the need for inventories to be taken in all cases.

Responsibilities for continuing care

Who is responsible for Raymond's continuing care? There are particular policy guidelines and procedures laid down by the Department of Health in the case of hospital patients. These relate to discharge, liaison with social services departments and the role of NHS personnel in providing further care. Note that these do not necessarily have the force of law, relating in some instances to the *Hospital Discharge Workbook* (Department of Health, 1994a) and in the following instances to extracts from circular LAC(95)5:

17. A minority of patients may need intensive support... Decisions about the discharge of these patients from NHS care and on how their continuing needs might best be met should be taken following an appropriate multi-disciplinary assessment of the patient's needs...
18. In all such cases social services staff should be involved at the earliest appropriate opportunity. Hospitals and social services staff should work together to ensure the most effective integration between social services assessments and care management procedures and hospital discharge arrangements.

On this basis, the consultant, in consultation with the multidisciplinary team, will decide whether the patient needs continuing NHS care or a period of rehabilitation, or can be discharged from NHS care.

Reasons for needing continuing care are set out in this circular; these include:

● ongoing regular specialist clinical supervision necessitated by the 'complexity, nature or intensity' of 'medical, nursing or other clinical needs' or the need for 'frequent not easily predictable interventions'
● the prognosis is that the patient is likely to die in the very near future and 'discharge from NHS care would be inappropriate'.

The circular states that patients can be discharged 'appropriately' with:

● either a place in a nursing home or residential home or residential care home arranged and funded by social services or by the patient and family

89

- or a package of social and health care support to allow the patient to return home or to alternatively arranged accommodation.

Local authorities and health authorities and Trusts should have clear agreements about how disputes are to be resolved. Patients and families should be kept 'fully informed about how procedures for hospital discharge and assessment will work' (circular: para. 25); and in particular:

- hospitals should provide simple written information about how hospital discharge procedures will operate and what will happen if patients need continuing care
- hospitals and social services staff should ensure that patients, their families and any carers have the necessary information, where appropriate in writing, to enable them to take key decisions about continuing care
- social services staff should provide written details of the likely costs to the patient of any option which he or she is asked to consider (including where possible and appropriate the availability of social security benefits)
- hospital and social services staff should ensure that patients receive written details of any continuing care which is arranged for them.

Furthermore:

26. Where a patient has been assessed as needing care in a nursing home or residential care home arranged by the local authority, he or she has the right, under the Direction in Choice (LAC (92)27 and LAC (93)18) to choose, within limits on cost and assessed needs, which home he or she moves into. Where, however, a place in a particular home chosen by the patient is not currently available and is unlikely to be available in the future it may be necessary for the patient to be discharged to another home until a place becomes available.

(circular LAC(95)5)

Delegating responsibility

General principles

What follows relates to Raymond's right and options in relation to property that he owns, including his own finances. Note, however, that if a trust is set up this effectively overrules his right to choose. His ability to act for himself would then be constrained by the precise terms of the trust.

Broadly speaking, setting aside the trust option for the moment, Raymond has three options:

- He could decide to deal with everything himself.
- He could delegate responsibility partly to someone else.
- He could delegate complete responsibility to other people.

In order to understand which of these choices is advisable, we need to start by exploring which is feasible; this in turn means getting to grips with some key legal principles. The important legal principles here are:

- If anyone delegates responsibility for their own affairs, it should always be possible to check and confirm that consent is freely given – consent here has to be continuous and the capacity to consent therefore has to be continuous.
- Everyone is capable of managing their own affairs unless and until it is proved that they are mentally incapable of doing so.

Let us take each of these in turn.

The statement 'consent here has to be continuous and the capacity to consent therefore has to be continuous' may seem on the surface confusing but is in practice comparatively straightforward. A straightforward everyday example may help to explain this.

Imagine booking a holiday. The Spanish sunshine beckons, Costasun Travel Agents make a tempting offer, and you succumb to the temptation, booking 2 weeks on the Costa Blanca. Booking a holiday involves entering a legal contract with the agent. The agent promises to act on your behalf in making certain arrangements, and you promise to pay them for making those arrangements. It is usual for the arrangements to be set out in a written contract, usually the 'Booking Conditions', but in addition to this there are certain principles that guide the transaction. Most relevant to our consideration are the following:

- The contract is specific and for a particular purpose.
- The contract is finite or, to put into contemporary language, a 'one-off'.
- You must be competent to enter into the contract.

Looking at each of these in turn, the specific aspect of the contract is obvious and would soon become apparent if the travel agent tried to arrange your house insurance for you without permission. You would rightly object on the grounds that the agent did not have the authority to do this.

Similarly, even if your holiday to the Costa Blanca were a roaring success, you would be somewhat disenchanted if the agent took it upon themselves to arrange the same holiday for next year. Only one transaction was authorised, and no agent is entitled to assume responsibility for making other arrangements.

In addition, what does 'competent' mean? It does not necessarily mean that you are doing something sensible or well advised; you may have booked the holiday on the spur of the moment, and it may be beyond your current budget or credit limit. But that is your problem. 'Competent' here refers to legal competence, that is, the ability to enter into a legally binding contract. Age, for example, might be a disqualification, since under-18s cannot be held as legally bound as an adult. A more complex issue is someone who does not really understand, someone who is in the manic phase of a mental illness, for example spending money freely and unwisely, or, as in this case, where there is a brain injury that might impede someone's capacity to understand the full implications of what they are doing.

Since the law assumes that adults are competent, at what stage does one become 'incompetent' with regard to entering into contracts? The answer to this is when:

> a person is incapable, by reason of mental disorder, of managing and administering his properly and affairs.
>
> (section 94(2), Mental Health Act 1983)

The law will assume competence unless these capacity conditions are fulfilled. Since they cannot be backdated, as it were, the unfortunate consequence for someone in a manic phase of a mental illness is that they are encumbered with the commitments they took on even if, in retrospect, they may not have been fully competent at the time.

However, there is one safeguard, namely that consent must be continuous. If you give friends instructions, for example, to look after your house while you are abroad, they can do so for as long as you remain competent to give them that instruction since this is technically a Power of Attorney. As soon as you become incapable of giving consent, the power to delegate ends since consent can no longer be demonstrated; this is what is meant by saying that consent must be continuous.

This last point is very important in social care work as people often take it upon themselves to run an ageing relative's affairs and, if challenged, claim to be doing so under Power of Attorney. The apt response to this is to ask for evidence that the person still, as of now, consents to that power being delegated and is competent to do so. If they are not, the power to delegate has ended and there can be no legitimate Power of Attorney.

This may of course not be a desirable state of affairs. Take, for example, someone who rightly anticipates that they may become incapable of managing their own affairs, someone with a long-term illness, for example. They may actually want power to be delegated under an agency arrangement or under a Power of Attorney and for this to last beyond the time they become incapable of managing their affairs. (Incidentally, the difference between agency and Power of Attorney is that whereas an agent has only a very specific power, as in our travel agent example above, a Power of Attorney is more general although still limited to what is actually delegated.) This is now possible by taking out an Enduring Power of Attorney, but this has to be taken out in written form before the person becomes incapable of managing their affairs. In other words, the incapacity must be anticipated in advance.

Having explained the principles, we now turn to specific ways of delegating responsibility.

Appointing an agent

If someone is capable of understanding their own affairs, it is open to them to nominate someone to collect benefits or pensions, or act in any other way on their behalf. The agent's duties are exactly as described in our example above. They are:

- specific, for a designated purpose or task
- for one occasion only, being renewed every time a request is given; that is, agents cannot just assume that they can collect benefit every week.

In some cases it may be possible to extend an agency arrangement further by having a signed mandate that allows a third party to deal with, for example, a building society account. This is subject to the voluntary agreement of all parties, including of course the financial institution concerned.

Appointeeship

Appointeeship is generally a longer-term arrangement particularly useful where Department of Social Security benefit payments are made to those who are not competent to handle their own money. The important elements of such an arrangement are that:

- its use is limited almost exclusively to payments for benefits
- its value is that a third person can receive benefits on the claimant's behalf and make arrangements for safe-keeping of the money, giving out small amounts at a time if need be
- it is relatively straightforward to apply for: a form is available from the Benefits Agency, which then, once satisfied that the claimant genuinely lacks 'capacity', makes arrangements with the person who is the most willing to collect the benefits (usually a relative).

In Raymond's case, appointeeship would have something to offer if he were incapacitated, but this would clearly be restricted to the collection and dispersal of benefit payments. However, appointeeship in conjunction with a trust might avoid the necessity of applying to the Court of Protection, and in other cases appointeeship might be all that is really required.

Power of Attorney

Power of Attorney is simply a formal arrangement whereby one person (the donor) gives someone else (an attorney) power to act on their behalf. It is possible to appoint more than one person to act as attorney, and these attorneys might act jointly or independently. Care therefore needs to be taken in making Power of Attorney arrangements, and legal advice will be essential in some cases.

The legal power derives from both common law (technically law of agency) and statute law, the current statutes being the Powers of Attorney Act 1971 and Enduring Powers of Attorney Act 1985. Cretney (1986) offers a comprehensive guide to these powers.

An ordinary Power of Attorney authority does not have to be in written form but does end as soon as the donor becomes 'mentally incapacitated'.

In contrast, an Enduring Power of Attorney does have to be in written form precisely because it is intended to operate after someone has become incapacitated. In order to be valid, an Enduring Power of Attorney has to be (Cretney, 1986: 19):

- made at a time when the person granting the power (donor) has the legal capacity to grant the power
- in a prescribed form.

While the donor remains 'fully mentally capable', the Enduring Power of Attorney is almost exactly the same in operation as the ordinary power. An Enduring Power of Attorney may be general or specific. If general, the attorney can do anything that the donor can do, except where the law requires that the action must be carried out by someone in person, for example when making a will. A specific authority obviously relates to what is prescribed in the original power.

Once someone becomes incapacitated, that is, unable to manage his or her own affairs, there is a precise procedure to follow in order to activate the 'enduring' aspect of the power:

- The attorney must give notice to the relatives of the intention to register the enduring power.
- The attorney must then apply to the Public Trust office of the Court of Protection for registration.

Once the Enduring Power of Attorney is registered, the attorney has the same powers as the donor did before becoming incapacitated. However, the Court of Protection also acquires certain functions. It can then:

- determine any question on the meaning or effects of the instrument granting Enduring Power of Attorney
- give directions regarding the management of affairs, accounting and remuneration
- possibly require the attorney to produce documents or information
- give authorisation to act that the donor could have given if mentally capable.

An Enduring Power of Attorney can be revoked if, for example, the donor of the Power regains his or her capacity and competence to handle personal affairs. The Court of Protection would have to agree to a request for revocation.

Court of Protection

The deficiency of the Enduring Power of Attorney procedures is that the donor of the Power must *anticipate* that at some future date they will become incompetent, and therefore the Power cannot apply retrospectively. So, what of the situation where someone has not granted an Enduring Power of Attorney but becomes incapacitated? The only way of dealing with this is to invoke the Mental Health Act powers of the Court of Protection. This is an office of the Supreme

Court and is responsible for the protection and management of property in cases where:

> the judge... after considering medical evidence is satisfied that a person is incapable, by reason of mental disorder, of managing and administering his property and affairs.
>
> (section 94(2), Mental Health Act 1983)

The law regarding the Court of Protection is to be found in the Mental Health Act 1983, which is interpreted by the Court of Protection Rules 1994.

Rule 9 of the Court of Protection Rules allows the Public Trustee, an agent of the Lord Chancellor's Department and accountable to the Court of Protection, to give directions in cases where relatively little money is involved. Such directions may only be given in cases where:

- there is medical evidence of a person's inability to manage his or her own affairs by reason of mental disorder
- the capital value of assets does not exceed £5,000
- no house is owned
- income does not come partially from stocks and shares, from a trust or from an occupational or private pension from which the annual income exceeds £1,200
- for some reason, the appointment of a receiver would be more appropriate.

The directions will take the form of authority to receive income, pay various fees (including residential homes' fees), deal with bank and building society accounts, dispose of furniture and effects, and so on (Public Trust Office, 1996a).

In all other cases a full application needs to be made to the Court of Protection itself. It may be worth noting that the mental disorder to which section 94 refers is not the same kind of mental disorder as is defined in section 1 of the Mental Health Act 1983 (see Chapter 7). A medical certificate is required, completed in some detail, but this is normally filled in by the patient's own GP. Specialist psychiatric opinion is not expected. In effect what is required is a much more general assessment of whether or not someone is capable of managing their affairs.

A relative will normally make the application, but in the event of no relative being available, or if this is inappropriate, anyone can actually make the application, although the court will expect a proposal of who should be nominated as receiver and will expect due notice to be given to the people concerned (Public Trust Office, 1996a). The receiver is the person who will deal with someone's financial affairs on their behalf in the future, and it is usual although not obligatory for the court to appoint one. The necessary forms can be obtained from the court, and communication with the court is normally through correspondence. Only where there is a challenge to the application does the court actually sit and have hearings.

The court will expect not only medical evidence, but also duly completed forms concerning the patient's property and their weekly needs since allowances will need to be paid out by the receiver, if appointed.

The court's role is quite wide ranging. Judges of the court may:

do or secure the doing of all such things as appear necessary or expedient

(a) for the maintenance or other benefit of the patient
(b) for the maintenance or other benefit of members of the patient's family
(c) for making provision for other persons or purposes for whom or which the patient might be expected to provide if he were not mentally disordered
(d) otherwise for administering the patient's affairs.

(section 95, Mental Health Act 1983)

When the court has become involved in a case it may exercise its powers in a variety of ways:

1. Where the Court of Protection does not regard the appointment of a receiver as necessary, it can make a short order authorising the administration of the person's property for their benefit. A major benefit of this kind of order would be the reduced costs of operating it.
2. Where speed is of the essence there may be an emergency application under section 98 (Mental Health Act 1983), and the court takes action over specific matters until the full hearing can be conducted: this might include appointing an interim receiver.
3. The court may act through a receiver. This may be a named person or 'the holder for the time being of an office so specified'.
4. The court may exercise those powers it takes on directly.

The role of the receiver, if one is appointed, is very important. The receiver will usually be directed by the court to collect income due and administer the property of the patient, keeping valuable property safely, including authorising minor repairs to property (Public Trust Office, 1996b), and generally act under the direction of the court during the patient's inability to do so. The receiver normally submits an annual account to the court.

If there is no-one apparently willing or able to be the receiver, it is possible for the Public Trustee to assume this responsibility (Public Trust Office, 1996a). While the receiver's role is wide ranging, the receiver is not permitted to make a will on someone's behalf. There are a number of reasons for this. First, it is conceivable that someone who is incapable of managing their affairs under the Mental Health Act might still be regarded as having the 'testamentary capacity' to make their own will. Second, if the person does not have testamentary capacity, it falls to the Court of Protection itself to make a 'statutory will' on the person's behalf if requested to do so (section 96(1)(e) of the Mental Health Act 1983).

The court may also request that the Lord Chancellor's Visitors assist by visiting the patient. These may be medically or legally qualified visitors, or lay (general) visitors, who visit in a welfare capacity and report to the court.

One criticism levelled at the court has been its expense (Gostin, 1983), and it should be noted that, in addition to paying the receivers' fees if they are professionally qualified and entitled to a fee, patients also have to pay an annual charge to the Court of Protection itself. Fees are assessed by reference to a person's cleared annual income after all deductions. They are levied on a sliding scale, currently ranging from £50 for net incomes of less than £1,000 per annum to £800 plus 5 per cent of income for annual incomes of over £15,000 per annum (Public Trust Office, 1996c). Specific tasks carried out by the court are charged for in addition to this.

The court's powers normally continue indefinitely, but receivership can be discharged if patients' mental disorder improves and they are able to resume management of their own affairs.

One final point to remember is that the Court of Protection only regulates the patient's financial affairs. It has no powers to require the person to live in a certain place or undergo medical treatment. Guardianship under the Mental Health Act 1983 can include stipulations on where someone should live and may even require that someone attend somewhere for the purpose of treatment (section 8 of the Mental Health Act 1983), but the grounds for guardianship are very different. For a fuller discussion of this, see Chapter 7.

Trusts

Although a detailed consideration of the value of various kinds of trust is beyond the scope of this book, it is worth pointing out that establishing a trust can be a valuable legal means of providing for someone's needs. A trust is essentially a formal agreement for administering money and property that is implemented by people who can be trusted, or are 'entrusted', with that person's care. A trustee might be related to the person who benefits from the trust, or be a professional person or body, for example a firm of solicitors or a bank. They might even be the charitable body that runs the residential home in which someone lives, although careful consideration would be needed if this were the case. As a general safeguard, there would certainly need to be more than one trustee (but not more than four), although it is in practice conceivable that one person would take the primary responsibility for ensuring that the individual's needs are met.

Trusts are sometimes used by parents of people with learning disabilities as a means of providing for the future once the parents die. The trust is therefore established by a will and can take various forms (Ashton and Ward, 1992: Ch. 9). Devising these kinds of trust requires professional legal assistance since a whole host of considerations need to be made: the rules regarding inheritance tax, the impact on social security benefits, the need to provide for other relatives, arrangements for access to capital, and the effect of the arrangements on local authority charges for community care services, for example.

In Raymond's case a trust might be considered as a means of administering the large lump sum awarded by the insurance company, since it is intended to provide an income for the rest of his life. Indeed, it is feasible that the insurance company might require this. Different kinds of trust can be established to meet varying needs, ranging from a life interest trust (to administer income from interest on capital) to discretionary trusts (trustees granted discretion to administer according to how they perceive need) and wholly charitable trusts (money going to a charity which then provides for needs). In addition a combination of trust arrangements can be used, and some organisations that are registered charities (MENCAP, Charities Aid Foundation, for example) also have umbrella schemes that may help in some cases.

The chief advantage of a trust in Raymond's case would be that it might remove the need for his affairs to be placed under the jurisdiction of the Court of Protection. This of course assumes that there are well-founded doubts about his ability to manage his own affairs. A secondary advantage of a trust is the greater flexibility that might be afforded for Raymond to take some responsibility for managing some of his affairs and ultimately to assume all of this if circumstances permit.

Social policy context

A sense of history sometimes gives clues to why people's needs are not met as comprehensively as they could be. In Raymond's case the distinction between NHS provisions and local authority duties is important. The role of different agencies in acting on his behalf is also of significance, as is the lack of clarity concerning how his needs can best be met. These features can be explained, although not always justified, by looking at the way in which law and practice have developed.

The foundation of the health service in 1947 reflected a clear, popular and political commitment to establishing a new system of health care that was free at the point of need. While over the years some of the basic principles underpinning the health services have been eroded, for example with the imposition of prescription and eye sight testing charges, several have not, and these remain cornerstones of the system. In the UK, visits to the GP are free, and while this is not unique, it contrasts with some other countries, for example Sweden, where welfare expenditure is generally higher but where charges are levied for primary medical care (Ginsburg, 1992: 58).

While local authority social services were established at roughly the same time as the health service, the principle of charging for services, especially residential care, has always been a feature of the system. Thus current regulations regarding charging for local authority services refer back to the National Assistance Act 1948.

In the case study outlined here, this became apparent when a decision was made to move Raymond from hospital to residential care, since while the hospital bed was provided free of charge, a place in residential care was not. This residential resource requires payment subject to a means test, and here the existence of a large lump sum from the insurance claim and inheritance may not be to Raymond's advantage, since it gives him substantial capital but no regular income. A trust might be a means of helping with this, but the point remains that this is an issue that has to be given careful consideration, and there may be unintended consequences of moving from health provision to social services department-organised care.

Differences in financial arrangements therefore make the dividing line between health and social care crucial. In some cases this may partly explain why there is resistance to discharge from hospital. It certainly means that health authorities' decisions to discharge patients are increasingly subject to scrutiny and challenge. Newdick (1996) has explored the role of the courts in cases where health authorities' decisions have been challenged, and the Health Service Commissioner has also been involved in a number of cases. The 'boundary dispute', as Newdick calls it, between the NHS and social services departments continues unabated, exacerbated by increasing pressure on resources for both branches of the welfare state. There is a growing body of case law concerning continuing care (Clements, 1996: Ch. 6) and a number of government circulars concerning this issue (LAC(95)5; LAC(95)17).

Turning to the property issues, one transparent feature of the law here is the potential gaps. For those who are able to plan ahead and are prepared to face up to the potential incapacity to make decisions, an Enduring Power of Attorney has a lot to commend it. Indeed it begs the question of why taking out such powers is not actively encouraged since it would potentially deal with a lot of problems. However, for those who do not, the ultimate power lies with the Court of Protection. Here some real limitations become apparent. The £5,000 limit, together with the bar on home-owners, severely restricts the potential usefulness of the Public Trustee in straightforward cases. This leaves us with the orders feasible under the jurisdiction of the Court of Protection itself. One major criticism of the Court is its dual cost: the fees charged by the court are additional to professional fees payable to the receiver. This means that a whole group of people who own houses but do not have sufficient resources to make the Court of Protection option worthwhile are effectively debarred from its protection. Trenchant criticisms of the operation of the court generally have been made by Gostin (1983), who concluded that, in his view, the court is necessarily overprotective, being a 'worthy' but essentially 'passive institution' (Gostin, 1983: 46). He also pointed out that the law assumed that people who became unable to manage their affairs became *totally* unable to manage any of their affairs; others have supported Gostin's view, pointing out that many people have difficulty with the more complex financial arrangements (social security benefits, annuities and so on) but can nevertheless still manage day-to-day budgeting.

Finally, the lack of integration of arrangements for vulnerable adults has been underlined by the Law Commission (1991), which has

101

proposed the appointment of personal managers for people no longer able to look after their own affairs, but with a presumption of competence even when a personal manager was appointed to avoid the current 'all or nothing' approach.

Conclusion

Besides examining the respective roles of health and local authorities, the chapter has also highlighted the divide between personal and property rights.

With the latter, different procedures apply in different contexts, and a number of historical reasons explain this. The origins of the Court of Protection, for example, are lost in the mists of time but certainly go back as far as the statutes of Edward I (Gostin, 1983: 11). The legacy is an unco-ordinated patchwork with large gaps.

Once again the crying need for a systematic approach to the needs of vulnerable adults is highlighted. Fortunately, some attempts have been made to produce workable reforms. Of particular importance and relevance in this respect is the work of the Law Commission, which has produced sets of proposals covering property rights and private law generally (Law Commission, 1993a), as well as the law regarding the protection of vulnerable adults and public law (Law Commission, 1993b). Some of these proposals have been very briefly summarised here; others will be highlighted where relevant in subsequent chapters.

The setting for the case study draws attention to another complexity in the service provision for vulnerable adults – that it is often based on a combination of services, some provided by the health authority and others by the local authority. We could complete the picture and add that increasingly the boundary between social services and housing is being blurred, many of the services once delivered by social service departments now being the responsibility of voluntary and commercial organisations. There is a clear message here for social workers with regard to developing skills of working with other colleagues from other disciplines. There might also be a long-term message about challenging existing lines of demarcation between professional groups.

The chapter is also about being clear and practical. Successfully responding to professional care and assistance can be as much about knowing that the 'every day' is being taken care of as it is about medication or community care. There is a role for the practitioner in identifying the practical courses of action that might be taken to protect resources, and users and carers might only explore these services if social workers alert them to their existence in the first place.

Further reading

Ashton, G. and Ward, A. (1992) *Mental Handicap and the Law*, Sweet & Maxwell, London.
Department of Health (1994) *Hospital Discharge Workbook*, Department of Health, London.
Public Trust Office (1996) *Making An Application; Duties of a Receiver; Fees; Handbook for Receivers; Information for Nursing Homes, Hospitals and Other Carers*, Public Trust Office, London.

5 Preparing to Live with Someone Else

Introduction

In this chapter the focus shifts to the issues that arise when vulnerable adults decide to set up home together. How can their new status as a couple be legally recognised? How do they set about finding appropriate accommodation? What practical matters arise? How can people be encouraged to do what they want to do yet also call upon help when it is required? What if special needs arise that are separate and distinct from the needs of each individual considered on his or her own?

These are just a foretaste of the kinds of question that spring to mind. It is not possible in one chapter to cover every possible scenario, but it is important to summarise the relevant legal framework sets and for some of its ramifications to be explored.

The chapter will use a case study in which two people with different kinds of need declare their wish to live together. In this example, some anxiety is displayed by professional staff who care for them, with an underlying concern that there is potential for exploitation. Although the precise scenario presented may be slightly unusual, the ambivalence felt by social care staff is not untypical. The case scenario described raises specific issues for:

- the statutory social care agencies, who have a duty to assess the needs of people with disabilities and now have to assess the needs of two such people living together
- bodies who have a duty to provide accommodation or may offer specialist accommodation appropriate to the needs of disabled people

- professional workers, who assume responsibility for safeguarding the interests of those who are particularly vulnerable
- the community, who are not always entirely enthusiastic about vulnerable people living together and may indeed be positively antagonistic, especially when people with learning disabilities set up home together.

Because the topic covered here is rather more general than in previous chapters, it takes a slightly different format. It starts by exploring the immediate issues concerning the status of the intended relationship. It then goes on to consider the role of professional carers, followed by an extensive discussion of a number of options. Understandably, these relate primarily to choice of accommodation. Options will be explored for their feasibility, with the intention of encouraging the consideration of a range of issues, indicating what kinds of legal question might arise. In this respect the chapter aims to be reasonably comprehensive. If, consequently, some professional or ethical issues are not fully explored, this results from limitations of space rather than deliberate oversight.

This chapter concludes with some brief comments. Additionally, some of the themes that emerge will be taken up and explored further in Chapter 9.

Memorandum

Date: 7 July 1997
To: Ms S Lloyd, Group Care Manager
From: Ms Anderson, Head of Care, Summerfields, multi-resource centre
Re: Relationships between residents

I write to inform you of a recent staff meeting discussion that may well have wider ramifications if some of the people concerned seek to raise it with a wider audience, as they are at present threatening.

The source of the dispute is the news from one of our more recent service users (Sylvia) that she intends marrying John Bundage who, as you know, has been with us for many years.

Briefly, the background to their circumstances is that John and Sylvia both live in Summerfields. They participate in the programme of activities in our day centre, as well as being residents.

John is 38 years old and has Down's syndrome, which has made him moderately learning disabled. John has lived in the adjacent attached unit

---

Memorandum *(cont'd)*

for adults with learning difficulties since it was opened. He has participated in some of the 'Skills for Independent Living' programmes, but a move to the Mencap group-care home was considered unrealistic because the level of support there was judged insufficient for his needs. The possibility of his moving has not been actively considered recently.

Sylvia is 32 and is a wheelchair user. With the redesign of the access arrangements to Summerfields last year, we were able to offer her a place in the Springfield Unit. Although she had lived alone in the community until then, she finds that the additional equipment available in Springfield for wheelchair users allows her more freedom and independence.

It is obvious to everyone who works here that John has developed a great fondness for Sylvia. Equally obvious is the fact that she likes to have John around because he is useful to her in lots of ways.

A few months ago there was a review with John, which he asked Sylvia to attend as his girlfriend. John's mother Mrs Kelvin, who was in her 70s, was present, and part of the review discussed John's future. Mrs Kelvin said that she had been talking to John about what would happen to him when she 'passed on'. When the discussion turned to financial matters, Mrs Kelvin explained that she had left the house, its contents and a considerable lump sum to John, who is her only relative, to ensure that he could be provided with the support he would need to enable him to continue to live as independently as possible.

Tragically, only a very short time after the review, Mrs Kelvin died. Within 6 weeks of the funeral, John and Sylvia announced that they wanted to get married. Sylvia says that she and John make a good team, that between them they can run a household that would give John a degree of independence that he has never experienced before. John constantly maintains that Sylvia is his girlfriend and that he loves her.

Some of the staff have strong suspicions that the question of marriage did not arise until Sylvia knew of John's inheritance. They are convinced that Sylvia did not profess her love for John until after his mother died, and they are worried about his vulnerability. They have raised the issue with John via his key worker, and subsequently Sylvia, who heard about it, became quite angry, complaining that staff have no right to make judgements about other people's 'private affairs'.

Other staff believe that John has developed new coping skills since his friendship with Sylvia started and see this as an opportunity for him to move safely into a situation where he would not have to rely on the all-encompassing support he gets in a residential environment. This group of staff are anxious to support Sylvia and John setting up home together and ask whether there is any way in which this can be facilitated. John has also asked his key worker, who belongs to this group of staff, for advice about contraception.

> ## Memorandum *(cont'd)*
>
> When the news was mentioned in the staff meeting in an incidental and congratulatory way, I was somewhat taken aback by the division of opinion within our group and the demand from some that I investigated the nature of their concerns in more depth.

What are the immediate issues?

At a time when the debates about normalisation, respect and the right for all clients to be treated with equal dignity and worth seem to have been won, it may strike us as odd that some staff still cling to more paternalistic and potentially stigmatising approaches when thinking about adults with learning difficulties or physical disabilities. Ashton and Ward (1992: 99), however, warn us that:

> It is not unusual for persons with a mental handicap to want to marry and they should have the right to do this just like anyone else, although until recently every effort was made to dissuade them.

It is sobering, therefore, to think through some of the implications of the objections being expressed by the care staff and see whether or not they do indeed have legal ramifications.

The immediate issue here is to do with the proposal to marry. Like the rest of the heterosexual world, John and Sylvia have two choices before them: they can either get married or they can cohabit. (Marriage is, in the UK, not an option for homosexual couples.) To marry is to enter into a legal contract, and this raises the subsequent issue about their capacity to do so. For them to cohabit may be easier, especially for the staff whose concern springs from a fear that this emergent love is likely to fade as quickly as it appeared, but it places the pair in a different legal relationship with each other, which could have significant consequences if their partnership survives.

The marriage option

Both parties in the scenario are over 18, and therefore the first possible impediment to tying the knot does not even appear on the horizon. Even in John's case we cannot argue that, despite his chronological age of 30, his mental age still keeps him in the 16–18 band, which would then require parental consent before he could slip the ring on Sylvia's finger. As it is a contract, both of the parties to the marriage must freely agree to and understand the nature of the duties and responsibilities that go with it. Concerned and supportive staff may have a useful role to play here. Although they are not the ones charged with the responsibility to check the capacity of either partner, they could usefully explore John's understanding of the situation – they could test out his ability to make such a choice, give him the opportunity to look at the alternative choices and see whether or not the one he seems to be making is indeed what he intends.

Having said that, there is no legal instruction as to what actually constitutes 'understanding', and we can only infer what might be meant by 'consent' from the negative. Thus consent has not been given if a person is under duress (an arranged marriage might qualify as such, although adequate attention would also be given to the cultural context in which it occurred and the expectations and understandings of the parents and child concerned) or if the ceremony was performed as a result of deception or mistake. Although the latter seems a particularly unlikely scenario, it was witnessed in 1997 when a student stood in for the absent clergy in order to help everyone out and not spoil the big day, thereby unwittingly almost invalidating the proceedings by doing so.

In the extreme, if staff (or anyone else for that matter) decide that John does not indeed have the capacity to enter the contract he is proposing, they can enter a *caveat* at the registry office or religious building where the couple intend celebrating their union and thus put a stay on the proceedings. This would have the effect of highlighting the need for proof of incapacity. The objector – and it could be a concerned staff member – would now have produce evidence for the claim that John did not understand the nature of the contract he was letting himself into.

If the marriage goes ahead, it is valid, as long as all of the formalities have been observed, and the couple are free to make the same mistakes as everyone else; going from paper to silver, golden and diamond jubilees, or legal separations and decrees nisi and absolute as the case dictates. Having said that, however, the couple face another potential challenge to their situation. Some perfectly happy unions are voidable. That is to say that unless challenged they are valid, but if the criteria are satisfied, the contract ends. The difference here between void and voidable relationships is more than one of semantics. If they fell into the former category, it would be *as if* they had never been married. Therefore, if one partner had their eye on the assets of another, they would find that they now had no claim because it were *as if* the legal contract had never taken place. Declaring a marriage void may also be a preferred option for members of religious faiths that do not accept divorce.

When we say that the contract was voidable, we recognise its validity up to that point, and the carpetbagger might have a claim on the estate before being sent on their way. The relevant criteria from the consolidating Matrimonial Causes Act 1973 and subsequent Marriage Act 1983 are that, as well as marriages being voidable if either partner did not give their valid consent, so they might also be challenged if either partner is incapable of consummating the relationship or refuses to consummate it. Here we understand the void/voidable distinction. John and Sylvia and Uncle Tom Cobbley and all could choose to have a marriage that did not involve full penetrative sexual intercourse. They would enjoy all of the legal rights and protections that other couples do. At some point in the relationship, however, one party or other could end the contract without the need for a divorce if any of these criteria were met.

John's own situation is alluded to even more clearly in the final definition of voidable. Had he consented to the agreement but was subsequently found to be unfit for marriage because of a mental disorder as defined within the 1983 Mental Health Act, the marriage could again become voidable. The same applies to Sylvia of course – she could also suffer from mental illness or psychopathic disorder and find the same charge brought against her. The reason we focus on John is because of the issues he raises about the multiplicity of definitions of disorder and disability between Acts and the possible points for confusion as one definition is applied elsewhere. If we are supposed to restrict ourselves to 'mental disorder' as defined in section 1 of the Mental Health Act 1983, John clearly comes within its boundary because the definition adds 'arrested or incomplete development of mind' to the above list and then throws in 'and any other disorder or disability of mind and mental disorder may be construed accordingly' – thus possibly capturing Sylvia on a bad day – for good measure! If, on the other hand, we are to take the precise definitions encompassed in mental disorder, the measure for John is 'mental impairment' or 'severe mental impairment', both of which require the necessary conditions of 'abnormal aggression' or 'serious irresponsibility' to be satisfied before they can apply, and from the notes we have these do not seem to be present. That John had a learning disability before the ceremony would not debar action under this heading. He might still have entered into a valid marriage contract, and it is only his subsequent deterioration that leads to this challenge.

Cohabitation

Trouble? Who needs it? Perhaps we should advise the couple just to live together; in fact, perhaps we should just look on them as we might our own children and allow them every opportunity to make their own mistakes. 'Doing nothing' here might put us at the forefront of social work intervention, allowing us to plead normalisation as our goal while at the same time avoiding some sticky legal culs-de-sac.

And so the largest room in Summerfields is vacated for the couple, and they cohabit. In an ideal world the pursuit of sexual gratification would be a right of all adults in the care system. Unfortunately, staff cannot rest easy. Just as the debate about the appropriateness of marriage tested the tension between normalisation and the concern of those who knew better, so the wish to allow John and Sylvia the same rights of sexual gratification raises questions for the staff as well. There is a tension here between the right to exercise choice in the matter of sexual relations and the need to protect vulnerable adults from exploitation and abuse. Much as we would wish otherwise, the staff still have to have an ear to the legal ramifications of the situation.

Staff in these circumstances might have concerns on two counts. They could be worried about their position under the Sexual Offences Act or they could be concerned about the possibility of John getting into a situation where he could be financially exploited by Sylvia.

Under the Sexual Offences Act 1956 offences can be committed against people who are described as 'defective'. Unpalatable as we might now find that label, its broader definition might encompass someone with John's limited abilities as it talks of states of arrested or incomplete development of mind, which include severe impairment of intelligence and social functioning. The degree of disability is crucial because it is a defence in all cases that the accused, whoever that may be, must have realised that the victim was within the definition and thus unable to give their consent.

It is worth noting here that, had this case been different and Sylvia been the one with the learning difficulty, the range of offences, and the consequent fear of staff who might wish to have control over the situation, would be greater as it is unlawful for a man to have sexual intercourse with a woman who is 'defective' (Sexual Offences Act 1956; for a further discussion, see Chapter 6).

If the couple are married, then intercourse is of course not unlawful, and no offence has been committed. This clearly has ramifications for the decision to either marry or cohabit.

What are the issues for professional workers?

The fundamental question is whether, as professional carers, they have a duty to care that overrides the wishes of the individuals concerned.

Let us compare the situation with that of hospital staff who are faced with a patient who wishes to discharge him- or herself against medical advice. In this instance, regrettable though the action may be from a nursing point of view, there is nothing that staff can do to intervene unless the client is mentally disordered within the requirements of the Mental Health Act 1983 or in need of life-saving procedures. Where there is a suspicion that the patient might require a mental health assessment, he or she can be held for up to 72 hours under section 5(2) of the Mental Health Act 1983, a restraining power that can be exercised over all inpatients in hospital. In the case of an immediate risk to life they have a common law power to detain for the minimum amount of time in which to provide the minimum level of care that is necessary to alleviate the situation (see Chapter 7).

Care staff in residential environments do not satisfy the levels of expertise and qualification necessary to invoke mental health procedures, and in this instance the urgency of their concern is not such that they feel that lives are being put at risk. The ultimate answer to whether the duty to care overrides individual wishes depends therefore on the status of the care offered.

The possibility of admitting adults to residential establishments such as Summerfields arises in a variety of circumstances. The degree of compulsion varies, as does the definition of the potential 'catchment' group. We have already seen that, under section 21 of the National Assistance Act 1948, local authorities may provide residential accommodation for people 'who by reason of age, infirmity and any other circumstances' are in need of care and attention that is not otherwise available. Furthermore, the power was extended by the Health Services and Public Health Act 1968 to enable authorities to enter into arrangements with other organisations for such provision in return for payment. This accounts for the existence of Summerfields and the availability of places there for both John and Sylvia. The nature of placements in these circumstances is that they are voluntary and residents can therefore theoretically leave whenever they wish, although in practice the majority of residents will recognise that it is in their best interests to be there rather than seek alternatives.

The National Health Service and Community Care Act 1990 now complements that legislation, and if as a result of an assessment under section 47 someone is thought to be in need of that service, a local authority must consider the extent to which the need is going to be met by itself or any other organisation. Note here that the Act empowers the local authority to carry out the assessment and not to remove a person against their wishes. Thus if that person subsequently declares their intention to leave, there is no power to prevent them.

Where individuals struggle to survive in the community and concern is expressed by others about their ability to live independently, the National Assistance Act also provides for compulsory admission to residential care under section 47 (see Chapter 7). Because of the seriousness of the consequences, it requires evidence to be presented at a court hearing, and the Power is a temporary one. At the end of the order, the person may return to the community; for some this will mean that they start on another cycle of questionable independence verging on self-neglect, or even deterioration to the point at which another admission is sought.

For those who are mentally disordered the Mental Health Act 1983 can be another route into some form of residential care. In addition to the opportunity for informal admission under section 131, people suffering from mental disorders can in some cases be admitted and compulsorily detained in hospitals and mental nursing homes. Again this issue is more fully explored in Chapter 7.

The Mental Health Act also operates in a more indirect manner. If someone is subject to the procedure known as guardianship (section 7 of the Mental Health Act 1983), one of the powers at the disposal of that person is to require the disordered person to reside at a particular place (section 8). Originally, it was mistakenly assumed that this enabled a local authority, through the guardian, to place in care those adults whom they thought would benefit from a residential environment but who failed to see that it was in their own best interests. In fact the guardianship power of removal is limited to the ability to require the police to return someone subject to it to their place of residence but not to transfer them to that place initially. Perhaps a variation on this theme will be one option to consider in attending to the concerns of Summerfields staff.

Some of these issues are clearly for the future. For the moment, let us return to the happy couple intent on carrying out their declaration to leave.

What are the long-term issues and choices?

Whether or not we hear the sound of wedding bells, John and Sylvia still present us with the intention of living together. Although for the moment they reside in a residential establishment that would claim to meet their needs, the fact remains that they are only there because they freely agree to be there.

Leaving Summerfields, where do they go? They go where anyone else seeking accommodation goes and face the same difficulties that other members of the public face. Having said that, we must note that their needs are for somewhere that is suitable for Sylvia, and this will inevitably narrow down the range of options.

The difficult context in which their search begins has been noted by the Disabled Persons Accommodation Agency (DPAA; reported in Rowntree Foundation, 1995a: 1). The research notes that:

> The lack of choice over housing options for people with a physical disability [is] due primarily to a lack of information on their housing needs.

Furthermore, the manner in which information about individual need and the facilities available in specific properties is recorded mitigates against making the best use of what are already meagre resources for a couple in this situation. In Kent, where the project operated:

> Information on adaptations funded by way of a grant was held under the individual property file and was not collated in any way that would assist in the 'recycling' of the adaptation should the property become available. On the other hand, information held by other agencies was based on individuals and it was difficult to identify properties that had benefited from an adaptation.
>
> (Rowntree Foundation, 1995a: 2).

The choices before them are:

- to find an alternative within the residential care system
- to seek accommodation with the local authority housing department

- to approach a housing association
- to look for private rented accommodation
- to buy their own property.

An alternative within the residential care system?

This possibility has already been dealt with in Chapter 3. John and Sylvia both have needs that the local authority must assess under section 47 of the National Health Service and Community Care Act 1990. When they marry their needs will change, and there can be a reassessment. This should include reference to their housing need, and the local authority will then have to consider the extent to which it involves the local housing authority in planning their response. The Departments of Health and Environment in LAC(92)12 and DoE circular 10/92 emphasise the need for co-operation in looking at housing need and press local authorities to go one stage further by also considering housing association provision. Regrettably there is still often a lack of co-ordination between the activities of health, social services and housing in meeting community care needs. In this instance the identification of the need of the couple will not produce the resource, but in some instances it may encourage authorities to consider whether there is any joint accommodation to which they could transfer.

The other outcome of the needs reassessment is that it should identify the range of support services and adaptations that are necessary for them to live as they intend, and this will be valuable when approaching the council or a housing association for accommodation.

Accommodation through the local authority housing department?

There is a tactical decision to be made here. Are John and Sylvia looking at the possibility of being rehoused within the general pool of housing available to the authority, or are they homeless within the meaning of the 1996 Housing Act and, because of the urgency of their need, seeking 'promotion' to the top of the waiting list?

The omens are not good. The tide is against them. The DPAA research mentioned above also estimated that, within its chosen county, only 6 per cent of public sector stock was suitable for people with disabilities (Rowntree Foundation, 1995a: 2). In addition:

The trend towards the residualisation of council housing has meant that local authority housing departments are already having to deal with an increasing proportion of vulnerable tenants. The move away from institutional care also means that many public landlords are finding a growing number of people with community care needs living as tenants in ordinary housing, or approaching the agency for housing through homelessness mechanisms, allocation procedures or through planned discharge programmes from institutions.

(Rowntree Foundation, 1995b: 2)

So if a residue of council property remains in the Midshires area where they want to live, they, like anyone else, can apply. They will probably face a long period on a waiting list, and where their position on that list is based on a points system, even though they might score heavily if lack of access to alternative sources of accommodation is one of the criteria, they will have little credit for the time that they have been registered.

It is interesting also to speculate on how a housing authority would look on their situation. As prospective tenants with limited earning capacity and very specific requirements in terms of adaptations to anywhere that was allocated, it might be that they are considered a high risk. The National Health Service and Community Care Act 1990 did not consider the role of housing agencies in meeting community care needs, yet there is clearly an argument for saying that the housing department should be involved in the community care plan from the start. Evidence from the Centre for Housing Research and Urban Studies (Clapham and Franklin, 1995) indicates that, where this does not occur, it is to the detriment of the user. Housing management staff often recognise that a degree of support is neces- sary in order to sustain certain tenancies, but there is then the unre- solved question of whether the task of the management of property extends to some form of personal contact with tenants. Housing departments can employ a variety of specialists, including tenancy support workers, resettlement officers, family welfare officers and concierges, who perform a variety of tasks that can sometimes overlap with social work. If care staff at Summerfields perceive housing management in these terms, it may be that they can work jointly with housing and not end up feeling that they have abandoned Sylvia and John in some way. All too often, however, it is reported that social workers do not see housing in this way and exacerbate what are already stressful situations by failing to share crucial information about tenants with housing staff in order to enable them to do their task effectively.

115

Also, let us not lose sight of the fact that, despite their needs for support, John and Sylvia also have preferences. It is not simply a question of them having to accept what we put before them. The report for the British Council of Organisations of Disabled People (reported in Rowntree Foundation, 1995c: 3) concludes disappointedly that:

> the introduction of the National Health Service and Community Care Act 1990 has not resulted in the purchasers and providers basing their services on the social model of disability; disabled people's organisations consider this to be essential if disabled people are to exercise choice and control in their day to day lives. Hence the provision of accommodation and support services continues to determine their lives rather than disabled people influencing the provision by exercising the choice and control which the 1990 Act was supposed to encourage.

The couple may well choose not to register on the housing list because of the stigma they feel is attached to council housing; they may find that, in line with the message above, housing staff start from the position that it is Sylvia's disability that is the problem rather than the obstacles that are put in her way by the built environment, and feel that this is not the place where their needs are going to be addressed. In Kent (see the research quoted above) 10 per cent of respondents indicated that they had been taken off waiting lists because they had refused accommodation that they had considered unsuitable for their needs. In a (public) landlord's market even the most deserving are expected to be grateful, and choice is seen as a luxury they cannot afford. While we can understand that housing authorities are anxious to maximise income from rents by getting the highest possible occupation rates for properties and need not tolerate delays when every property can be let twice over, we should still be sensitive to the plight of our prospective new tenants in this scenario. Much is made of the trauma of integrating children who have been accommodated by a local authority back into the community, where they may have the support of their families and peers. Just because the movement of adults into residential care is less likely to be a two-way process does not mean that they avoid similar uncertainties. John and Sylvia have never lived together as a couple; they have not managed without supportive staff around them for a considerable period of time. They plan independence but cannot forecast when they will be put to the test. Hardly surprising, then, that the sudden reality of a one-way key to a flat that does not quite match their rose-covered cottage ideal is turned down. This is an understandable knee-jerk response, but in the housing world it can rarely be set aside and an alternative offered in its place.

Perhaps all is not lost. Could they pursue the alternative strategy? They might qualify as being homeless under the 1996 Housing Act. As with the 1985 Act that it replaced, the 1996 Act hinges on the three crucial definitions: those of 'homelessness', 'intentionality/unintentionality' and 'priority need'.

John and Sylvia may be 'homeless', even though they have for the moment somewhere to live, because the relevant section 175 of the 1996 Housing Act brackets together 'homelessness' and 'threatened homelessness'. If the possible homelessness arises in the next 28 days, the local authority's obligation to them is exactly the same as if Ms Anderson and the staff dumped their things in the car park and returned the deposits on their room keys. So moves can be made, although for the moment they have a roof over their head. They can inform the authority of their impending plight when they move out 4 weeks hence.

Remember that there are no compulsory powers detaining them at Summerfields. John and Sylvia are perfectly entitled to leave whenever they wish, and if they say that the accommodation is no longer suitable for their needs, they may do so. In these circumstances section 175 of the Housing Act 1996 states:

(1) A person is homeless if he has no accommodation available for his occupation, in the United Kingdom or elsewhere...

(3) A person shall not be treated as having accommodation unless it is accommodation which it would be reasonable for him to continue to occupy.

But do they or do they not have accommodation available for their occupation? Section 176 throws light on this and raises the expectation that the agency responsible for homelessness might have a statutory responsibility to do something for them. The wording here is critical:

Meaning of accommodation available for occupation:

Accommodation shall be regarded as available for a person's occupation only if it is available for occupation by him together with –

(a) any other person who normally resides with him as a member of his family, or

(b) any other person who might reasonably be expected to reside with him.

(section 176, Housing Act 1996)

On the declaration of their intent, when the wedding bells are ringing or at some time in between, the point arises that they have created a situation in which they would normally expect to reside with each other. It may therefore be argued that they are homeless and that the local authority has to respond to their need.

The hard-hearted authority could, of course, respond by raising the issue of intention. Section 191 warns that where the loss of accommodation is a result of the applicant's deliberate act (and we hope the decision to get married is just that), or even failure to act, the authority's duty is limited to providing advice and assistance to support their attempts to secure housing, which may in reality mean little more than supplying a list of local landlords.

But this is to judge the powers that be too harshly. John and Sylvia have a case – they are threatened with homelessness because of their change in circumstances and consequently of need, and we are not going to let that be part of a narrow-minded view of 'intention'.

If that is the case, the next step is to establish whether the applicants fall into one of the priority categories. Only then will the local authority have to provide anything because to do so effectively means that, in a period when council housing is scarce, recognising the needs of the homeless means allowing them to leapfrog to the front of the waiting list.

The priority categories recognised in section 189 replicate the position established in the Housing Act 1985. The section continues to endorse the claims of households in which someone is pregnant or in which there are dependent children, and this will therefore continue to be a hunting ground for politicians anxious to pinpoint scapegoats for housing shortages. As far as this couple are concerned, their needs are covered:

(1) The following have a priority need for accommodation...

   (c) a person who is vulnerable as a result of old age, mental illness or handicap or physical disability or other special reason, or with whom such a person resides or might easily be expected to reside...

(section 189, Housing Act 1996)

Definitions, we can see, are beginning to multiply. In the absence of precise criteria for establishing 'mental... handicap, physical disability or other special reason', we will assume that John and Sylvia could indeed make out a convincing case, and then we would have the local authority in a corner. But we are rushing ahead. Before building any thresholds to be carried over, let us reflect on what has happened in the process of working under the Act. The need to satisfy priority need criteria has forced us back on to a defensive medical model of disability: prove the extent of their physical needs, and something may be available. But perhaps John and Sylvia just want somewhere to live. They want clear information about options and the same chance to reflect on what might suit them as anyone else. Then they would want to deal with the physical environment that hindered their smooth(er) passage through life. The homelessness strategy does not allow this. It reinforces the discrimination that they may have met elsewhere; it confines them rather than liberates them.

Still, the happy couple may wish to compromise and accept the keys that may be offered. If so, we next need to consider any other hurdles. Under the Housing Act 1996, when we get to the stage at which the authority has to provide accommodation, its responsibility is limited by two restricting clauses:

Duty to persons with priority need who are not homeless intentionally:

(3) The authority are subject to the duty under this section for a period of two years ('the minimum period')... After the end of that period the authority may continue to secure that accommodation is available by the applicant, but are not obliged to do so.

(section 193)

Of course, many of the staff suspect that the relationship will not last 2 years anyway, but, however strong the bond, we can see that this might only be a temporary solution.

That sense of its being temporary is underlined by the other clause:

Duty where other suitable accommodation available: Where the local housing authority... are satisfied that other suitable accommodation is available for occupation... in their district... their duty is to provide the applicant with such advice and assistance as the authority consider is reasonably required to enable [them] to secure such accommodation.

(section 197)

Where the applicant then fails to take 'advantage' of this advice, the authority ceases to have a duty to them, even though their needs remain a priority and they are homeless.

In defence of the housing department, this final decision has to take into account personal circumstances, which in this case will almost certainly offer the couple some protection, and they also have to consider the extent to which the local housing market can provide something akin to their needs. But the tone is set, and one more hurdle looms – the need to establish a local connection that will hope-fully pinpoint which local authority will pick up the responsibility. Let us just hope that, in fulfilling its responsibilities under section 47 of the National Health Service and Community Care Act 1990 by buying in care from a residential establishment outside their borders, Midshire do not claim that the couple have more of a link with the accommodating area than the assessing area, which thereby transfers the above responsibilities to that authority.

Why not approach a housing association?

Prospects here may be better as the housing association movement has traditionally concerned itself with special needs. Associations can respond with offers of support either within their general housing stock or within those projects designated for tenants with special needs.

Unfortunately, government housing policy may frustrate that goal. With the contraction of council housing, the expectation has been that associations step up their provision. This can be financed by borrowing on the open market, which in turn means that rent levels rise as unsubsidised interest rates have to be repaid. While this is in line with the general proposition that housing subsidies (in the rented sector, if not the mortgage sector) be reduced and that rents should reflect the market rate for the property, it hardly opens up opportuni-ties for couples with special needs that are in all probability going to require further investment if they are to be met.

For the moment there is still a grain of hope. Housing associations interested in supporting people with special needs in their *general* housing stock are able to use 'floating support' to provide services to help them to live independently. That floating financial support is theoretically for short-term needs, and it 'floats' because as the needs of one tenant are met, so the money can be used for another else-where. At one time the money was linked to specific properties, in which case it could have been very helpful for getting John and Sylvia out of care but would have created another housing dilemma once they achieved independence, because the accommodating association would have been under pressure to move them on in order to enable someone else to take advantage of the additional assistance connected with that tenancy. Now the fund floats either between properties or tenants, and the 1996 Act has fortunately neither curtailed that nor set any time limits on how long a tenant might benefit from it.

The benefit in this case is that it creates slightly more opportunity for the couple in the housing association 'market' and is an opportunity in with 'ordinary' tenants – they do not have to be seen as a 'special need' in order to be housed, yet any special needs they might have when they get their accommodation can be met.

What does the private rented sector hold in store?

As we move into the open housing market where money alone determines occupancy, an additional set of questions comes to the fore. They have been there in the past because even subsidised accommodation has rules, but now they are unavoidable. We need to ask four questions.

Can they afford it?

Putting aside any expectations we might have of private landlords either being prejudiced against tenants with the level of need of John and Sylvia or, recognising their vulnerability, seeing them as an opportunity to make profit from the benefit system, we still need to consider whether or not they will be able to meet the market rent.

The landlord might be satisfied that the tenancy is secure because much of their income is made up of benefits, which means that it is reliable. The landlord may equally be wary of taking them on because some housing departments are slow at processing housing benefit claims from the private sector, giving priority to tenants in their own properties in order to prevent the accumulation of rent arrears.

Additionally, if they are dependent on housing benefit, the rent officer will have to assess the rent level. This power was granted in section 121 of the Housing Act 1988. Having abolished rent control, the government was concerned about the possibility of private landlords making substantial rent increases in the expectation that the difference would be met by central government through the housing benefit scheme. With new housing benefit claims, rent officers assess private rented properties to see whether they are unreasonably expensive or unreasonably large for the claimant's needs. The question then is whether or not the particular needs of vulnerable clients, who may not be able to consider the full range of housing in the area and find that they are restricted to those with rents above the market level, are taken into account. This takes us back to the role of the housing department and the interface with social support. Does the housing benefit unit have a policy for dealing with clients who are vulnerable and likely to be exploited by the private landlord? Does the rent officer recognise that awarding full benefit entitlement to vulnerable people may have a community care value over and above savings that could be made by an assessment that did not consider 'vulnerability'?

Can they enter into such a contract?

If the couple are not married, they can still both have their names on the tenancy agreement. The ability to enter into a contract is something John is considered to be able to do until we have evidence to the contrary. The special needs of the couple do not affect their rights and duties as tenants or mortgagees in any way. Although mental disorder may influence the judgement on whether or not someone is incapable of holding property, it does not of itself indicate incapacity. Therefore, in John's case in particular, if he has entered into the contract to rent or to buy, that is binding. If mental disorder were to disqualify him, it would be at the time of the signing of the contract. Had it been known then that he was so disordered and that the disorder in turn made him incapable of entering into a valid contract, it would be invalid.

Where the disorder does not lead to that judgement, his ability to enter into the contract stands. For it to be subsequently taken away from him, his affairs would have to be put in the hands of the Court of Protection. Adding to the list of specific powers already given in Chapter 4, we see that the court might make a variety of decisions in relation to people's property:

> Powers of the judge as to patient's property and affairs. (1)... the judge shall have power to make such orders and give such directions... for –
>
> (a) the control... and management of any property of the patient
> (b) the sale, exchange, charging or other disposition of or dealing with the property of the patient
> (c) the acquisition of any property in the name or on behalf of the patient.
>
> (section 96, Mental Health Act 1983)

The Mental Health Act 1983 uses property in its most general sense; we are interested in the implications of these powers for the more confined definition, that is, the bricks and mortar that John and Sylvia struggle to find and the ramifications of the contract they have entered into with the landlord should one of them fail in their obligations. Clearly, if either party had difficulty in managing their affairs because of any kind of mental health problem, it would be possible for their interest in the contract (whether it were a contract with the landlord or, in the case of house purchase, the other party and any mortgage lender) to be safeguarded by the Court of Protection.

How secure will their tenancy be?

Tenancy arrangements are complicated. We will assume that if John and Sylvia set out now, they are assured tenants under the 1988 Housing Act, but in this area of work you must always clarify the nature of a tenancy before giving any advice. In this instance, the tenancy could be held jointly, or Sylvia might feel more competent at dealing with the landlord and effectively establish herself as the sole tenant. Does it matter? After all, they are in love.

It does matter – and if John and Sylvia get to the point of renting, they need careful advice about the situation they are putting themselves in. As joint tenants they have joint responsibilities. Both of them have an equal right to remain in the property should the relationship run into difficulty: neither can force the other to leave. Both of them are responsible for the rent and will continue to be so even if they find the situation intolerable and move on. If the tenancy is fixed term, it will take both of them to get the landlord to agree to its premature ending; if it is not fixed term, either of the joint tenants acting independently of the other can bring it to an end – and they will need to ensure that they do formally end that tenancy with the landlord; otherwise they will be understood still to be joint tenants and be liable for all the costs that fall on a tenant.

If, on the other hand, Sylvia's name were the only one on the rent book, she would be the sole tenant and John's future would be very different. Living together as man and wife, sharing cooking and accommodation, he would probably be a 'licensee', which would offer him very little security. The ramifications of that status are discussed below in the section on owner occupation.

'Sub-tenancy' is the alternative for the non-sole tenant – hardly a happy prospect as it is not protected by any Rent Act. Should tenant and sub-tenant go their separate ways, the amount of notice is only the equivalent of the period for which they normally pay rent. Settle your bill weekly and you might be out within 7 days. The tenant remains in control here, and if they decide to go, the sub-tenant, even though wishing to stay on, has no particular claim on the tenancy.

A lack of attention to these matters at the outset is compounded by the death of either party. In joint arrangements the survivor can inherit the tenancy, but on the death of one's partner who was the sole tenant, the survivor has no right to stay.

All of this emphasises the contractual nature of entering into tenancy agreements and the obligations that fall on people as a result. The other side of that coin is, of course, the landlord who lets the property. Landlords are also party to the contract and responsibilities fall on them as well, the major one being the responsibility to respect the terms of the contract. Thus if a landlord has a change of heart, deciding that the presence of John and Sylvia in the building has an adverse effect on the letting of other properties, he or she cannot just evict them. 'Assured tenants' can only be made to leave the property if the landlord serves them notice of his or her intention to go to court and seek repossession:

(1)   An assured tenancy cannot be brought to an end by the landlord except by obtaining an order of the court...

(section 5, Housing Act 1988)

In doing so, the landlord must make out a case by fulfilling one or more of the grounds for possession. The grounds divide into two categories: those which are mandatory, and those which depend on the discretion of the court. Thankfully, 'not liking the tenants' is neither a mandatory nor a discretionary basis for getting people out. However, if the struggle for independence proves too much for John and Sylvia and they fall into rent arrears, that can be the basis for seeking a court order under both the mandatory and the discretionary conditions. Three months rent arrears at the time when the landlord serves notice and on the date of the court hearing means that the court has no option but to award the landlord possession. As a mandatory power the landlord does not have to demonstrate the 'reasonable-ness' of the request to have them vacate the property as he would with discretionary ones. If John and Sylvia received notice from the landlord of the intention to seek possession on this specific ground, they would be well advised to pay something off before the hearing in order to avoid automatic eviction.

Under the discretionary conditions, landlords can seek possession for non-payment of rent without the strict time limits mentioned above applying. Having been persistently in arrears but not necessarily on the date of the hearing, or in arrears when the landlord served notice, could be sufficient for the court. However, 'discretion' means just that: the court will look at the facts but also consider circumstances in which the arrears had arisen. If the arrears were out of character, possession might not be granted; alternatively, the occupants might be granted a longer period of time before they had to move out or even be allowed to stay on the condition that they accepted certain conditions.

Other discretionary grounds, described in detail in Schedule 2 of the 1988 Housing Act, also exist. The couple had better not:

- fail to fulfil all their other tenancy obligations
- cause the condition of the property to deteriorate
- be guilty of misconduct that is a nuisance to neighbours
- ill-treat the furniture

because these all fall within the discretionary category.

The legislation is clearly about protecting the rights of the landlord as it was part of a deliberate policy to try to solve the housing crisis by encouraging private landlords back into the market. From the tenants' perspective, the judgement might be rather different. It might lead them to conclude that any toe-hold in the mortgage market is better than the uncertainty or straitjacket of renting – which might equally be part of government thinking.

John and Sylvia might find that the reality of the private rented sector was not quite as comforting as the law at first made it appear. The unscrupulous landlord, uncertain of a result in court, might pressurise them into leaving. That landlord would be committing an offence of harassment under section 29 of the Housing Act 1988 even though the tenant did not get to the point of leaving. It would be sufficient that the landlord or the landlord's agent had interfered with the peace or comfort of the residential occupier to the point at which they might be likely to leave. If they were evicted without a court order, there is the further offence of unlawful eviction:

Damages for Unlawful Eviction:

(2) This section... applies if... a landlord or any person acting on behalf of the landlord...

    (a) attempts unlawfully to deprive the residential occupier of any premises of his occupation of the whole or part of the premises, or,

    (b) knowing or having reasonable cause to believe the conduct is likely to cause the residential occupier of any premises... to give up his occupation of the premises... does acts likely to interfere with the peace and comfort of the residential occupier or members of his household, or persistently withdraws or withholds services reasonably required for the occupation of the premises as a residence,...

(section 27, Housing Act 1988)

In this instance an injunction could be taken out against the landlord and he or she could be made to pay the hapless tenants compensation.

Hassle could come from fellow tenants. If other residents cause them trouble, the landlord needs to be alerted to the fact then that behaviour can be used as the basis of a case for removing the troublemakers, as we have seen in the discretionary powers of the court above.

These are undoubtedly important protections but are meaningless when taken out of the legal vacuum in which they are set down and placed in the context of the real world. People want somewhere to live. Our pioneers want only to find out whether they have anything to offer each other and get on with their lives. How can they do this in an atmosphere of hostility in which a landlord is alert to every opportunity to remove them?

To what extent can the place be adapted to meet their needs?

It may be that the National Health Service and Community Care Act 1990 did not anticipate the impact it was likely to have on the number of people seeking to move from residential care living into supported accommodation in the community. The fact that the Act did not consider the role of housing agencies in the assessment of community care needs meant that the barriers existing between those two departments have often remained, to the detriment of service users. A consequence of this policy is clearly that there has been inadequate planning of the provision for adaptations in accommodation.

Before we look at the possibilities of adaptation we need to consider its place in the general pattern of decision-making in which the couple are engaged. One of them clearly has needs that will require adaptations to most properties. This in turn will raise questions about:

- 'permission': that is the permission of the owner/landlord to allow those changes to be made, especially if in the future this might influence the future renting of the property
- 'finance': for even where public money is available, it may be that the initial outlay is by the purchaser, and it therefore assumes a degree of financial independence
- 'suitability': are there criteria attached to the kind of people who can qualify for assistance, and does their applicability in this case need to be established before all else?

The Chronically Sick and Disabled Persons Act 1970 establishes the fact that local authority social service departments have a statutory duty to make adaptations that are necessary to someone's home if it fails to meet needs that arise from their disability. Adaptations may include minor works such as the additions of hand rails or the provision of special taps; they could equally be extended to cover the widening of doors for access or the provision of ramps, special baths, stair lifts and so on. Many of these facilities might be necessary to meet Sylvia's needs.

The Local Government and Housing Act 1989 moved some of the responsibility for support to housing departments with the introduction of the Disabled Facilities Grant. This grant can be used to cover work to be done on privately owned or even rented properties. Thus the fact that they went into council housing or housing association accommodation, or tried their luck in the private rented sector, need not necessarily disqualify them from this form of assistance. However, bearing in mind that the permission of the council or association, and in the case of private renting that of the landlord, will have to be sought, it would be worth clarifying at an early stage in any discussion of housing plans.

The Disabled Facilities Grant comes in two forms:

1. A means tested, mandatory grant, with an upper limit for adaptations that would ease access to the dwelling and allow the use of key facilities. The means test applies to the disabled occupant and anyone else intending to live in the dwelling. They do not have to be married or related to each other. In the case of private dwellings, the financial assessment takes no account of mortgage repayments. For the grant to be made there have to be recommendations from the welfare authority and the housing authority, which can result in delay and a feeling that it is the applicant rather than the environment that is being assessed.

2. A discretionary grant, which may be added where changes entail greater expenditure. This can only be added where the works are necessary and appropriate to the needs of the disabled person. Department of the Environment circular 10/90 defines 'necessary and appropriate' and yet again brings to the fore the place that housing fills in community care. The carrying-out of any work must be necessary for the implementation of the care plan and enable the person to maintain independence in the community. The circular suggests looking at:

● the assessed needs of the individual, including his or her medical and physical needs

- the psychological needs of the claimant and the carer
- the extent to which the work would increase the independence of the former and ease the burden on the latter.

In making application for grants it does not matter who owns the property (so it could have been bought outright by John) as long as the intention is that the disabled person making the application will live there. Neither it is necessary for Sylvia to be registered as disabled, only that she would satisfy the requirements for that should she so choose.

Although 60 per cent of the cost of adaptations comes from government subsidy, the remainder has to be found by the local authority. This might mean robbing Peter to pay Paul where they take money from their budgets for repairs and the improvement of poor-quality accommodation. It might also be found in social service and health service budgets (where the cost of the provision of suitable adaptations might be weighed against the cost of employing occupational therapists) or the resources of housing associations. Not surprisingly, the level of local authority support for adaptations is reported to vary by a factor of up to 100. John and Sylvia's future may hinge simply on where they happen to live.

Local authorities show varying degrees of imagination in extending help over the provision of adaptations. Where they are willing to take into account housing need in community care assessments, some offer a top-up scheme for those who cannot meet their assessed contribution (Rowntree Foundation, 1994).

Now can they go ahead? No; as always there is a need for evidence, in this case a certificate of future occupancy. With privately owned property, they must intend living there for at least a year, and if they did that but then left within 3 years, the local authority might require the repayment of at least some of the grant. With the rented accommodation the commitment is even more challenging. Assuming that the landlord agrees to the changes, the certificate of future occupancy is on the landlord's behalf: he or she has to state that it will be available for dwelling as a residence for 5 years. In many cases this will discourage landlords from agreeing to the let in the first place.

The final solution: house purchase?

Owner occupation is something to which many aspire, and there is no reason why John and Sylvia should not share the same ambition.

They might find it difficult to locate a suitable property, and as we have seen above in the collation of information about adapted properties in the public rented sector, it is unlikely that they will find that estate agents can point immediately to places that have been adapted or might be suitable for adaptation. The irony of the private market is that expensive property adaptations are often seen as a hindrance to a sale and are therefore removed beforehand.

Can they buy?

If they need a mortgage as individuals or a couple reliant largely on state benefits, they have the advantage of being able to demonstrate a reliability of income that many others could not match, so as long as the mortgage request falls within the borrowing requirements that can be met by that income, they should stand a good chance of finding a supportive lender. There may be problems raised by lenders in the form of a health guarantee before they are willing to lend money, and it could even be that as more building societies become banks with shareholders to answer to, the sense of mutual assistance becomes even more remote.

Who is to get the mortgage and who is to be the owner?

Imagine a scenario in which Sylvia chose to pool her resources with John and together they bought a property: they would then be joint owners. In the absence of evidence to the contrary, joint owners are assumed to have equal shares in the property, and if one dies the survivor inherits all, regardless of any will.

Suppose, however, that they had not split the purchase price down the middle. They would then be 'tenants in common', and the same assumptions could not be made. John and Sylvia would be well advised to set up a trust deed to cover all eventualities. (Trusts are described in detail in Chapter 4.) In this case it would state the proportions in which the property was divided, the circumstances in which they might choose to sell it, the process by which they would have it valued – everything, in short, that might cause friction if they got to the point at which they could no longer live together. On the death of either 'tenant in common', the remaining partner would only inherit if there were a will to that effect; otherwise their share would be disposed of under the rules of intestacy, and the survivor could end up living with a stranger or being forced to sell in order to avoid that.

Without wanting to linger unnecessarily on the nature of the relationship between this couple, we can see that staff might have genuine fears about the possible exploitation of one by the other.

If the arrangement for purchase is that John owns the property and Sylvia then goes to live there as his partner, sharing rooms and with no part of the home as her exclusive domain, they have created a 'licence' and Sylvia has become a licensee. If they then split up, Sylvia's future is dependent on whatever agreement they made over the licence. It may be that this was formal and guaranteed her future occupation of part of the property; if there were no agreement, she would be at John's mercy. As the owner of the property he would have discretion over how to treat her and he could ask her to leave. In due course Sylvia might have redress. The courts could recognise her as having an 'equitable right' to live in the property, but this would be judged on the length and nature of their relationship and the nature of the understanding under which they had first chosen to live together.

Personal loyalties could be with either of the pair; professional advice should be offered to both, recognising that there may well be conflicts of interest. One of the first questions that was asked was whether or not the couple should marry. In this instance we can see that Sylvia would have more protection if she did. As John's wife, even if her name were not on the deeds, she would have the right to live in their home. In the event of the relationship breaking up and John deciding to exclude her from the home, Sylvia could seek a court order forcing him to let her return under the Matrimonial Homes Act 1983 (now re-enacted in Part IV of the Family Law Act 1996). But perhaps this is becoming too calculating and too pessimistic about John and Sylvia's future together.

Conclusion

For the moment we are bound to conclude that the passage from care to the community is not going to be as smooth as some might have supposed at the original staff meeting at Summerfields. This not so much a commentary on the competence of the staff but more a reflection of the difficulties inherent in adapting and applying legislation to the specific needs and wishes of vulnerable adults.

In other chapters the need for a systematic approach to the needs of vulnerable adults is highlighted, and the situation described here certainly echoes this. However, we have here also been outlining how a natural desire expressed by two people with special needs can be accommodated within the existing legal framework. In some ways this may disadvantage John or Sylvia, or it may close off certain options to them. Whichever is the case, it is improbable that anyone would argue for separate and distinct laws that only applied to people with disabilities who wanted to set up home together. Consequently, we must pay attention to general laws applicable to everyone, being mindful of the specific needs of vulnerable adults.

The chapter has concentrated on marriage and accommodation. Other factors raised in the case study, for example the potential vulnerability of John to possible financial abuse, are addressed elsewhere (particularly in Chapter 6). Despite the specific focus of the chapter, readers may have been surprised by the range of factors that need to be considered. It may be that the overwhelming impression is that everything is so complicated, but we must never lose sight of people's rights to live as they would wish and for workers to facilitate this desire wherever possible. Certainly in this case, the more we can iron out potential complexities with an understanding of the law involved, the better we might be in a position to help Sylvia and John plan for the future.

And out of this meander through welfare rights issues, housing legislation and contract law, what emerges for the social worker?:

- a further encouragement to resist the temptation to look only to disability law for service users who are vulnerable
- a reminder of the burden of responsibility of the social worker who takes the 'normalisation' agenda seriously. Informing service users of their legal rights and opportunities may create difficulties in the long term not only for those users, but also for staff who work with them
- an awareness that the problem of accommodating the aspirations of adults with special needs can be accommodated within the existing legal framework. In this instance the law appears to close off options as much as it opens up choices for them.

Further reading

Cooper, J. and Vernon, S. (1996) *Disability and the Law*, Jessica Kingsley, London.

Rowntree Foundation (1995) *The Effect of Community Care on Housing for Disabled People*, Housing Research Paper 155, Joseph Rowntree Foundation, York.

6
Protecting Adults from Abuse or Harm

Introduction

In this chapter we shall be examining the important issue of the abuse of vulnerable adults. This topic has only really come into prominence in the past 10 years or so with Eastman's (1984) publication on old age abuse and a handful of articles and books on the abuse of people with learning disabilities (Williams, 1995). Since that time thinking on this subject has developed with concerted efforts to move away from the abuser/victim approach (Department of Health, 1993) towards one which explores dependency as a key factor and relates this to issues of ageism and sexism (Eastman, 1994). The awareness of abuse of people with learning disabilities has lagged even further behind.

The abuse of adults, especially the abuse of older people and people with learning disabilities, is challenging. It tests the adequacy of the whole care system since there is no fixed system adopted nationwide for responding to the abuse of vulnerable adults. This stands in marked contrast to the child care system, which, in social work terms at least, has clear objectives and procedures, a point to which we will return at the end of the chapter.

The abuse of vulnerable adults also challenges assumptions about what happens within families and indeed within care establishments. For a long time assumptions were made about family care to the point at which the abuse of adult family members was automatically discounted as being inconceivable. Now this is no longer the case, but there is a residue of reluctance to take this whole issue seriously, and this runs alongside difficulties with the legal framework, which tends to assume that adults can protect themselves or can at least seek redress unaided. Institutional abuse adds a further dimension to this since vulnerable adults rarely know how to complain about abuse and may well be reluctant to do so for fear of reprisals.

This is compounded by the fact that relatively little is known about the true extent of the abuse of vulnerable adults. Research into the incidence of abuse of older people suggests that 5 per cent of over-65s reported having been verbally abused by a member of their family, 2 per cent claimed to have been physically abused and 2 per cent said they were financially harmed in some way (Ogg and Bennett, 1992). More comprehensive research in Canada suggested an incidence frequency for physical violence of 5 per 1,000 older people; for neglect the incidence was 4 per 1,000 people; for psychological abuse this figure rose to 11 per 1,000, the most common form of abuse being financial abuse, for which the incidence was cited as being 25 per 1,000 (for a summary of the research, see McCreadie and Tinker, 1993). Information specifically about the abuse of people with learning disabilities is even more scant, much of it being anecdotal (Williams, 1995).

Attempts to measure accurately the incidence of abuse are hampered by a lack of agreed definitions on what exactly constitutes abuse. Indeed one commentator has suggested that:

> It seems unlikely that there will ever be agreement on a single all-embracing 'authentic' definition of abuse.
>
> (McCreadie, 1994: 4)

Official guidance has skirted this issue by suggesting that social services departments should adopt an interagency approach to a definition (Department of Health, 1993). Nevertheless, there is some agreement that abuse takes different forms, the most common typology distinguishing physical abuse from psychological harm, sexual abuse, neglect and financial abuse. Even within these categories, however, there is still potential debate: financial abuse, for example, can take several forms:

- straight theft, taking items without the vulnerable adult's consent
- money being misappropriated; that is, someone is told that money is being used for one purpose but it is in fact used for quite another
- money being withheld, for example money that was specifically given for one person's needs being pooled and lost in a more general fund, for example in a group care setting
- money being obtained by extortion, that is, threats being made that will be acted upon unless money or goods are forthcoming

- money obtained by deception, for example grossly inflated charges being made for repairs that are either not completed or are carried out in a very cursory fashion
- undue influence or pressure being brought to bear to ensure that 'gifts' or even legacies are made where they would not normally have been considered
- people being 'persuaded' or cajoled into parting with money or property
- most contentiously of all, arrangements for gifts to be made in order to avoid liabilities for charges for care services.

While all of these activities are morally dubious to a greater or lesser degree, it does not automatically follow that they are all criminal offences. The owner of property is of course entitled to give it to another person, and even with vulnerable adults the assumption has to be that donors know what they are doing: they are sufficiently competent to understand the nature of the act of giving and its consequences, namely the loss of goods or money to themselves. Similarly, in agreeing to pay a wholly excessive price for roofing or other repairs, it is assumed that even vulnerable adults have entered into a legally binding contract. Only if it can be shown that the other party knew about the vulnerability can there be any suggestion that the contract is not legally valid (and legal advice would definitely be needed if this were a real issue, since the law on this is complex and, interestingly, in Scotland the legal position is rather different). In addition, difficulties will arise if a person cannot remember making a gift or cannot recall events accurately enough to be a reliable witness if the incident does result in court action.

The potential inadmissibility of evidence from a vulnerable adult does of course graphically demonstrate why financial abuse is so pernicious. Unscrupulous individuals may knowingly take advantage of the vulnerable confident that a successful prosecution will be impossible to mount.

The prevention of financial abuse is therefore important, and social workers will be keen to empower people in order to alert them to potential situations where abuse might occur and where there is the possibility of being exploited.

Furthermore, the abuse of vulnerable adults brings into focus a whole range of questions about social policy more generally. What should be the balance between the desire to protect vulnerable adults and their rights to self-determination? To what extent should social workers and others intervene in families where there is abuse? Should there be any difference between the response to abuse of vulnerable adults and the response to child abuse?

These are some of the issues that this chapter aims to address. The legal context here is important, not so much for the protection that it provides but more for the lack of a systematic approach to the whole issue. Consequently, clarifying roles and actions in cases of abuse of adults involves picking a careful path through a range of laws none of which was directly intended to address this issue.

The purpose of this approach is to highlight how and where aspects of the law might be relevant to the case and to provide a focus for social work practice. At the same time it is recognised that direct referrals to social services departments of suspected abuse are rare and that it is more likely that a sensitive observer will become suspicious of abuse; thus the approach to abuse may have to be indirect. This will be the case particularly if abuse within a care establishment itself is suspected. Nevertheless, the same principles of practice and legal framework will apply.

The first part of the chapter takes the reader through cases in which abuse or harm is the primary object of attention. The first case highlights physical abuse and the second possible sexual abuse, while the third focuses on financial abuse. It may seem odd to suggest that someone can suffer financial *abuse*, but it is becoming apparent that financial abuse may be quite widespread (McCreadie, 1994) and it is certainly true that relatively little attention has been directed to this form of abuse.

The second part of the chapter explains what remedies are currently available in situations in which abuse is suspected, and this will inevitably lead to consideration of the adequacy of the current framework. Here the comparison with child care law may be relevant, the Law Commission proposing a model that imports child protection responsibilities and procedures into work with vulnerable adults (Law Commission, 1993a) although this has not been without its critics (Penhale, 1994).

The cases described highlight several key issues for:

- agencies receiving an allegation that someone is being abused
- the professional workers involved
- the person who may have been abused
- policy relating to family care where help or care may be needed but has not been requested
- the legal system itself.

All of these aspects will be highlighted in this chapter, which takes the following form:

- a discussion of the relevant issues for professional workers
- the roles of the various agencies involved in the case
- responding to the immediate needs
- the legal context
- the broader policy issues and need for reforms in this area.

The cases

In the first case, the social services department receives a letter that outlines some very real anxieties about an older person.

Telephone: 01115 437999
                                                43, South Street
                                                        Monkton
                                                        Midshire

                                            21 November 1996

To the Director of Social Services,
County Hall, Midshire

Dear Sir/Madam,

I am writing to you about a neighbour of mine, Mrs Hilda Bates, who lives at number 41.

As you are aware, or at least I assume you are aware, Mrs Bates is in her 80s and is cared for by her daughter, Rosalind Bates, who took early retirement from her job in British Telecom in order to care for her mother.

I am very concerned about Hilda as she is totally dependent on her daughter and has no-one to turn to except me when things are going wrong, as they are at the moment. And they are going very wrong at the moment. Please, please, you MUST do something. I have heard Hilda screaming with pain because of the way her daughter is treating her. Several times I have heard Rosalind shouting at her mother, and I am sure I heard her being slapped the other day. It is easy for me to hear as I live next door and this is a terraced house. Last night was the worst ever. I heard Rosalind shouting for ages at her mother and this was followed by the sound of several very hard slaps. I am sure I heard Rosalind shouting that that will teach you a lesson or something like that. This was just before the 9 o'clock news. I couldn't concentrate afterwards. I didn't know what to do. I couldn't sleep for worrying so I decided I just had to do something. This morning I telephoned the Citizen's Advice Bureau and they suggested I write to you.

cont'd

When Rosalind first retired 2 years ago, things seemed fine, but I have to admit Hilda is getting more demanding. She has taken to wandering at night, and the last time I saw her in the garden she did not recognise me but wanted to know what I thought I was doing in Betty's garden, which was a bit much as I am Betty and this is MY garden. Even so, it does not excuse Rosalind striking her mother.

When is your department going to do something about this? I know one of your social workers has visited, but Hilda told me nothing came of it as they were told she could go to a day centre but they would have to pay. Is that really true? It seems a bit much that people in desperate need have to pay just to go to a day centre for a meal and a chat. Instead they are forced to stay at home, and if someone doesn't do something quickly poor Hilda is really going to suffer. You see, there are no other relatives at all. Poor Hilda's only sister died a couple of months ago and there are no other children. We have always been quite friendly, but I just never see her now as she rarely goes into the garden and she never pops round for a chat.

I am sorry if this letter is rambling but I am VERY, VERY, VERY concerned about Hilda and insist that you do something or else I will have to write to the MP. Please do not tell them I have written to you as Rosalind has a fiery temper and we do not really speak to each other since our disagreement about that tree of hers which was overhanging into my garden.

Yours sincerely,

Betty Smith

What are the issues for professional workers?

The arrival of this letter is likely to have an immediate impact on professional workers. A number of conflicting emotions are aroused. If the allegations are well founded, there is:

- obvious sympathy for the victim of abuse
- abhorrence at the thought of vulnerable adults being abuse victims at all
- a desire to 'rescue' Hilda Bates
- yet at the same time, sympathy for the abuser: how did this situation come about, how can someone demean themselves by assaulting another human being?
- workers might also want to reflect on the stresses and tensions created by this situation.

Whatever workers' individual feelings might be, it is important to be honest and open about these and to take time to reflect on them. It is comparatively easy either to over-react or to 'under'-react to cases such as this; getting the balance right involves reflective thought and careful consideration.

In addition there are some issues that lie just beneath the surface:

● Workers who are honest about their feelings might admit to a lurking doubt about the letter: is there an ulterior motive hinted at by the reference to the dispute about the tree? Is the letter entirely accurate? What is the relationship between the neighbours?
● What about issues of confidentiality? Is it really possible or desirable to adhere to Betty Smith's request for anonymity?
● What about rights to self-determination? Is it really acceptable to interfere in people's private lives to the extent to which the letter assumes? Can social workers intervene at all if an adult has not specifically requested this for themselves?
● Given the whole range and mixture of emotions, how should one proceed to unravel this request?

Role of the social services department

In this case, the responsibilities of the social services department are not as clear cut as one might assume. Specifically:

● There is no statutory duty to investigate allegations of abuse of vulnerable adults as such.
● There is no entitlement to information from other agencies.
● There is no clear national procedure set out for responding to abuse, although some social services departments, Kent and Enfield for example, have set out their own procedures (Pritchard, 1995, Appendix 1 and Appendix 2).
● The only specific duties relate to the assessment and provision of services (see Chapter 2).
● Consequently, the local authority has to rely on its duty to identify vulnerable adults in need and to offer services, duties that derive principally from the Chronically Sick and Disabled Persons Act 1970 and the National Health Service and Community Care Act 1990.

Responding to allegations of abuse

The letter from Betty Smith could be responded to in a number of different ways. Each strategy has its own merits and disadvantages. It may be useful to demonstrate this with a diagram.

Table 6.1   Response options

Action	Advantages	Disadvantages
Go to see Betty Smith, who wrote the letter	Is an immediate response to concerns raised Could help to clarify a number of issues Involves complainant in decision-making about what happens next	Ethical issues: is it right to discuss this without the Bates' permission? There might not be any more information to give Could put Betty in difficult position
Go to see Hilda Bates on her own	Would be able to ask about abuse Might be able to assess whether being abused Would be able to offer services	Explaining response without breaching confidentiality Reticence about confiding abuse Hilda may not be able to talk about it anyway
Go to see Rosalind Bates on her own	Would be able to ask about abuse Might be able to secure her co-operation Would be able to offer services	Explaining response without breaching confidentiality Reticence about confiding abuse May be refused permission to see Hilda, which would place the social worker in a dilemma
Go to see Hilda and Rosalind Bates together	Would be able to ask about abuse or at least observe mother and daughter together Appears more respectful of their rights Would be able to offer services	Explaining response without breaching confidentiality Reticence about confiding abuse One person may be inhibited about talking in front of the other

Table 6.1 (cont'd)

Action	Advantages	Disadvantages
Refer case to the police	If abuse has occurred, this is an offence, and it is the duty of the police to investigate offences Interrogation skills Emphasises seriousness of abuse	Have not been asked to do this 'Heavy' intervention In any case, what would one expect the police to do?
Refer case to the health services	Access to help needed May be more acceptable to family Health professional probably already known to family	No remit to do this Ethical issues: health professionals may well refuse because of this Social care and assessment for services are not the responsibility of health services

There are in fact a number of preliminary actions that one could consider. This assumes that the option of doing nothing, which ignores the needs of a vulnerable adult who is possibly being abused, is discounted.

1. Ask Betty Smith for more information. Although it may be that there is not much more information for her to give. Nevertheless, this would indicate that the letter is being taken seriously and reassure her that the department wants to respond. It may be at this stage that one has to be honest about the limitations of a possible investigation, given the strictures that Betty Smith has laid down.
2. Ask Betty Smith for permission to share information. Again this provides reassurances that the complaint is being taken seriously, at the same time clarifying exactly what can and cannot be done, given the contents of the letter. It may be that the social worker has to be quite open about the limited possibilities of action unless Betty withdraws some of her provisos. If Betty were still reluctant to allow information to be shared, one consequence could be for an agreed plan of action to be negotiated. Although it may not be totally reassuring, this would at least make clear the boundaries within which social workers can operate and why the scope for action is so limited.

3. Find out what other agencies know. This might seem an obvious first step in any case, although the ethical considerations concerning breach of confidentiality are still relevant and the point about lack of entitlement to information, even in cases of abuse of vulnerable adults, needs to be reiterated.

4. Call a case conference. This is the plan of action favoured by most social services departments that have set out clear guidelines for staff. It mirrors the general approach taken in child abuse cases, although the possibilities of action are necessarily less wide ranging. This is of course not being suggested as a course of action on its own, but would run alongside or follow on from one or more of the actions listed above.

The fact that there is no obvious strategy that commends itself underlines the difficulties that social workers face in this area and the reasons why commentators have suggested the need for greater clarity. A number of social services departments have set out their own codes of practice and procedures (see, for example, Pritchard, 1995: Ch. 3), but it must be recognised that these are codes devised voluntarily by departments for their own staff and lack the legal backing that exists for social services departments in children's cases.

In the second case, the manager of a day care centre for people with learning disabilities receives a complaint about the activities of someone who attends the centre.

Twelvetrees Manager: I have asked for this urgent staff consultation because, as you know, we have just received a complaint from Belinda Jones that her daughter Sarah was 'touched up', as she put it, by one of the men who attends the centre. This apparently happened on the way home on the transport. Before I do anything about this, I would like some agreement among the staff on what we should do about this.

Deputy Manager: It's obvious. We call the police in straight away.

Assistant Manager: No, we do not. It's true we cannot investigate this ourselves as we are a voluntary organisation, so we have to report this to the social services department. But first of all, shouldn't we find out if Sarah

cont'd

---

	wants to make a complaint? You know how protective Belinda Jones is, and this may just all be a misunderstanding, or alternatively Sarah might have enjoyed it.
Deputy Manger:	I disagree. If we take that line, we'll be accused of colluding. After all, we have a duty to stop this kind of thing happening.
Manager:	But we don't know yet whether anything did happen.

What are the issues for professional workers?

The dilemma for the workers comes across from their discussion and is a very real one. Are care workers really equipped to carry out investigations of this nature? Is there a danger that they may not do so impartially, since they may not want the adverse publicity that comes from incidents of this nature? In any case, what is the purpose of the investigation and for whose benefit is it to be carried out? This reflects back on to some more fundamental issues:

- Care workers may resist the idea that they should be involved in discussing people's sexual activity.
- Consequently, it is tempting to assume that people with learning disabilities are entitled to engage in sexual behaviour just as all other adults do and that this is no-one else's business.
- Conversely, care workers can also be overprotective and start investigating all sorts of trivial incidents.
- Thus the question is raised of whose interests are being protected here.

These are all, of course, significant ethical issues, and there are no easy answers. However, a first preliminary step is to ask how the legal framework fits this case.

142

What are the roles of those involved in the case?

Twelvetrees

We are told that Twelvetrees is a voluntary organisation, but the status of the organisation does not actually matter greatly. While it is important to be clear on what exactly is alleged, it is also important to recognise that, if the allegation is that someone has been assaulted against their wishes, doing nothing is not really an option. It is a common law principle that every citizen has the duty to report a crime, and it is certainly not open to an organisation to mediate or filter the victim's right to report what has happened to them.

The local authority

The assumption that the social services department has greater power to carry out an investigation may be a myth since the department does not have the same duties or powers regarding vulnerable adults as it does in relation to children. In fact, many social services departments would not have set procedures in cases such as this, although there are some notable exceptions (London Borough of Greenwich, 1993).

The police

Interpreting the complaint, it may be that what is alleged is indecent assault. If this is the case, it would be open for the police to investigate. (Certain lesser degrees of assault are deemed to be private matters in which individuals might mount a private prosecution.) Indecent assault is, according to case law, in 'contravention of the standards of decent behaviour of right thinking members of society in regard to sexual modesty or privacy' (Cross *et al.*, 1995: 272). The assault must be intentional, and if the other person is incapable of consenting, it must be proved that the assailant knew that the victim was unable to consent (section 14 of the Sexual Offences Act 1956). There is further consideration of the law relating to abuse later in this chapter.

For the third case, we explore the issue of financial abuse when it is suspected to have occurred in a residential establishment.

Florence Carpenter, aged 82, lives in Beechwood House, a 20-bed residential home run by the Munificent Association of Cordwainers and Scriveners. The home is run by this registered charity on a non-profit-making basis, with a mixture of self-financing and 'sponsored' residents. Its standards of care are considered by the inspectorate to be 'exemplary'.

Mrs Carpenter, who moved into Beechwood House 2 years ago (3 months after being widowed), meets the cost of her own fees. She is in fact comparatively well off since she is entitled to a pension in her own right as she worked all her life in local government, and she also has a widow's pension from her husband's employer's scheme (who was of course a cordwainer, hence her entitlement to a place in the home). In addition two large lump sums have come her way from her husband's life insurance policy and from the sale of her home shortly after she moved into residential care.

The manager of the home has recently contacted the local authority inspectorate for advice as she was horrified to discover that Mrs Carpenter has been giving away large sums of money, to the extent that she will shortly be encountering difficulties meeting the charity's charges for accommodation. The manager does not know who has benefited from Mrs Carpenter's largesse, except in one case where the issue apparently came to light when a member of staff casually mentioned receiving £50 from Mrs Carpenter for tidying her room. As this was clearly in contravention of the home's rules, the staff member was dismissed and the manager began further inquiries. From this it emerged that Mrs Carpenter has offered payments to other staff members, which they have rightly refused.

When challenged about this Mrs Carpenter pointed out that she was entitled to do what she wanted with her own money and that this did not matter 'as I am not for this world for very much longer anyway'.

The residential home have asked their doctor for advice; this doctor spoke to Mrs Carpenter for some time and concluded that she was really quite depressed and did not really understand what she was doing.

The manager asks for advice on what to do next. 'Will the social services department be prepared to offer financial support for this placement when Mrs Carpenter becomes unable to meet our charges?', she asks.

What are the immediate needs?

There are a number of issues that need addressing here, which do not just relate to Mrs Carpenter herself, but may also extend to management arrangements and supervision within the home. However, the immediate need is for:

- clarification of what is happening to Mrs Carpenter's money; this may include some multidisciplinary consultation on the extent to which she is currently competent to control her finances
- a review of the financial arrangements if the possibility of Mrs Carpenter's not being able to meet the home's charges is real
- some assessment of need if the local authority is being asked to take on financial responsibility.

Interestingly, there is no specific legal remit for conducting an investigation of abuse, and as was mentioned earlier, the law relating to vulnerable adults in no way equates with the systematic framework of legislation and guidance that pertains to children. However, there are some initial grounds for the local authority social services department claiming a right to investigate the following:

- A general power to promote the well-being of older people in accordance with approved schemes (section 45 of the Health Service and Public Health Act 1968), implemented by circular 19/71, which lists services, including the provision of advisory services and social work support.
- There is a specific duty to protect a person's property under section 48 of the National Assistance Act 1948, and this might apply here.
- A request to take on the responsibility for meeting the cost of the placement in Beechwood House is in effect a request to meet costs for services provided under the National Health Service and Community Care Act 1990, and the local authority is, after assessing need, entitled to charge for the service (section 17(3) of the Health and Social Services and Social Security Adjudications Act 1983), and is indeed under a duty to charge the people it places in residential homes (section 22 of the National Assistance Act 1948).
- If the financial abuse is potentially serious, it may necessitate referral to the Court of Protection, and this can be initiated by anyone, although the court will expect some plan to be proposed, including who should be appointed as receiver.
- In relation to Beechwood House itself, the local authority might claim that an overview of the supervision of staff is necessary and that this could be related to the standards of care that inspection units require, although it has to be said that enforcing specific standards and practices is a contentious issue, and more specialised

145

information may be needed if this is a real issue (McDonald and Taylor, 1995).

● If the abuse is really serious, this may be a police matter since a criminal offence may have been committed and it is the duty of any citizen to report offences to the police, so this duty could apply to the local authority as well as the manager of Beechwood House, who may not have reported the theft by her ex-member of staff.

What are the issues for professional workers?

It has already been suggested that professional workers might feel appalled at the prospect of an older person being abused, particularly where physical abuse is concerned. With financial abuse one important factor to recognise is the reluctance of care agencies to take the issue of financial abuse sufficiently seriously, and there is also the temptation to be overwhelmed by the complexities of involvement in people's financial affairs. Workers may also feel that delving into older people's personal finances is particularly intrusive and insensitive, leading to considerable upset and embarrassment. Confiding to a stranger the intimate details of one's financial affairs can be especially difficult for older people brought up to believe that this is exclusively a personal affair, and in some cultures this may be reinforced very strongly. It is also possible that care workers may feel that this is not an area in which they should anyway be involved; they may claim to lack knowledge and expertise, and may not feel sufficiently assertive in tackling those who may be implicated in the abuse.

For these reasons it is especially important to be clear about the roles of the professional care agencies and also to be aware that there are some measures that can be taken to protect people. Financial abuse does not simply have to be condoned.

What are the roles of those involved in this case?

In contrast to cases discussed earlier, the roles of the various agencies are not so clearly defined, and this may also explain the initial reluctance among workers to become involved in cases of this nature. However, there is a need to make some kind of response.

The local authority

In this case the local authority social services department was not responsible for the initial placement at Beechwood House but may still have a duty to respond to the information that it has now been given. There is a clear distinction between what the social services department *must* do and what it *could* do if it wished.

Given that Beechwood House is a registered home, it would be subject to inspection by the local authority, and while the local authority would not be involved in the day-to-day running of the home, local authority inspectors might nevertheless wish to reassure themselves that sufficient safeguards are in place to ensure that similar events do not recur. Ultimately, if very severe financial abuse has taken place and if the managers are implicated in this, registration of the home could be withdrawn.

Beechwood House

If Beechwood House is part of a voluntary organisation that is charitable, the organisation is subject to rules regarding the operations of charities, as well as being subject to the Registered Homes Act 1984 (or Registered Homes (Amendment) Act 1991 if it is a smaller home run for fewer than four people).

Generally, the law relating to charities lies outside the scope of this book, but suffice it to say that charities are legally constituted bodies that can be held responsible for their actions. If negligence can be proved against them, they are as liable as any other person or body. Vicarious liability, that is, the trustees' liability through their employees, and responsibility to third parties (such as Mrs Carpenter) for their actions applies to the organisation. It cannot somehow exempt itself from these responsibilities by virtue of its charitable status, although charities could if they wished stop providing services. They are not subject to legal statutory duties and responsibilities in quite the same way as are local authorities (Ashton and Ward, 1992).

Police

The role of the police here is much less clear than in cases of severe physical abuse or indeed where a definite crime has been committed. Nevertheless, the misappropriation of money, or taking money under false pretences, contravenes the Theft Act 1968, and it is the duty of the police to investigate crime. It may therefore be that it is appropriate to refer any malpractice to them, although it would certainly be prudent to talk first with Mrs Carpenter to establish what exactly may have happened.

It may be worth noting that if clear evidence of theft or fraud is uncovered, there is an obligation to report this to the police. While it is quite common practice for employers not to report theft by employees, but simply rely on dismissal as an appropriate penalty, this is not strictly in accordance with the duty to report offences to the police.

Legal advisors

Legal advisors would have a potential role here, depending on the outcome of the initial investigation. If Mrs Carpenter is not aware of her legal rights and is at risk of being exploited by a relative, it may be important for her to instruct a solicitor to act for her. This would certainly become important if Mrs Carpenter were to be placed under the care of the Court of Protection.

If a local authority social worker were involved in the initial stages of the investigation of Mrs Carpenter's circumstances, it is highly probable that they would need advice from the local authority's own legal department since issues of financial abuse can become complex and it is not anticipated that social care workers generally would have sufficiently wide legal knowledge to be able to deal with this kind of case unaided.

The Court of Protection

The Court of Protection is potentially involved in this case as it is possible that Mrs Carpenter is no longer competent to manage her affairs and that the court needs to protect her from exploitation. The Court of Protection has in the past been the subject of some criticism (Gostin, 1983), which has tended to focus on the formality of its system, the delays involved in decisions and the costs involved. However, the court is the only means of protecting people from financial abuse where they are unable to protect themselves through loss of capacity to handle their own affairs. The principal safeguards that the court offers are:

- legal authority to take over someone's affairs, including not only obvious matters such as running bank accounts, but also the ability to make wills ('statutory wills') on behalf of someone who comes under its jurisdiction

- the appointment of a receiver, or in some cases the Public Trustee, who will be able to take decisions and make practical arrangements on a day-to-day basis
- supervision of the receiver's handling of property, including a requirement to submit poorly drawn up accounts
- the appointment of visitors to ensure that various other matters, such as the person's general welfare, are attended to.

A fuller discussion of the role of the Court of Protection was set out in Chapter 4.

The second part of the chapter sets out the relevant legislation as it applies to all these case studies and to abuse of vulnerable adults in general.

Which law is relevant here?

Duty to investigate abuse

Some constructive and imaginative use of the legal framework may be necessary here, but a number of pieces of legislation could be relevant.

First, the local authority social services department is empowered to provide social work support and assistance to older people by virtue of a government circular of 1971 that refers to the Health Services and Public Health Act 1968. Section 45 of this Act states that a local authority:

> may with the approval of the Secretary of State and to such extent as he may direct, make arrangements for promoting the welfare of old people.

This Act, as implemented by DHSS circular 19/71, gives approval to the arrangements by local authorities for any of the following purposes to meet the needs of older people:

1. to provide meals and recreation in the home and elsewhere
2. to inform the elderly of services available to them and to identify elderly people in need of services
3. to provide facilities or assistance in travelling to and from the home for the purpose of participating in services provided by the local authority or similar services
4. to assist in finding suitable households for boarding elderly persons
5. to provide visiting and advisory services and social work support

6. to provide practical assistance in the home, including assistance in the carrying out of works of adaptation or the provision of any additional facilities designed to secure greater safety, comfort or convenience
7. to contribute to the cost of employing a warden on welfare functions in warden assisted housing schemes
8. to provide warden services for occupiers of private housing.

(DHSS circular 19/71)

Here one could logically argue that the local authority is being asked to provide advice and support, so there is no reason why a social worker cannot visit either Sarah Jones or Mrs Carpenter and discuss matters with them. More problematic is the right of the local authority to pursue matters if its social workers became suspicious that they were being exploited. At this point it might be important to refer matters for legal advice. If the evidence of abuse is very clear, the police should be informed. The fact that government guidance has been issued to local authorities and others may be taken as indicative of implying an expectation that they will respond to such issues (Department of Health, 1993).

Physical abuse as an offence

It is not often realised that an assault is technically a threat to inflict an injury, whereas 'battery' is the actual striking of a blow. Assault is both a criminal offence and grounds for civil action: the extent of redress in a civil action hinges on damage caused, and this is explored further in Chapter 8. In certain circumstances assault/battery can be lawful, for example when related to an arrest, self-defence or if consent is given (for example in a sport, or for medical purposes). In both the examples cited above, if abuse can be proven, an offence has been committed, but it should be noted that this would have to be proved 'beyond reasonable doubt', and there are special difficulties in securing convictions where vulnerable adults are the victims. Again, this point is explored in further detail in Chapter 8.

There are several gradations of assault within a range including assault with intent to rob (section 8 of the Theft Act 1968), indecent assault (discussed earlier), assault occasioning actual bodily harm (section 47 of the Offences Against the Person Act 1861) and malicious wounding/causing grievous bodily harm (section 20 of the Offences Against the Person Act 1861).

It is also worth noting that it is a specific offence to ill-treat or neglect any person suffering from a mental disorder while in one's custody or care (section 127(2) of the Mental Health Act 1983). Likewise, it is an offence for staff of a hospital or mental nursing home 'to ill-treat or wilfully to neglect a patient' who is either an inpatient or outpatient (section 127(1) of the Mental Health Act 1983).

Case law cited in McDonald and Taylor (1995: 152) suggests that ill-treatment requires proof of intent or recklessness and is deliberate conduct 'which could properly be described as such whether or not it had caused or was likely to cause harm'. Ill-treatment need not result in actual injury; it includes bullying and the use of harsh words. The presence of mental disorder in the victim does not have to be specifically proved.

Sexual abuse

Offences under this category include:

- indecent assault (sections 14 and 15 of the Sexual Offences Act 1956)
- indecent exposure (section 4 of the Vagrancy Act 1824)
- gross indecency (section 13 of the Sexual Offences Act 1956)
- incest (sections 10 and 11 of the Sexual Offences Act 1956)
- procurement (using threats or intimidating someone into having intercourse) (section 2 of the Sexual Offences Act 1956)
- buggery (section 12 of the Sexual Offences Act 1956 as amended by section 143 of the Criminal Justice and Public Order Act 1994)
- rape (section 1 of the Sexual Offences Act 1956 as amended by section 142 of the Criminal Justice and Public Order Act 1994).

A number of legal texts (for example Cross et al., 1995; Smith and Hogan, 1996) offer concise summaries of these laws.

In addition to offences outlined above, there are some specific legal provisions worth noting that might relate to someone with severe learning disabilities, although the legislation often uses totally outdated terminology, referring to people with severe mental impairment as 'defective'. First, it is a specific offence to abduct a woman 'who is a defective' for the purpose of sexual intercourse (section 21 of the Sexual Offences Act 1956). Williams (1995: 4) points out that, besides using outdated language, the law does not cover the abduction of men, the abduction by a woman or situations where a woman lives independently and not 'in the possession of her parent or guardian' (section 21(1) of the Sexual Offences Act 1956). Similarly, using equally outmoded language, the Sexual Offences Act 1956

151

makes those who are responsible for running establishments guilty of an offence if they knowingly allow a women with severe learning disabilities to have sexual intercourse (section 27(1) of the Sexual Offences Act 1956). Williams (1995: 6) also points out, in discussing sexual offences, that 'existing research suggests a bias towards offences in service settings… One of the most dangerous places, as far as sexual crime is concurred, is a care setting.' He points out that mental health legislation in this respect covers group homes as well as hospitals. The Mental Health Act 1959 (section 128) is relevant here; this lays down that it is a specific offence 'for a man on the staff of, or employed by, a hospital or mental nursing home to have extramarital sexual intercourse with a woman who is receiving treatment for mental disorder in that hospital or home… or who is subject to guardianship or is otherwise in his custody or care (Jones, 1996: 332).

Financial abuse as an offence

Most forms of financial abuse are, strictly speaking, offences that quite often fall under the ambit of the Theft Act 1968, but the problem is proving that there was an intention to take advantage of the vulnerable adult. This has to be proved 'beyond reasonable doubt'. Here we run straight into the issue of the reliability of Mrs Carpenter as a potential witness. Even if she is consistent in what she says about what has happened to her, it may well become a matter of interpretation. Suppose an unscrupulous relative claims that Mrs Carpenter gave them her diamond engagement ring. If Mrs Carpenter is confused or uncertain about this, it is unlikely that there can be even a remote prospect of bringing the matter to court. It is for this reason that financial abuse is a difficult issue for all professionals and why a police investigation may not result in prosecution. However, the involvement of the police may be sufficient to warn off any potential abuser, making it clear that people outside the family know what is going on.

Direct intervention to protect vulnerable adults

It is not really possible to use current legislation to protect vulnerable adults from abuse, except when certain very special and unusual circumstances arise in relation to the vulnerable adults themselves. These extremely rare occasions fall into the categories covered by the National Assistance Act 1948 section 47, which relate to:

- grave chronic disease
- living in insanitary conditions
- not receiving proper care and attention.

For specific details of the criteria set out in the legislation see Chapter 7.

In addition, in certain very extreme cases, the Police and Criminal Evidence Act 1984 (section 17) authorises the police to act in 'life and limb' situations, which are also discussed further in Chapter 7.

The provisions under this Act might be used where vulnerable adults are found in very urgent need of medical treatment. Using the legislation to protect a vulnerable adult from abuse from a carer or other person would seem highly questionable, although there might be some extreme cases in which it could conceivably be justifiable.

Remedies for people who have been abused

One remedy not mentioned so far is the possibility of orders obtained under domestic violence legislation. Previous legislation was confined to assisting people who were married or cohabiting, but the Family Law Act 1996 extends this to people who live in the same household (providing this is not as a tenant, lodger or employee) or are relatives (section 62(3) of the Family Law Act 1996). More controversially, under the same section, orders can be applied for by children or by people who have agreed to marry, and it may be possible in future to apply on behalf of someone else, subject to rules and regulations to be made by the Lord Chancellor under section 65 of the Act.

The two kinds of order that the court can make are:

- occupation orders to enforce an applicant's entitlement to live in the home and regulate its occupation by, for example, stopping someone entering it for a period of time (sections 30–41 of the Family Law Act 1996)
- non-molestation to protect from further violence or harassment (section 42 of the Family Law Act 1996).

A power of arrest may be attached to the orders if 'the respondent has used or threatened violence' (section 47(2)(b) of the Family Law Act 1996). Alternatively, undertakings may be made (section 46), but courts may not accept these as appropriate in all cases.

These remedies are available through any court to any person who can show an 'association'. Domestic violence is no longer to be associated exclusively with married or cohabiting women.

The Protection from Harassment Act 1997 extends the opportunity for seeking a non-molestation order and thereby provides further protection. Under this legislation the victim does not have to be 'associated' with the attacker and the harassment may fall short of physical assault.

There is also the possibility of using the law of trespass and assault in order to secure compensation. However, the potential for deploying the law in this way in relation to family members is limited. First, any injunction is a temporary means of responding to a situation while the amount of damages are assessed by the court (*Patel* v. *Patel* [1988]; also cited in McDonald and Taylor, 1995: 153). Second, there is no statute law that readily fits the bill to cover a vulnerable adult who is the victim of an assault. In other words, this aspect of law is intended to provide compensation for a legal wrong; it is not designed as a means of protecting people, and certainly not on a long-term basis.

Remedies for people who have been neglected

What if someone has been abused as a consequence of a lack of care or supervision by someone else? Here, the law does allow for claims for damages because of failure to protect, but the remedy is limited. First, the legal presumption that parents care for their children, enshrined in the Children and Young Persons Act 1933, does not apply the other way around; in other words, adult children, are not automatically legally responsible for their ageing parents. The duty of care must be proved.

As far as institutional abuse or neglect is concerned, staff do have a general duty of care and must exercise this consistently with the standard that applies to the ordinary skilled person in that professional capacity. By general legal principles, employers are vicariously responsible for the actions of their employees, so actions for damages against a member of staff can also be brought against their employees, whether the employer is a private employer or a local authority.

Abuse as an indicator of need

Perhaps of more immediate relevance to both cases is the potential for taking abuse as an indicator of need rather than as the grounds itself for some legal action. Betty Smith's letter could simply be treated as an indication that someone was in need of an assessment, and a positive intervention in this case could then be guided by the need to consider providing services. The carer's needs could then be considered alongside this. There is no requirement that someone in need of services must ask for these services themselves, nor indeed is there anything to limit the means whereby a local authority discovers that someone is in need. The obligation on the local authority is to assess needs where it 'appears' that 'any person for whom they may provide or arrange for the provision of community care services may be in need of any such services' (section 47(1) of the National Health Service and Community Care Act 1990).

Rights to assessment

As we saw in Chapter 2 there is a distinction between people with disabilities who are entitled to an assessment under the National Health Service and Community Care Act 1990 and other vulnerable adults whose needs the local authority might be prepared to assess. Clearly then, it might matter whether in two of our cases the people concerned were registerable as disabled. However, this might be facilitated by the general obligation the local authority has under the Chronically Sick and Disabled Persons Act 1970 to ascertain the extent of general need in their area.

In all the case examples the victim of abuse may be entitled to an assessment of their needs under the National Health Service and Community Care Act 1990. In addition the carers are entitled to an assessment by virtue of section 2 of the Carers (Recognition and Services) Act 1995, providing the local authority agrees that the victim of abuse needs an assessment. The Carers (Recognition and Services) Act 1995 does not convey independent rights to an assessment.

As far as Mrs Carpenter is concerned the whole point about the National Health Service and Community Care Act 1990 in essence is to ensure that residential care is used only where necessary, and the policy means of achieving this is by subjecting all claims for financial support to the full assessment procedures envisaged in the Act.

In this case Mrs Carpenter would be entitled to ask the local authority to assess her needs under section 47 of the National Health Service and Community Care Act 1990. The purpose of the assessment is obviously to anticipate that the local authority will say that her needs are best met by the provision of residential accommodation in Beechwood House. Having made that declaration, the local authority is then obliged to meet the costs, taking into account Mrs Carpenter's means and requiring a financial contribution from her.

It is of course possible that the local authority social services department might say that Mrs Carpenter's needs can be met in the community and that the cost of meeting those needs would be lower than the charges for residential accommodation. Providing that assessment relates to her needs, it would be difficult to argue with that conclusion. However, it is also possible that it might agree that her needs are extensive enough to warrant their being met by the provision of residential accommodation, but the local authority might dispute that Beechwood House, with its higher than average charges, is the only way of meeting those needs. In this case the local authority would be entitled to meet the need in an alternative way, providing it did meet the need and despite the fact that Mrs Carpenter and her family might not agree with this. This is the effect of the Court of Appeal decision in June 1996 in a case involving Lancashire County Council.

Meeting the costs of care in the independent sector

Legal authority for meeting the costs of Beechwood House derives from the National Assistance Act 1948 and the Health and Social Services and Social Security Adjudications Act 1983. Section 22 of the National Assistance Act 1948 lays on the local authority a duty to charge for the accommodation it provides.

This is relevant here since if, after assessment, Mrs Carpenter is considered to be in 'need' of care that can best be provided by Beechwood House, the local authority is empowered to make arrangements with the voluntary organisation to provide care under section 21(10) of the National Assistance Act 1948. This power to provide care through voluntary organisations was extended to private organisations by virtue of section 42(1) of the National Health Service and Community Care Act 1990. As this is an arrangement for residential care, the local authority, having made the arrangements, then has a duty under section 22 of the National Assistance Act 1948. This duty requires the local authority to levy a standard rate that reflects the full cost of the accommodation. The resident's means are then taken into account, and contributions towards the cost of accommodation are required on this basis.

Incidentally, the position of people who moved into accommodation prior to 31 March 1993 is different in that they may have benefited from social security payments for their accommodation, and there is therefore provision for protection in relation to the full implementation of the community care regime. In effect they may have preserved rights in relation to their contributions.

Advocacy/empowerment

Assuming that Mrs Carpenter, our third case example, has become confused about financial matters and is really not able to cope with her affairs, what then could be done?

First, it may not be possible to do very much with regard to the money that has been given away, although it may still be worth seeking legal advice on her behalf about this.

Second, however, some steps can be taken almost immediately to prevent any further attempts to exploit her. A solicitor's help could be enlisted in order to make application to the Court of Protection; in an emergency an urgent application can be made and provisional arrangements made by the judge (section 98 of the Mental Health Act 1983). It is unlikely that the local authority will want to make the application since the Court of Protection will anticipate a proposal in terms of who is going to act as a receiver. In the majority of cases a relative will act as receiver. If the fear is that it is these relatives who are responsible for the financial abuse, another person could be appointed, including a solicitor or accountant, although they would obviously charge for their services. It is possible for the Director of Social Services (but not a named person in the social services department) to act as receiver, although local authorities are generally reluctant to take these duties on. If all else fails, there is provision for the Public Trustee to act as receiver, and it is not always necessary to appoint a receiver if someone's affairs are relatively straightforward. While care workers would not normally be involved in making applications to the Court of Protection, it is worth knowing the general principles that apply to the court's functions; these were set out in detail in Chapter 4.

Third, for the long-term future, would it be advisable in cases of potential financial abuse for people to make a will? In some ways the value of this would be limited as it does not actually prevent abuse in the meantime, but on the other hand, the act of setting down someone's wishes on paper is important, clarifying what property they own and expect to pass on to the next generation. The law regarding making wills can be quite technical, pushing it beyond the scope of this book. Nevertheless, it is worth noting that, although professional legal advice may be required, this need not be prohibitive if the will is reasonably straightforward.

Social policy context

This discussion leads us neatly into the wider framework and the limited recognition of the abuse of vulnerable adults. It is not altogether clear why this has been such a neglected subject, but it appears likely that this has followed on from the recognition of child abuse as a feature of contemporary society and a break with a romanticised notion of family life.

In discussing the issue of abuse of older people, observers have frequently commented on the demographic changes that have indeed been dramatic during this century. The rise in life expectancy has led to an increasing proportion of dependent older people, and this may partly explain the apparent increase or emergence of elder abuse. Changing perceptions of family life and increased openness and honesty about abuse within families have also been cited as explanations for the increased publicity afforded to the abuse of older people. However, it is difficult to sustain the view that abuse within families itself is new or is a particular feature of contemporary society. What is not in dispute is that, belatedly, increasing attention is being paid to this whole subject.

At the same time it is important not to create a moral panic about the abuse of vulnerable adults but to keep the issue in perspective. To this end there have been some attempts to define abuse and also to devise a system that acknowledges its occurrence and responds to it.

An often repeated definition of abuse derives from Mervyn Eastman's seminal work on the abuse of older people:

> The systematic maltreatment, physical, emotional or financial of an elderly person... this may take the form of physical assault, threatening behaviour, neglect and abandonment or sexual assault.

> (Eastman, 1984: 23)

This definition was taken up by the Law Commission (Law Commission, 1993a), who have undertaken a reappraisal of the whole legal system for protecting vulnerable adults. It is worth looking at the Commission's proposals in detail since these give a framework for intervention, with suggested changes in the legal system that now operates.

The Law Commission recommended that section 47 of the National Assistance Act 1948 and the National Assistance (Amendment) Act 1951 should be repealed and replaced by a new scheme giving clearer and more appropriate powers to local social services authorities to intervene to protect incapacitated, mentally disordered or vulnerable people. In order to achieve this it was important to be clear about which group of people the legislation should cover.

The Law Commission proposed that an *incapacitated* person is one who is either:

(a) suffering from mental disorder, within the meaning of the Mental Health Act 1983 and unable to understand an explanation in broad terms and simple language of the basic information relevant to taking the decision in question, including information about the reasonably foreseeable consequences of taking or not taking it, or unable to retain that information for long enough to take an effective decision; or
(b) unable by reason of his mental disorder to make a true choice in relation to that decision; or
(c) unable to communicate the decision in question to others who have made reasonable efforts (taken all practicable steps) to understand it.

The Commission proposed that a *vulnerable* person is one who is:

by reason of old age, infirmity or disability (including mental disorder within the meaning of the Mental Health Act 1983) unable to take care of themselves or to protect themselves from others.

It recommended that powers to protect vulnerable adults should be available to protect incapacitated or mentally disordered or vulnerable people aged 16 and over.

As regards investigation, assessment and short-term intervention, the recommendations of the Commission were as follows:

1. The local social services authority should be the agency responsible for investigating allegations of neglect or abuse of an incapacitated, mentally disordered or vulnerable person
2. The local social services authority should be responsible for initiating proceedings in relation to the care and protection of incapacitated, mentally disordered or vulnerable people
3. Where a local authority has reasonable cause to suspect that a person is incapacitated, mentally disordered or vulnerable and is suffering or is likely to suffer significant harm or serious exploitation, they should be under a duty to make such enquiries as they reasonably can, including taking steps to gain access to that person, and to decide whether they should take any action to provide community care services for that person or otherwise protect them from harm or exploitation

4. The Commission wondered whether, in addition, there should be guidance on suitable case conference procedures and whether it was desirable to set up registers of vulnerable adults about whom the local authority were concerned because they may not be receiving adequate care or may be being abused.

In order to implement these duties, the Commission recommended that local authority social workers should have the power to enter premises where any vulnerable adult was living if there was reasonable cause to suspect that that person was suffering, or was likely to suffer, significant harm. There would be back-up legal force to this by making the obstruction of local authority officials a criminal offence and by authorising entry into the premises by force if necessary. This last power would be subject to authority being granted by a court or magistrate and would be exercised by the police. In this respect the power to force entry would be similar to the power that already exists in relation to mentally disordered people (section 135 of the Mental Health Act 1983).

Finally, the Commission recommended that the local social service authority or its officers should be able to apply for an emergency protection order 'authorising them to remove to a place of safety a person believed to be incapacitated or mentally disordered or vulnerable where there are reasonable grounds to believe that that person is likely to suffer significant harm... if not removed and, in the case of a vulnerable-person, that they would not object to the order being made' (Law Commission, 1993a: 49). In addition the Commission floated the idea that local social services authorities might have the power to assist an incapacitated, mentally disordered or vulnerable person to bring proceedings for a non-molestation order or ouster order under private law.

So far these proposals have not been implemented. There are various reasons for this that are tied in to the whole debate about the protection of vulnerable adults. These issues are explored in greater depth in Chapter 9.

Conclusion

The issue of advocacy is complicated by the fact that adult victims of abuse do not have clearly laid down rights and it is therefore difficult to see how they are 'entitled' to protection. Indeed it is not even clear that family members owe them a duty of care, so this whole issue is fraught with confusion. What we can say is that there is an ethical duty on social workers and others to protect vulnerable adults, and it is important in this area to use the limited potential of the law as constructively and as imaginatively as possible. It is very easy to shut one's eyes and ears to the possibility of vulnerable adults being abused, and when resources are scant, and workers hard pressed, it is tempting to do so. However, it needs to be borne in mind that the abuse of children is accorded high priority in social services departments' work, and some lessons can be learned, or rather adapted, from the system devised to protect children. Specifically good practice would commend:

- the need to listen to abuse victims and to respond to what they are saying
- the notion of working in partnership with families even when abuse has definitely occurred
- a multidisciplinary approach that involves shared information and decision-making
- clarity about what is and is not abuse, and how and when to intervene.

Finally, it is important to be more open about the whole issue of abuse and to encourage a wider discussion of it. Greater honesty is needed in order to examine why it is that some families find the pressure of caring too much and what steps can be taken to prevent abuse occurring.

Further reading

Eastman, M. (ed.) (1994) *Old Age Abuse: A New Perspective*, Chapman & Hall, London.

Pritchard, J. (1995) *The Abuse of Older People*, 2nd edn, Jessica Kingsley, London.

Williams, C. (1995) *Invisible Victims*, Jessica Kingsley, London.

7 Protecting People from Themselves

Introduction

In this chapter we shall be exploring the ultimate dilemma in social work. At what point can someone's rights to make their own decisions about their own care be overridden? When is it right to deprive someone of their liberty in order to protect them from themselves? At what point should caring professionals intervene to oblige someone to accept help even if they have declared that they do not wish to receive this help?

It is this aspect of social work practice which raises the greatest concern for individual rights and civil liberty. Here we are considering circumstances and situations in which someone is incapable of looking after their own health or caring for themselves properly. The reasons for the incapability could be related to a mental illness or some kind of 'disorder', or it could simply be that someone does not have the knowledge or ability to understand the danger that confronts them.

The chapter starts with an example of where these issues might arise. The example relates to an older person in the community who is clearly not managing to care for herself. The situation described occurs quite frequently in various guises. Although each case has to be assessed individually, there are some general principles that underpin all work in which major civil liberty issues arise, and the legal framework is clear about circumstances in which professionals can consider intervening, even if it is not always clear about the circumstances in which it is appropriate to intervene.

The case scenario described raises specific issues for:

- the statutory social care agencies who have particular duties and responsibilities in relation to the care of people who may be mentally disordered
- the role of medical staff who have to determine whether or not someone is mentally disordered
- other agencies, such as the police, who may be called upon to assist where someone appears to be unable to care for themselves
- carers, who are often perplexed by the apparent inadequacy of the law to protect people from themselves
- the community, who perceive the danger that someone poses and assume that 'someone' ought to do something about this.

Intervening in people's decision-making rights is an important issue, which predominates in this chapter. The emphasis will be on assessment and decision-making in which co-operation is unlikely and in which there is a particular need to be clear about the boundaries of professional roles and the rights of the individual. The chapter starts by exploring the immediate needs and roles of the various organisations involved in assessing those needs. It then goes on to consider the legal aspects most relevant to social care practice and intervention in this case. The discussion will also include references to the duties of different agencies involved and the legal context in which they operate. In this area it is important to understand the limits of professional and social care agency accountability, and that individuals do have the right to live as they choose even if this does not accord with what others consider to be in their best interests.

As with previous chapters the intention is not to 'solve' the case but to make readers aware of the serious issues at stake and indicate how one might respond to circumstances in which those issues arise. Readers are again reminded that the book is not an authoritative statement of the law, but references are provided wherever possible so that further information can be obtained if necessary.

At the conclusion of the chapter will be found a discussion of the broad social policy context within which the law and social care practice operate, raising issues that are explored further in the concluding chapter on the need for a comprehensive review of law and practice.

Mrs Edith Harrison

Monkton Social Services Department receives a telephone call from a local GP:

'This is Dr Stewart here. I am the GP for Mrs Edith Harrison, a woman who lives alone and who is becoming very confused. She is posing an extreme danger to the community and to herself, and I think she ought to be in hospital or receive some kind of care, probably under an order. She is 75, with no near relatives as far as I know, but I should stress that I've only been her GP for a few months. Her husband died 2 years ago. According to records passed on to me, the couple coped together perfectly adequately, but since that time she has become increasingly confused. This has gone on to such an extent that she is now posing a serious threat to the community and to herself. She is in the habit of lighting fires at all times of the day or night, usually in the garden, and showing no concern when these get out of control. She is now deluded, and convinced that people are breaking into her house and stealing her possessions. Three nights this week she has been found wandering in the streets; the police have been involved in returning her and have contacted me. All that happens is a few minutes later she leaves the house again. The police are exasperated with her and, frankly, so am I. Mrs Harrison is really not *compos mentis* enough to agree or disagree to leaving her home, but for her own sake she cannot be left where she is.'

There is only a scant social services department file on Edith Harrison. All previous visits seem to have been made in response to neighbours' demands for her removal; when she has been seen, no such action has been seriously contemplated except on one occasion when a previous social worker was thinking in terms of her removal under section 47 of the National Assistance Act 1948 in view of the squalid conditions in which she was living. All offers of domiciliary services have been refused in the past.

A home visit is arranged.

Mrs Harrison is initially reluctant to open the door but eventually does so. She does not always speak clearly but mutters to herself constantly, so obtaining direct answers to questions is not easy. However, she does express quite forcefully her conviction that neighbours are stealing her money and other possessions. When asked to show the social worker the food she has in the house, she opens a cupboard to reveal nothing except digestive biscuits – and launches into a stream of abuse against Mr Patel, the next-door-neighbour, whom she accuses of stealing her groceries.

She denies wandering at night but she cannot say what day of the week it is, nor the time of day. She cannot recall the GP's last visit or her three recent dealings with the police. She remembers the names of her son and daughter eventually, but cannot remember where they live.

Mrs Edith Harrison *(cont'd)*

This prompts her to tell the social worker about the time that she took her daughter to see the changing of the guard at Buckingham Palace at the time of the King's Coronation, an event she recalls in vivid detail, repeating some parts several times.

She declares that she is looking after herself quite well, although she admits to missing her husband. She does not want anyone coming into her house, so she declines the offer of domiciliary services. She certainly does not wish to leave her home, saying she is perfectly all right, or would be if the neighbours would stop coming in and taking her money.

The house itself is chaotic, with piles of newspaper, magazines and clothes everywhere. The kitchen is filthy, with flies crawling over the remains of old food. The floor throughout the house has particles of food stuck to it or squashed into the carpets. It is only too apparent in the bedroom that Mrs Harrison is incontinent.

On her dressing-table is a massive pile of buttons, coins, matches and knick-knacks that people are angrily forbidden to touch. Outside in the garden there are signs of a bonfire having been blazing perilously close to a neighbour's fence, which is scorched.

What are the immediate needs?

Physical/medical

It might be considered that there are no immediate physical needs, assuming that the fire is not still burning in the garden, but this view would be wrong. It is easy to assume that things have gone wrong gradually over a period of time and that any further deterioration will be slow. However, this need not be the case. There are certainly clear danger signs here:

- Edith is not eating properly.
- However confusion might be defined, she is confused about what she is doing and, more significantly, about time.
- There is a link between the two: failing to eat properly will compound and may aggravate the confusion and this may trigger a sudden deterioration.
- There may be a specific cause, such as a urinary tract infection, to explain the confusion; it would be a mistake to assume that the confusion is due to a long-term problem.

165

- If she does have an acute confusional state, this may become very severe, with the risk of her wandering at night and consequent risks.
- She appears to be unaware of her own needs.

In these circumstances the GP might conclude that she needs an urgent medical assessment. The GP might, for example, arrange hospital admission or referral to a community psychogeriatrician.

Emotional/mental health

It is difficult to tell to what extent Edith is distressed by her condition since it is not clear to what extent she understands it. However, it is fairly safe to conclude that no-one would want to be deprived of nourishment or would want to be unaware of time or events, so some consideration has to be made of her mental health. At the same time it is important not to jump to conclusions. It is tempting to label the behaviour described as symptomatic of dementia, yet all guidance on this subject would say that dementia must be a diagnosis of last resort. A multiplicity of the factors, ranging from blood disorders to acute isolation, can cause confusion, and none should be automatically discounted.

The difficulty posed by cases such as this is not persuading people that something should be done but deciding what should be done and how the reluctant co-operation of people like Edith can be secured. Given that dementia ought to be a diagnosis of last resort, referral to the psychiatric network appears premature. Yet it is only admission to a psychiatric hospital that can be imposed. A comprehensive physical examination and assessment would seem more appropriate, but how is this to be effected? The indications are that it might be neglectful to leave Edith Harrison where she is, but what alternative is there if she refuses to go to hospital? Is assessment in the community possible?

What are the issues for professional workers?

All of the civil liberty issues raised by the case are fundamental in any society. They raise all sorts of questions about individuals' rights to decide for themselves. They trigger dilemmas concerning the role of the state and the role of the individual. Above all, they challenge professional power and decision-making. To whom are professionals accountable, and are they competent to make decisions for people that cut across people's own declared avowed preferences?

At the same time it cannot be right to let people suffer if they are so confused or 'disordered' that they do not understand how serious their situation is. It is not right to let people suffer when they simply cannot understand the implications of their own decisions. Yet these are inherently value statements, moral statements almost, that do not fit easily with the usual professed beliefs of social work: empowerment, advocacy, asserting one's own wishes and beliefs. Nevertheless, denying the possibility of compulsory care, to use a short-hand phrase, is to deny some people the care or treatment they need (need, here, as opposed to want), and in some very extreme cases implies condemning people to death.

The case raises many of the general concerns we have already expressed about the social workers' rights to intervene in the lives of adults who have reached a stage bordering on 'incapacity' or 'incompetence'. In this context incapacity means being unable to understand and act on one's own primary needs, for example for safety or food. Incompetence means being unable to meet those needs appropriately, not being able to make effective choices. The justifiability of our intentions does not, unfortunately, provide the necessary sanction for any intervention that has not been consented to by the person themselves. At least in the case of children we are able to fall back on the explanation that they are not yet able to understand the ramifications of some of the decisions they might be faced with, and thus we act on their behalf or ask their parents to decide for them. With adults this is not so.

This general concern is backed up by some thoughts and fears more specific to this instance:

- With older people the care worker might be particularly alert to the fact that admission to hospital or any residential facility might undermine their ability to reassert themselves in the community and thus be the start of a process that can only end when they die. In this instance, the house being left unattended for any period of time eventually raises questions about what might happen to it. The outcome of that decision might then close down a range of future community care options. Thus it is a question not just of whether or not we can provide some temporary accommodation, while a detailed assessment of needs takes place, but also of the possible long-term impact of that move.
- Furthermore, there is a natural concern here for the public interest. Unfortunately, as is all too obvious, individual and public interest

do not necessarily coincide. From Mrs Harrison's point of view we argue for independence and the concomitant need to take risks so that people might assert it; from the point of view of the public, and particularly the neighbours, the demand is for control and prevention. The social worker can see that, only too easily, they will lose out either way. They will either be criticised for imposing their values on Edith or will be faulted for displaying a lack of concern for public safety.

- There is a slight sense of unease here about the place that relatives might have in the decision-making process. For the moment they remain a distant memory and, for all we know, might not even be alive or, if they are, may not be concerned about the fate of their mother. Any action by the care worker at this point has an impact on their future involvement. If decisions are made without trying to contact them, they may at a later stage accuse the worker of usurping their rights and presenting them with a *fait accompli* regarding the care being offered; if establishing contact is placed high on the agenda, the worker might find that the decision-making process is encumbered by their concerns or interests.

- There is also unease about the position of the neighbours. Do we take what Edith Harrison says about Mr Patel at face value? Do we challenge her interpretation of how she came to have no food? Do we confront her apparent racism (assuming that Mr Patel is Asian and she is not)? If not, do we indulge her fantasy (assuming that it is a fantasy of course, not forgetting that confused older people occasionally really are the victims of theft by neighbours) and ignore the assumed racial undercurrent of her accusations? All of these are potent dilemmas for the worker operating in accordance with anti-discrimination principles. At the same time the worker does have a moral obligation to the neighbours, at least to protect them from the potential fire hazard. Should the worker arrange to see them, to reassure them, to gain information, to seek their views? But what then of Edith's rights to privacy and confidentiality? If a social worker talked to your next-door-neighbour about your state of mind, how would you like it?

- While being alert to the dangers of ageism, the social worker may find that his or her views on anti-discriminatory practice are not always shared by others. The danger in cases such as this is to interpret everything in terms of immediate needs and assume that this somehow disqualifies an older person from opportunities that care workers would normally extend to others. For example, the loss of her husband 2 years previously might be a major unresolved issue for Mrs Harrison. Neither age nor experience necessarily brings with it protection from pain, and just as we might offer a younger adult counselling, so it should also be considered here. The question is whether or not that concern is also shared by the other professionals we work with.

● Labelling: the case also raises the question of how an initial response then determines all subsequent courses of action. At this stage, if we emphasise the mental health aspects, linking these to the fears of the local community, we run the risk of labelling this case as a 'mental health problem' and of subsequent actions all being interpreted through that lens. If we place emphasis on the physical nature of the problems, we find the potential for action circumscribed by issues of consent and also by a medical approach that may overlook the social psychological causes of Edith Harrison's apparent distress.

There is also the more complex issue of assessing a case in which a multiplicity of factors are relevant. Specifically, Mrs Harrison could be experiencing a combination of physical, mental, emotional, psychological (including bereavement) and practical problems. On this last point, it may be that she is short of money or that the accommodation may be under threat of repossession. How would this combination be assessed? Good practice would clearly indicate the need for a multidisciplinary assessment, but this may have to be very wide ranging, involving a number of agencies such as housing providers and welfare rights advocates. This point is worth making since it highlights the difficulty of broadening assessments in practice; some professionals are most reluctant even to consider such a broad approach. In some areas, combined social and medical assessment (as carried out, for example, by a local authority social worker, GP or psychiatrist) is still not routine practice, but in this case the lack of such an assessment could have serious repercussions.

If the initial reaction is to proceed down the mental health road, this might propel us towards psychiatric hospital admission, which might mean that other causes were ignored or at least considered irremediable. This might eventually lead to further deterioration and a very real possibility that Mrs Harrison would become a long-term patient.

On the other hand, if the assessment were purely social, this might play down the physical causes and thereby cause unnecessary suffering. A further consideration is that such an approach might underestimate the extent of the danger posed, either to the person concerned or to other people.

Responding to cases such as this ultimately involves balancing risks, and there is certainly no easy answer in deciding what might be the best approach. All that we can say is that it must be acknowledged that confusion and disoriented behaviour have many causes and that anyone carrying out an assessment must be open to all possibilities. Jumping to conclusions about causation is certainly dangerous, and no two cases are identical.

What are the roles of those involved in this case?

Community health services

The NHS (General Medical Services) Regulations 1992 sets out conditions under which GPs provide medical services to their patients. This now includes a specific responsibility to visit all patients over 75 at least annually (Regulations, Schedule 2: para. 16), which now applies to Mrs Harrison.

There are some general principles worth noting about the provision of community health services:

● There is no distinction between psychiatric and other specialist medical services as far as the means of accessing those services are concerned.
● The GP is always the first port of call for securing medical services.
● A GP could therefore refer someone to a psychiatrist or to a geriatrician, depending on the preliminary assessment of that person's medical needs.
● GPs are self-employed and in some cases have delegated powers to purchase services for their patients (fund-holding practices), whereas hospital doctors are the employees of hospital authorities or Trusts.

Specialist medical services

This case study indicates a potential need for specialist medical opinion, and this raises the difficult question of whether that should be provided by a psychiatrist, by a geriatrician who specialises in the care of older people, or by a psychogeriatrician who deals with older people with mental health problems. The principle still remains that requests for specialist medical care have to be routed via the GP, who clearly has a role in assessing someone's needs in the community. Other principles that apply are as follows:

- While in hospital, patients become the responsibility of the consultant in charge of that medical specialism.
- In the case of psychiatry, the consultant, as the Responsible Medical Officer, has additional special legal duties in relation to the operation of the Mental Health Act 1983: these primarily relate to treatment (which can be given despite the patient's wishes in some cases – see Part IV of the Mental Health Act 1983) and discharge under the Mental Health Act 1983 as amended by the Mental Health (Patients in the Community) Act 1995.
- After discharge from hospital the responsibility for the patient reverts to the GP, who has access to community nursing support services, including community psychiatric nurses.

In the case study there is reference to powers under section 47 of the National Assistance Act 1948 (see below). These powers can only be invoked if the community physician considers this necessary. The community physician is appointed by the local health authority.

Social services department

Whatever the diagnosis of Ms Harrison's condition might eventually be, social services are presented here with a request by the doctor to which they have to respond. The doctor puts further pressure on the care worker with his or her indication that an institutional response is in order. Why does the social services department have to respond?

1. The person concerned may be in need of services, and the fact that there are serious safety issues does not remove the need to assess under the National Health Service and Community Care Act 1990 rather than the Mental Health Act 1983.
2. There is a moral obligation on anyone to intervene in any case where there is a potential threat to life and limb.
3. There are duties and powers to provide services following on from an assessment. It may be possible for a social worker to link Mrs Harrison into a network that might ease some of her problems.
4. In extreme cases compulsory powers may be required, and it is the

social services department that is under a duty to provide approved social workers who are qualified and authorised to do this.

Therefore, as regards the social services department's role, we are faced with a distinction between powers granted to all care workers and those which require the specific involvement of Approved Social Workers, that is social workers who are specifically appointed under section 114 of the Mental Health Act 1983 to discharge the functions of a local authority with regard to compulsory admissions and detention. The intention in this chapter is to focus on the range of responsibilities of a local authority towards mentally disordered people rather than provide a practice guide for Approved Social Workers with a more specific remit. However, there will be some reference to functions that are exclusive to Approved Social Workers.

The case raises a set of concerns similar to those identified in other chapters but in a more extreme form. There is the intertwining of concerns around the person's physical and mental state, and it is initially difficult to decide which might be uppermost. Again we have to consider whether to use powers under the National Assistance Act or Mental Health Act, and we are also faced with the difficulty that much of what the doctor might offer is dependent on the willingness of Edith Harrison herself.

Police

It may seem odd to include the police here, but they have been asked to return Mrs Harrison home at least three times very recently. It is recognised that, in many cases, it is the police who will first encounter people with serious mental health difficulties. Consequently, there are special police powers covering probable emergency situations.

Under the Police and Criminal Evidence Act 1984, police officers have the power to enter and search any premises without obtaining a warrant if such action is required to save 'life and limb' or to prevent 'serious damage to property' (section 17(1)). The provisions under the Police and Criminal Evidence Act 1984 are occasionally used where vulnerable adults are found in need of urgent medical treatment, especially where they are on their own. The question might be raised of what the police would do once the person is removed. The answer to this is that common law permits them to take any reasonable action that would prevent the threat to life, so securing urgent medical attention would clearly fall into this category.

Police officers also have the power to remove people to a 'place of safety' in certain circumstances:

> If a constable finds in a place to which the public have access a person who appears to him to be suffering from mental disorder and to be in immediate need of care or control, the constable may, if he thinks it necessary to do so in the interests of that person or for the protection of other persons, remove that person to a place of safety...
>
> (section 136(1), Mental Health Act 1983)

that is to say:

> residential accommodation provided by a local social services authority under Part III of the National Assistance Act 1948 or under paragraph 2 of Schedule 8 to the National Health Services Act 1977, a hospital, as defined by this Act, a police station, a mental nursing home or residential home for mentally disordered persons or any other suitable place the occupier of which is willing temporarily to receive the patient.
>
> (section 135(6), Mental Health Act 1983)

A person removed to a place of safety:

> may be detained there for a period not exceeding 72 hours for the purpose of enabling him to be examined by a registered medical practitioner and to be interviewed by an approved social worker and of making any necessary arrangements for his treatment or care.
>
> (section 136(2), Mental Health Act 1983)

Arrangements for treatment or care are generally assumed to mean deciding whether someone should be admitted to hospital under the Mental Health Act 1983. However, this is rather a narrow view, and it could be argued that the assessment should be much broader than this. Nevertheless, it must be carried out by an Approved Social Worker.

Which law is relevant here?

Duty to assess

That both medical and social services have responsibilities towards Mrs Harrison alerts us to the fact that both have a role in assessing her. However, it is the social services department that has the major responsibility in deciding how to proceed in two respects.

First, the social services department has duties in relation to both the National Health Service and Community Care Act 1990 and the Mental Health Act 1983. The community care duties relate primarily to assessment for the potential provision of services and were comprehensively covered in Chapter 2. It is not, therefore, intended to repeat these here, but it is important to assert the right of people to an assessment when they are in need on the grounds of an inability to care for themselves. The suspicion of serious mental health problems does not disenfranchise someone; that is to say, worrying behaviour should be grounds *for* a community care assessment rather than grounds *against* attempting one. After all, there may be resources or networks that could be relatively easily deployed to help diminish Edith's confusion.

Second, social services departments have duties derived from the Mental Health Act 1983 (primarily sections 114 and 13). These centre on the potential need to arrange for Edith to be admitted to hospital, and although application for admission can only be made by an Approved Social Worker, all those working in caring agencies ought to be familiar with the boundary between care and control. These are set out in the next section.

The question to be considered here is to what extent the social services department *has* to respond. The department is not obliged to send a social worker to assess simply because the GP requests this, but our sources of information about Mrs Harrison might clearly go beyond what the GP can say. For example, the social worker might already have made an assessment of the degree of risk she represents that leads them to hesitate over the need for institutional provision. Having said that, there is also a difference between what *must* be done and what *should* be done, and just as the doctor owes a duty of care to patients, so the Approved Social Worker has a similar duty (Jones, 1996: 65–6). Therefore the request has to be given serious consideration, and if the social worker chose not to respond, the reasons for this would have to be recorded.

There is also the issue of who should respond within the social services department. If it is a clear request for a mental health assessment and there is a possibility that there might be a call for compulsory detention, as the GP is indicating, the response must include an Approved Social Worker, who is the only person entitled to make such applications. There is of course no legal reason why the Approved Social Worker should not undertake an assessment under the National Health Service and Community Care Act 1990.

Moving on a stage, if one does respond, the Mental Health Act gives a clear indication of the direction of that response. The fact that the doctor has already made a tentative judgement about the outcome of the assessment should not determine the actions of the social worker. The doctor's request indicates that it would be most appropriate for the case to be handed to an Approved Social Worker, but that person's remit is to decide whether or not an application (for compulsory detention) ought to be made. The medical recommendation is clearly a significant component in the decision, but the responsibility of the two professionals (the social worker and the doctor) is quite separate and the Approved Social Worker makes a judgement about the medical evidence along with other information.

There is a safety issue in the case, and that alerts us to the criteria for admission to hospital for either assessment or treatment of mental disorder under section 2 and/or section 3. In both instances there is mention of the health or safety of the person or the protection of other persons. However, we must remember that these are necessary and not sufficient conditions. Thus we must not fall into the trap of thinking that, because there is an issue about safety, the mental health legislation can automatically be used. For detention in these circumstances it would still be necessary to satisfy all of the other criteria, which are set out below.

Mental health assessment

There is sufficient in the behaviour of Edith for us to feel that some kind of assessment is required. The lack of attention to her wellbeing, the carelessness with which she plays with fire, the urgency with which she senses that others are out to take advantage, all suggest the possibility of a mental disorder without denying the possibility of a physical dimension to her difficulties as well.

What we have to do here, however, is to ensure that care arrangements are made in a manner that is consistent with the spirit and the fact of the law. The 1983 Mental Health Act encourages social workers to seek solutions in the 'least restrictive' way possible, although, interestingly, the phrase 'least restrictive alternative' never actually appears in the Act itself. In the first instance, therefore, we need to look at the possibility of conducting the assessment in the community rather than in hospital. Thus the doctor needs to be pushed to explain why this is not possible. Convenience and established working practice are not suitable answers here if there is pressure to use compulsion.

Should we concede that hospitalisation is necessary, the argument still does not automatically end with detention. A combination of the strength of the entitlement to informal admission (although not an entitlement to demand hospitalisation in the first place) and the rigorous testing of the criteria for compulsory detention under section 2 should ensure that the power to detain Edith against her wishes is only to be used as a last resort. The Mental Health Act states unequivocally that:

> Nothing in this Act shall be construed as preventing a patient who requires treatment for a mental disorder from being admitted to any hospital or mental nursing home... without any application, order or direction rendering him/her liable to be detained.
>
> (section 131, Mental Health Act 1983)

The significant words here are 'nothing' and 'without', and in the majority of cases the wording should be sufficient to ensure that, in the first instance, mental health patients enter hospital with the same status as people with physical problems. Note that 'informal' does not mean the same as 'voluntary'. Voluntary consent would imply a declared wish, an active expression of agreement. In contrast, 'informal' may imply passive consent, that is, consent which is not declared but merely assumed on the basis that there is no active objection. This issue came to the fore in December 1997 when the courts had to consider whether it was right to regard a patient as being admitted informally when he did not have the capacity to give active consent (*L. v. Bournewood Community and Mental Health NHS Trust*).

The distinction is important since it is possible for patients admitted 'informally' to find themselves, if the criteria are satisfied, detained under the compulsory powers of section 5 of the Mental Health Act 1983 with a view to a full assessment being undertaken in accordance with section 2 of the Act. It also has, as in the Bournewood case, an impact on relatives' rights to discharge a patient kept against their (the relatives') wishes.

The informal admission is informal for the caring authority as well as the patient. It does not require the involvement of an Approved Social Worker, although if, as in this case, informal admission might be considered an alternative to detention in hospital, the expertise of an Approved Social Worker could prove invaluable.

How pressing is the requirement that the social services department makes an assessment? If the request comes from the nearest relative, the responsibility is clear:

> It shall be the duty of a local social services authority, if so required by the nearest relative of a patient residing in their area, to direct an approved social worker as soon as possible to take the patient's case into consideration under subsection (1) with a view to making an application for his admission to hospital.
>
> (section 13(4), Mental Health Act 1983)

The obligation here is beyond dispute, but in many instances the request will not materialise in this way. In most situations the power to act is given by implication:

> It shall be the duty of an approved social worker to make an application for admission to hospital or a guardianship application in respect of a patient within the area of the local social services authority by which that officer is appointed in any case where he is satisfied that such an application ought to be made...
>
> (section 13(1), Mental Health Act 1983)

The duty of other care workers, therefore, is to mobilise resources, pass on the request for the interview to the Approved Social Worker and explain procedures.

There is, of course, no reason why some preliminary assessment should not be made. For this purpose it is worth noting that there is general guidance covering the circumstances in which informal admission is appropriate and those in which it is not (Department of Health, 1990c: paras 2.7–2.9; Jones, 1996; 338–42).

The outcome of all of this is that each case must be assessed with care: clear judgements must be made based on sound reasoning, and above all, an individual's rights must be determined according to an objective assessment of their need. Need in this case may conflict with what someone says they want (usually 'to be left alone!'), and in this context, but only in this context, it may be necessary to act in accordance with someone's needs rather than their wishes. Such action must be in strict accordance with the legal grounds stipulated in the Mental Health Act 1983 or elsewhere, to which we now turn.

Grounds for compulsory care: National Assistance Act 1948

Under the National Assistance Act 1948, any person of any age may be forcibly removed from their home in certain specified circumstances. The purpose of removal is in order to 'secure the necessary care and attention' if they:

(a) are suffering from grave chronic disease or being aged, infirm, or physically incapacitated, are living in insanitary conditions; and
(b) are unable to devote to themselves, and are not receiving from other persons, proper care and attention.

(section 47, National Assistance Act 1948)

The 1951 Act introduced an emergency procedure whereby the law can in effect be used either where there has been a gradual deterioration or where someone needs hospital admission or immediate care and is refusing.

If the first is the case, the community physician is empowered to certify to the local authority that the removal is necessary in the interests of the person themselves or in the interests of 'preventing injury to the health of, or serious nuisance to, other persons'. The local authority then applies to the court, which can make an order that lasts for 3 months, revocable after 6 weeks.

If it is an emergency, the community physician can apply directly to a single magistrate and need not give 7 days' notice, in which case the order, if granted, lasts for 3 weeks but can be converted to a longer order by application to the court (National Assistance (Amendment) Act 1951).

In practice, the National Assistance Act 1948 is used very rarely and in some local authority areas not at all. The significance of the legislation is that it is not tied to the mental health of the individual concerned but instead relates to the public health threat that their condition may pose to others. It is unlikely to be appropriate in cases such as Edith's unless the circumstances are very extreme, far worse than have been indicated so far. Living in unpleasant or squalid conditions does not *of itself* pose a public health threat. Bear in mind also that compulsory removal that is vigorously opposed but nonetheless carried out might lead to traumatic reactions resulting in premature death.

178

Grounds for compulsory hospital admission under the Mental Health Act 1983

Here we will consider the main sections under which non-offenders who are mentally disordered might be detained against their wishes. The care worker should know that the principal grounds on which someone might be taken to hospital against their will are:

(a) that they are, or may be, mentally disordered
(b) that they ought to be detained in the interests of their own health or safety, or with a view to the protection of other persons

(section 2(2), Mental Health Act 1983)

Both criteria need to be substantiated, and to this end responsibilities are clearly delineated: medical staff provide recommendations to satisfy the first criterion, on which others might then act. Doctors cannot themselves apply to detain people; applications can be made either by an Approved Social Worker or by the nearest relative of the patient, who must determine whether criterion (b) is satisfied. 'Nearest relative' is a title with specific meaning in mental health law and is not the same as next of kin or the person the patient feels closest to: the nearest relative is identified by reference to legal rules contained in section 26 of the Mental Health Act 1983 rather than by choice. Medical staff interview (prospective) patients prior to applications being made. The two doctors statutorily required can interview either together or separately, but in the case of separate interviews there can be no more than 5 days between the days on which the interviews occur (section 12 of the Mental Health Act 1983).

The significance of this in Edith's case is that, should we get to the point of considering detention, contact with the nearest relative becomes a live issue. Any failure to make contact potentially denies the assistance of someone who could:

● stop the application in the case of admission for treatment under section 3
● exercise the power to discharge after admission for assessment or treatment (that is after a section 2 or section 3 admission).

Applying the criteria for section 2 admission, we could point to a number of salient factors:

● danger to her own health posed by not eating properly, by the health risks in the house and by a lack of basic care, which includes incontinence

179

- danger to her own safety posed by wandering at night, and loss of memory about where she is and what time of day it is
- danger to other people through risk of fire and possible paranoia.

Section 2 of the Mental Health Act 1983 allows for detention for assessment, or assessment followed by treatment; in an emergency this can start by an application based on one medical recommendation under section 4. Used in the case of Edith it could lead to her detention for a period of up to 28 days during which time a decision on continuing care will need to be made: discharge, remaining in hospital as an informal patient, detention under section 3. It would have to be demonstrated that she required assessment in a hospital, that the assessment could only be done if she were detained, and that it was in the interests of her health or safety, or the protection of others. For the care worker the importance lies in noting the sufficient conditions. Thus it is the:

- need for assessment *and*
- that it has to be in hospital *and*
- that she has to be detained in order to achieve it *and*
- that her health is at risk *or* that there is a risk to her safety *or* that there is an issue of the protection of the public.

Section 3 might provide another avenue for care. Section 3 of the Act authorises detention for a period up to 6 months, renewable in accordance with the provisions in section 20. For section 3 to apply, the medical condition would need to be that she has been diagnosed as suffering from one of the forms of mental disorder defined in section 1 of the Mental Health Act 1983:

Mental disorder means mental illness, arrested or incomplete development of the mind, psychopathic disorder and any other disorder or disability of mind and mentally disordered shall be considered accordingly.

(section 1(2), Mental Health Act 1983)

In Edith's case, if we are only considering assessment, it is sufficient that her behaviour amounts to mental disorder as defined above. For the moment we do not need to know which of the categories she fits into, and it is interesting to note the generality of the last part of the definition, which will almost certainly create the opportunity to detain her should we be so inclined.

With section 3, the diagnosis needs to be clear, and Edith has to fall into one of the four forms of disorder if she is to satisfy the first of the criteria. Mental illness, interestingly enough, receives no further definition in the Act. Jones (1996: 6) comments wryly on this omission:

> The Government abandoned its search for a definition of mental illness partly because of the difficulties of producing a definition which would be likely to stand the test of time and partly because of the fact that there apparently had not been much evidence that the lack of definition of mental illness leads to any particular problems.

In addition to mental illness, the other 'disorders' (defined in section 1(2) of the Act) are:

- Severe mental impairment: a state of arrested or incomplete development of mind which includes severe impairment of intelligence and social functioning and is associated with abnormally aggressive or seriously irresponsible conduct on the part of the person concerned
- mental impairment which is similar to the above but does not amount to the severe condition in its state of arrested or incomplete development of mind
- psychopathic disorder: a persistent disorder or disability of mind (whether or not including significant impairment of intelligence) which results in abnormally aggressive or seriously irresponsible conduct on the part of the person concerned.

Section 1, Mental Health Act 1983

For the moment we can see that Edith might possibly fit into a general category of mental disorder, but we do not have sufficient information on the background to her problems to say that it is one of the others. Furthermore, there is a very real debate concerning dementia as a form of mental disorder. If dementia is the root cause of Edith's problems, remembering that dementia is always a diagnosis of last resort, is it then a mental disorder as defined in the Mental Health Act 1983? The debate in medical circles centres on whether it qualifies as a mental illness, a mental impairment or neither of these. If it is a mental disorder, compulsory powers can be invoked; if not, detention under the Act is simply not legally feasible. The Mental Health Act Commissioners have commented that there is no 'hard and fast rule' and that each case should be judged individually (Jones, 1996: 340). Social work texts tend to assume that psychiatric care is rarely appropriate for people with dementia and that other approaches are more valuable (Marshall, 1990; Chapman and Marshall, 1996).

181

This is important because, for section 3, there would have to be certainty about assigning Edith to one of the four states, and both medical recommendations would have to agree on at least one category. In addition, and in common with section 2, the Approved Social Worker would have to be satisfied that detention in hospital was the only way in which treatment could occur, and thus by implication the alternatives – of allowing her to be an informal patient and of allowing her to be treated as an outpatient or by visits to the surgery – would be ruled out.

Although in all of the above instances the primary responsibility for assessing and deciding on a care plan lies with the Approved Social Worker, other care workers can play a significant role, not least because they may hold important information that helps doctors and Approved Social Workers to reach their conclusions.

Community orders and the Mental Health Act 1983

The complaint is often made that the Mental Health Act ought to include a community order. In one sense the complaint is unjustified since the Act does include provisions for guardianship, but it is true that guardianship cannot compel someone to accept treatment against their wishes. Therefore there is no community treatment order, but there is a kind of community care or supervision order.

The grounds for 'being received into guardianship' are similar to the grounds for detention in hospital under section 3, except obviously for confirmation that a community approach rather than hospital treatment is appropriate (section 7 of the Mental Health Act 1983). But what does being 'received into guardianship' entail? First, nothing at all in relation to the person's property. Second, a general expectation of supervision, with a specific requirement for social work visits at least once every 3 months (rule 13 of the Mental Health (Hospital, Guardianship and Consent to Treatment) Regulations 1983). Third, three specific powers (section 8(1) of the Mental Health Act 1983) to require:

- residence at a place specified
- attendance at 'place and times so specified for the purpose of medical treatment, occupation, education or training'
- access to be given to medical practitioners, Approved Social Workers or any other person 'so specified'.

In this case it would have to be confirmed that Edith was suffering from a stipulated form of mental disorder before guardianship could even be contemplated. It is not possible to use guardianship as a means of securing a full assessment, and there would inevitably be problems if the danger to the neighbours and others became persistent. Nevertheless, guardianship would offer supervision and would provide access to the home. It might also facilitate Edith attending day care resources, although to what extent she participated would be a matter for her.

Rights of relatives

This section refers specifically to relatives' rights under the Mental Health Act 1983. Rights of carers under the National Health Service and Community Care Act 1990 were dealt with in Chapter 2.

For those who know, the powers of the nearest relative of a mental health patient are considerable. Although the identification and location of that person is the responsibility of the Approved Social Worker, and therefore need not detain us here, it is important to remember, as discussed above, that the term 'nearest relative' has a strict definition and is not the same as next of kin nor is it the person to whom the patient might feel closest.

The nearest relative, as defined in section 26 of the Act, has some major decisions to make, and it would be good professional practice for any worker already involved with the family to inform them of their rights and support them in making appropriate decisions. Specifically the nearest relative has:

1. The right to make the application for detention under section 2 (including section 4 in an emergency) or under section 3 of the Act. Nearest relatives also have the right to apply for guardianship under section 7. The code of practice rightly points out that, in the majority of cases, the Approved Social Worker is going to be the preferred applicant, but we can imagine situations in which social services are not involved with the case and the suggestion to sign an application comes from a GP or consultant. Alternatively, we might have a scenario in which one member of the family feels that he or she should take direct responsibility for a decision that will restrain another, and the making of the application is the open acknowledgement of that. The task of the care worker in these

circumstances might be to inform the person of this right and provide a sounding board for the merits or otherwise of doing it.

2. The right to apply for the discharge of the detained relative. In the majority of cases detained patients will be discharged by the hospital managers as soon as it is thought advisable to do so. However, there might be situations in which one feels the review process has failed to take account of changing circumstances, and then the nearest relative can give the hospital 72 hours' notice of their intention to discharge the patient and the responsible medical officer has to produce a report for the hospital managers on the advisability of acting in that way (sections 23 and 25 of the Mental Health Act 1983).

3. The right to transfer their responsibility to someone else who is willing to take on the duties. The intention of the Act appears to be to locate someone who has a real concern for the well-being of the patient. In many cases this will be the person they live with, but the operation of the section 26 rules may mean that that person is not the actually legally defined nearest relative. In keeping with the 'concern' theme above, however, that person usually takes precedence over other claimants, but when this is not the case the nearest relative can inform another person in writing of the transfer of their powers to them. This account supposes that everyone is supportive and the motives of relatives are always honourable. In real families this may not unfortunately be the case, and in those circumstances one might have to resort to a court hearing in order to have that unhelpful person removed and someone else named in the place (section 29 of the Mental Health Act 1983).

4. The right to be informed of the pending discharge of a detained person from hospital. This is useful when the nearest relative is going to be involved in after-care although when either of them (that is, the nearest relative or the patient themselves) objects, this information will not be given (section 133 of the Mental Health Act 1983).

5. The right to be informed about the opportunities to apply for a tribunal, which is a body set up to hear appeals against detention under the Act. The patient can appeal to the tribunal within the first 14 days of detention under section 2 or at any time if detained under section 3 (section 66 of the Mental Health Act 1983). This provides another avenue that would lead to a review of the case and might result in early discharge. Nearest relative powers are limited here and often by proxy. The nearest relative

cannot seek a tribunal hearing themselves in section 2 cases but can with patients detained under section 3. These powers are in addition to the patient's rights of appeal.

Preparing reports

Preparation of reports for people who receive psychiatric care is a task that is not exclusive to Approved Social Workers. Having said that, Approved Social Workers would normally complete a background report to any admission that they undertake, but there are other circumstances in which the Approved Social Worker may not have been involved.

If an admission is carried out on the application of the nearest relative, the social services department is required under section 14 of the Mental Health Act 1983 to prepare reports for the hospital. This is often a neglected task, since the patient is after all already in hospital and the ethical issues around detention have been side-tracked for social workers by the action of the nearest relative. However, we would argue that this task is vital because it is the only way in which some of the requirements of the Mental Health Act 1983 concerning people's rights and wishes can be respected. It also facilitates an assessment of the troubling behaviour in context and may enable a social worker to assess needs in terms of the National Health Service and Community Care Act 1990 rather than just the Mental Health Act 1983.

Specifically, section 14 requires a report on social circumstances, which Jones (1996: 76) considers could include an account of the patient's family and social relationships, employment record, financial situation and accommodation. The report should also cover the circumstances of the admission and, if the nearest relative's application was made after an Approved Social Worker has refused to make one, the reasons for the Approved Social Worker's decision.

Finally, under this heading should be noted the requirement for reports to be submitted to mental health review tribunals. These concern arrangements for the proposed discharge of a patient from hospital. Again, it is not essential for these to be undertaken by an Approved Social Worker, but they should reflect a broad knowledge of the resources available in the community to meet the ends of discharged psychiatric patients.

Care plans

Section 117 of the Mental Health Act 1983

This section lays on health authorities or Trusts and social services departments a duty to provide after-care services for people who have been detained under section 3 and certain other longer-term orders. Although it would apply to a comparatively small number of people, the model of multidisciplinary planning implied by section 117 for after-care is often used for a wider range of patients.

This now also needs to be seen in conjunction with requirements for the supervision of people discharged from special hospitals and regional secure units, to whom restriction orders may apply (sections 37 and 65 of the Mental Health Act 1983), and also alongside additional supervision requirements of the Mental Health (Patients in the Community) Act 1995. Briefly, these relate to requirements for supervision and extensions of the period during which discharged patients can be recalled to hospital. Additional powers are conferred on supervisors to order the recall of patients allowed leave when subject to certain detention orders.

Need for services: community care

In affirming people's entitlement to an assessment as part of a care plan, the amendment to the definition of disabilities in the National Assistance Act 1948 to include mental disorder is important (this amendment being generally attributed to circular LAC13/74). It is significant because the diagnosis of a mental disorder attached to someone who has been a psychiatric patient automatically means that they qualify for inclusion as a disabled person, and this in turn entitles them to an assessment of need under the National Health Service and Community Care Act 1990 (section 47).

This does not mean that services have to be provided, but it does mean that the local authority is obliged to assess and consider to what extent services should be provided (for a fuller discussion, see Chapter 2). Co-operation with hospitals with a view to carrying out assessments is encouraged by circular LAC(95)5 in particular, which was summarised in Chapter 4, and also by guidance to hospitals (Department of Health, 1994).

What are the broader issues?

Oppression and potential discrimination

This case study was introduced as it demonstrates specific aspects of practice that relate to assumptions made about older people with mental health problems. There is a very real sense in which Edith Harrison is in double jeopardy: there is a risk of her behaviour being interpreted as indicating a mental disorder, and ageism may also be a factor. Worse still, some might connect the two, assuming that her age explains her confusion, linking this to dementia and implying that this dementia is inevitable and irreversible. Careful assessment that avoids stereotyping will unpack these various strands and may offer alternative explanations or strategies for responding to her behaviour.

Leading on from this, there is little doubt that the Mental Health Act itself could be oppressive in its operation. The potential is considerable. The Act could lead to the lengthy detention of people who have not committed any kind of criminal offence. The criteria for detention are open to interpretation by professionals, and reliance must be placed on their integrity in deciding whether to deprive someone of their liberty. Significantly, decisions to admit people to hospital or guardianship are not open to challenge in the courts. The mental health tribunal has a role in hearing requests for discharge, but civil actions for damages caused by inappropriate detention will only be heard with permission of the High Court and then only where it is likely that actions were taken in 'bad faith' or 'without reasonable care' (section 139 of the Mental Health Act 1983). This arrangement perpetuates a long-standing approach to mental health that sees mental health as a public order matter with severely limited rights of redress through the courts.

The most obvious points for potential discrimination are:

- at the time of admission
- at the commencement of treatment
- during the preparation of care plans for discharge.

At the point of admission the debate may easily centre on the need for detention as opposed to testing out alternative approaches or indeed to the possibility of informal admission under section 131 of the Mental Health Act. Furthermore, some research has suggested that black people are at greater risk of being formally detained and that generally there are more women than men inpatients in psychiatric hospitals (Barnes and Maple, 1992; Skellington, 1992: 83–4).

Once people are involved in the treatment process, there is a danger that the urgent need to do something overrides concerns about the effects of the treatment under offer. While the code of practice makes it clear (Department of Health, 1990c: section 15) that consent should be obtained for treatment, the Mental Health Act 1983 allows a course of medication to be prescribed and administered to detained patients for up to 3 months without consent and without formally overriding consent (section 58(1)(b) of the Mental Health Act 1983). Refusal to agree to electroconvulsive therapy (ECT) can also be overridden by the provision of a second opinion by a Mental Health Act Commission doctor (section 58(1)(a) of the Mental Health Act 1983). Some research has indicated that this latter form of treatment may be overused for black and Asian patients (Fernando, 1988: 74).

As far as discharge is concerned, it will be noted that the whole tenor of mental health legislation, and the Mental Health (Patients in the Community) Act 1995 in particular, is on the control and supervision of discharged patients. It is easy to see how this may actively disadvantage some groups of people who are perceived to be a particular threat to society. Certainly, a diagnosis of schizophrenia would compel professionals to be especially wary of premature discharge, and intrusive controls over discharged patients' lives may be instigated. It is also worth noting that formal supervision arrangements only apply on a legal basis to longer-term detained patients, and this may discriminate against informal patients, who are consequently accorded less priority in access to support services.

Empowerment

Empowerment would be facilitated by an Act that set out clear entitlements to support services and had an emphasis on a preventative approach to mental health difficulties. Sadly, the Mental Health Act 1983 offers no such approach. The Act is primarily about protection, centring on hospital admission as the way of responding to mental health crises. Assessment plays a crucial role, not with a view to ascertaining people's needs for services (as in section 47 of the National Health Service and Community Care Act 1990) but rather to determine whether someone needs to be detained in their own interests or for the protection of others. There is no doubt that safety and health needs are sometimes paramount, but the scope and range of the Act is in effect quite narrow. The power of the professionals called upon to operate the Act, including local authority Approved Social Workers, should not be underestimated. Accountability is severely circumscribed.

So what can social workers, care workers, relatives and others do to ensure that people's rights are respected and that, wherever possible, people do participate in decision-making?

First of all, it is important to be alert to the discriminatory practices that might arise. Knowledge of the law, with all its flaws and limitations, is important, and knowledge of mental health law should not be seen as the exclusive preserve of the Approved Social Worker. With regard to the precise areas for potential discrimination outlined, there may be actions that social workers should consider.

At the assessment for admission stage, there may be a real need for the worker to be prepared to advocate the less immediately restrictive alternative to admission. This may imply pushing the medical professionals to question their routine practices in responding to particular disorders or behaviours.

When forms of treatment are being offered, it may be that a social worker has a formal contribution to make. If the doctor is to undertake treatment without the patient's consent (assume for the moment that it had been withheld), the social worker might be called on as one of the people whom the Mental Health Act Commission doctor should consult before proceeding (section 58(4) of the Mental Health Act 1983). If consulted, the social worker would be asked to comment on the ability of the patient to understand 'the nature, purpose and likely effects of that treatment' (section 58(3)(a) of the Mental Health Act 1983). The responsibility here is not a medical one. Care workers cannot testify to the appropriateness of the medication on offer, but they can test out the understanding of the person concerned, asking the kinds of question of the doctor that they themselves might ask if they were to receive the treatment in question.

At the discharge stage the social services department potentially has a key role to play since it should share the responsibility for rehabilitating former psychiatric patients into the community and should ensure that community care resources are made available to them. As explained above, discharged patients would be entitled to an assessment or reassessment of their community care needs.

Care or control?

The underlying issue here is ultimately whether law and practice focus on the care or the control of people who are not looking after themselves. For a number of reasons the conclusion has to be that the Mental Health Act 1983 emphasises control, while the National Health Service and Community Care Act 1990 assumes a market-orientated approach to care with assessors of need as purchasers of services, and a potential array of services for purchase. The difference in approach reflects different priorities and approaches, with a long history of mental health legislation having been concerned with control (Scull, 1982; Barham, 1992).

The practice consequence of this distinction is that practitioners may need to be reminded that Edith is not automatically a mental health 'case'. She also has clear needs in terms of physical examination and the assessment of corresponding needs under the National Health Service and Community Care Act 1990. This entitlement may be foreshadowed by the urgency of the mental health assessment but still has to be addressed, and if she is not admitted to hospital, it will be necessary to assess her needs and decide on the extent to which social services will be involved in catering for them. She and her relatives should also be kept fully informed of the assessment process since withholding information from people disadvantages them in securing either their freedom or their entitlement to the best possible form of care.

The case also raises the issue of the supervision of people in the community. No-one wants to force Edith to reside anywhere else, yet we would like to have a remit to watch over her without waiting for another crisis to precipitate Draconian actions. Unfortunately, there is no legal provision that quite meets this need, although guardianship may partly fit the bill.

Financial

It may seem curious to include this, but people in Edith's position quite often have considerable resources at their disposal. If Edith owns her own house, the rise in property prices may mean that she has considerable assets. As with any other community care assessment, this will become a factor in the equation once we get into the question of financing her requirements for services.

For older people housing is often a major issue. The pressure to sell is only too apparent, revealing the tension between buying the best service that someone needs and the natural desire to preserve savings or wanting relatives to inherit.

There is also Edith's own stated concern about other people taking her money. While her accusations may or may not be well founded, these issues together may raise the question of the advisability of putting decisions about her financial future on a firmer footing. So, once more we have to look at the possibility of using the Court of Protection and other means of protecting property outlined in Chapter 4.

Conclusion

The interplay of mental health, ageing and social isolation described in the case study underlines some of the strengths and weaknesses in the current legislative framework. The preciseness of the Mental Health Act 1983 and specific role of the Approved Social Worker point to some clarity when civil liberty issues arise. However, the accent on protection means that the Mental Health Act is not strong on securing services, and there is consequently the potential for discrimination. There is also the dilemma about which avenue to pursue: full medical assessment, psychiatric assessment, community care assessment. The outcome may depend on crucial decisions taken at the pre-assessment stage.

The case also underlines that only two Acts address compulsory removal and intervention: the National Assistance Act 1948, which is very rarely used, and the Mental Health Act 1983, which is used much more frequently. There are no others. Compulsory care cannot be secured by reference to community care legislation, and if someone falls outside the (admittedly wide) filtering process of the Mental Health Act 1983, compulsory powers simply do not exist. In practice it is sometimes difficult to convey this to anxious relatives who sometimes believe that local authority social services departments have reserve powers by which older people can be compelled to enter residential care. They do not.

The mix of mental health and ageing poses challenges to some social services departments who employ social workers who specialise in work with older people and also employ Approved Social Workers who may not. The potential for demarcation disputes is apparent, but of equal concern is the limitation in the value of the assessment.

Approved Social Workers are in difficulty carrying out their assessment if they are not familiar with the resources available to meet the needs of older people, but only they can carry out an assessment if compulsory admission to hospital is a real possibility. This situation is compounded and reinforced by the legislation. In such cases a joint assessment may be advisable or, even better, more specialist workers who are Approved Social Workers trained.

Finally, given that organisations may have difficulty coping with dual sets of needs, what happens if additional factors are added? For example, what if someone has an additional physical disability or there are race and culture factors that are of significance? The complexity of the assessment is potentiality limitless, but it is worth pointing out that the very complexity challenges the adequacy of services to meet needs. It also challenges the notion that people have to fit into certain categories before action can be taken to respond to their needs. Should mental health needs be met primarily through inpatient hospital treatment? Should the extent of supervision or support services depend on a specific psychiatric diagnosis? Should there be such a clear distinction between medical needs and social needs? Should compulsory care be confined to people whose mental health poses a potential threat to themselves or others? These are the general kind of question raised in this chapter, which inform the current debate about how the law can both promote people's well-being and protect them from themselves.

Further reading

Barnes, M. and Maple, N. (1992) *Women and Mental Health*, Venture Press, Birmingham.

Jones, R. (1996) *Mental Health Act Manual*, 5th edn, Butterworths, London.

Marshall, M. (1990) *Social Work with Old People*, Macmillan, Basingstoke.

8 Adults who Become the Victims of Crime

Introduction

In this chapter we shall be examining the issue of vulnerable adults as victims of crime, focusing on the victim–crime relationship. There is inevitably some common ground with Chapter 6, which focused on protecting vulnerable adults from abuse and harm. The key difference is that, whereas Chapter 6 addressed the role of social services departments and others as preventative and protective agencies, this chapter concentrates on people's rights as victims of crime and the specific issues that arise when a vulnerable adult is the victim.

As in previous chapters the discussion is initiated by a case scenario, here represented by a fictitious event presented in a fairly typical way by the local press.

This topic is important for all those engaged in social care as the full implications of what happens when a vulnerable person becomes the victim of crime are not always obvious. The incident is often viewed as simply a matter for the police and law enforcement agencies, support at the time of crisis being provided by victim support schemes. There are a number of reasons why this response for vulnerable adults may not be adequate.

First of all, the statutory social care agencies may have particular duties and responsibilities to reassess need and to decide, in the light of the incident, what additional response ought to be made. These needs may be overlooked or even delegated to another agency, such as the victim support scheme, and this may not always be appropriate or advisable for adults with special needs.

Second, there may be a lack of willingness to tackle this sensitive issue. It may be that there is a temptation among professional workers to protect vulnerable adults from the law enforcement process, and rights to redress may also be overlooked. This in turn may be a reflection of the way in which vulnerable adults are perceived by professional workers. These aspects form the focus of the first part of this chapter.

The second part of the chapter examines the roles of the different agencies involved and the legal and social policy context in which those agencies operate.

Finally, since there is a need to think more widely about these issues, some consideration is given to the very broad social policy context and the limitations of current arrangements for responding to vulnerable people's needs as the victims of crime. It will be suggested that there are certain inherent weaknesses in the legal system that the case highlights, some specific ways in which the path to securing proper provision for vulnerable adults as the victims of crime is impeded.

The case described therefore highlights several key issues for:

- the people or agencies involved in providing care for people with learning difficulties
- the professional workers involved
- the victims of the crime
- policy relating to community care for people who are vulnerable and who become the victims of crime
- the legal system itself.

All of these aspects will be highlighted in this chapter, which takes the following form:

- a discussion of the relevant issues for professional workers
- responding to the immediate needs
- the roles of the various agencies involved in the case
- the legal context
- the broader policy issues and need for reforms in this area.

What are the immediate needs?

Physical/medical

The newspaper report of our case (Figure 8.1) indicates that the immediate physical needs of Pauline and Anne, the victims of the crime, were attended to by the hospital, but some follow-up medical help may be required. Primary responsibility for the medical treatment of patients in the community clearly rests with the GP, and incidents such as this demonstrate the importance of registering with a GP.

Netherthorpe Weekly Echo

Saturday 9 March 1997

CRUEL HOAX AT CARE HOME

Con men forced their way into a RehabCare group home last Wednesday and robbed residents of their savings.

Two female residents were at home when the thieves called. The men apparently told residents they had a water leak and then tricked them into opening the door. They forced their way past them, knocking both residents out of their way. It is not known how much money was taken.

Both residents of the home were reported to be very shocked and bruised after their experience. Both needed medical treatment but were not detained in hospital.

A RehabCare spokesperson told the *Echo*: 'It is shocking that people with learning disabilities should be robbed in broad daylight like this. We are currently liaising with the social services department to examine this case and to see if there are any lessons to be learned for the future. Elmlea Road is an unstaffed group home: residents live in the community and look after themselves.

There are staff visiting regularly and, of course, residents are warned about checking visitors' identities. In this case, it seems the men forced their way in.'

RehabCare is an organisation which provides homes and care for disabled people. It started in 1982 when patients were discharged from Netherthorpe Manor into the community. Fears were expressed at the time that people who used to be at The Manor were too vulnerable to be able to live in the community. Elmlea Road resident Fred Smith told the *Echo*, 'Residents are not surprised this happened. It was only a matter of time. These people are too vulnerable to be left unsupervised. The social services never visit and it was obvious something would go wrong sooner or later.'

On Thursday two men were helping police with their enquiries.

Figure 8.1   Press report

195

At a later date, the GP may be involved in providing reports for the Criminal Injuries Compensation Authority. It is the physical harm which provides evidence that the Authority needs and on which its decision will be based, so proof of this obtained as soon as possible after the incident is important.

Accommodation

It is of course possible that, as a consequence of this incident, Anne and Pauline will decide that they no longer wish to stay at Elmlea Road. An immediate assessment, or reassessment, of their needs may therefore be called for.

Even if they do not request a change in accommodation, immediate consideration will have to be given to their safety, and Rehab-Care will need to conduct an evaluation of the home's security arrangements. There are certain other issues that might be raised concerning the running of the home. For example, was enough information given concerning what to do in an emergency? What access to help do residents have? What support is available? Is the management of the home adequate? These are questions for the social services department's inspectors or advisors to address.

The review of these issues inevitably brings into question the extent to which Anne and Pauline's needs are being fully met by the current placement. The primary duty to carry this out rests with the social services department, whatever the status of Rehab-Care and the financial arrangements relating to the current placement. Even if it is only a consideration of how a recurrence of this event can be avoided, the need for some kind of reassessment may well be indicated.

Emotional

Any kind of physical attack, which is in effect what this was, can be traumatic, and the psychological harm such an incident can cause cannot be overrated. Indeed, on the Holmes–Rahe social adjustment scale, which assesses stress factors on a comparative basis (on a scale of 1–100), physical injury rates at 53, higher than dismissal from work and just lower than death of a close family member (Fontana, 1989: 32). An organisational question is, who is going to take responsibility for this: the GP, social services, independent sector or a voluntary agency? In a number of areas in the UK, victim support schemes would be prepared to offer assistance in this kind of case.

At the same time it is important to note a potential clash between needs of the victim for counselling and support and the need of the police and law enforcement agencies for valid evidence. In children's cases, this stops counselling for fear of evidence being dismissed as tainted: the victim may be regarded as having been coached in what evidence to give to the court.

Police investigation

The newspaper report indicates that police investigations are well underway in this case. However, it needs to be acknowledged as a general principle that it is important for police inquiries to begin as soon as possible after the incident. In cases involving vulnerable adults it is easy for caring agencies to overlook this, perhaps because of a misguided view of the likelihood of success of a police investigation. The point to remember is that everyone is entitled to have offences against them reported to the police, who have the sole authority to record and investigate offences. It must also be remembered that it is a civic duty, that is, a declared moral but not legally enforceable duty, to report crime when it is committed.

What are the issues for professional workers?

At this point it would be useful to take some time to think about how professional workers might themselves respond emotionally to the issues raised here. Dealing with such cases is likely to rouse in all of us some or all of the following feelings:

● Abhorrence at the thought of vulnerable adults being crime victims at all.

If workers are honest about their feelings, it is not surprising that they feel angry about attacks on vulnerable people, and immediate thoughts of retribution are not unknown. In fact, they are quite healthy for, if social workers and carers stop responding emotionally, they have probably lost the ability to respond at all. It is important to acknowledge these feelings, discuss them openly and then move on to a more considered professional response to the incident: prevention of its recurrence and empowerment of the victims.

- Objection to the publicity that attaches itself to such cases.

Again it is only natural to want to try to protect people from publicity, from their names appearing in the paper, but this may sometimes be beneficial. It implies public recognition of the importance and awfulness of the incident and acknowledges that the incident did happen and has important consequences. Alternatively, there may be real dangers in publicity yet a feeling of powerlessness when requests to play down the publicity are ignored by journalists.

- Feeling powerless to help, especially when there is a conflict between the judicial process and justice as perceived from the victim's point of view.

Dealing with cases like this can sometimes feel like being in a car that is speeding out of control. The law enforcement agencies could take over, insisting that Pauline and Anne give evidence against the two men 'helping with enquiries', and pleas to make allowances for their vulnerability may go unheeded. This underlines the importance of knowing what the agencies' respective roles are and also of being realistic about the extent to which people can or ought to be protected. The very real limitation in the extent to which the courts can accommodate vulnerable adults in the course of judicial process is obviously a live issue. Once more, it is important to know what these limitations are and to be prepared for probable responses.

- Potential defensiveness: should this have happened at all to someone for whom the caring services had a responsibility? What if they say the worker or their agency is partly to blame?

Feelings of guilt are, to some extent, inevitable since it is so easy to say that this incident should not have happened. However, blaming people will not help: it is more fruitful to examine systems to identify weaknesses and to work on enhancing networks in order to prevent the recurrence of such incidents.

There are also a number of implications for professional workers, questions that immediately spring to mind when confronted with an incident such as this:

198

- Could this incident have been prevented?
- Is this the right kind of placement, and is it properly managed?
- Is a reassessment of need going to be required?
- How can the victims be empowered and helped to re-establish themselves?
- How can the victims seek redress for what has happened to them?
- Do the victims need an advocate?

In terms of anti-oppressive practice, workers would obviously want to ask whether the two people concerned had sufficient knowledge and skills to protect themselves against possible abuse or exploitation. In other words, empowerment is of paramount importance here. How can this be addressed?

One approach is for those who have the principal responsibility for caring to gain greater knowledge themselves of the procedures for responding to the crime. Carers can then work alongside vulnerable adults in helping them secure their rights, bearing in mind that there are significant limitations to what can be achieved.

What follows is an attempt to do this, first by exploring the roles of the agencies who will be concerned with the incident, and second by examining the legal context that lies behind this.

What are the roles of those involved in this case?

The unfortunate incident outlined on the report from the *Echo* needs to be tackled on a number of different levels and in a number of different ways. It may be useful to demonstrate this with a diagram (Figure 8.2).

Social services department

In this case the social services department may well have specific responsibilities. These could arise if:

- the local authority is responsible for the running of the group home
- the local authority is responsible for the placement arrangement, in other words does not provide services itself directly but is involved in co-ordinating and/or financing these
- the local authority is responsible for the registration and inspection of the home.

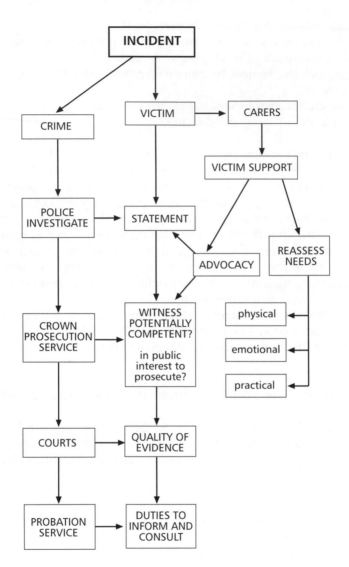

Figure 8.2   Response to crime where a vulnerable adult is the victim

These specific responsibilities might arise from, for example, accommodation arrangements made following on from an assessment under the NHS and Community Care Act 1990, which could relate back to duties under section 21 of the National Assistance Act 1948 or even section 2 of the Chronically Sick and Disabled Persons Act 1970. Registration and inspection duties would derive from the Registered Homes Acts 1984 and 1991.

Both probation officers and local authority social workers have responsibilities to help prevent crime (Pitts, 1990; Jones, 1992), and empowering victims or potential victims is a clear example of this. However, direct work with victims of crime, where there is no other reason for social worker involvement, is unusual, and it is presumably for this reason that victim support schemes have evolved.

RehabCare

The role of RehabCare is clearly crucial since they are responsible for the running of the home and thus for the provision of services on a day-to-day basis. The legal status of the organisation is important, as is the precise contractual arrangement between the organisation and Pauline and Anne. It may well be that the arrangement is one which is mediated through the social services department. It could be, for example, that the contract for provision of services is between Rehab-Care and the social services department. Pauline and Anne's placement may be a consequence of implementation of community care policies, and this may well be supported financially by the social services department. They may not therefore have a direct contractual arrangement with RehabCare itself; this brings into focus the question of what should happen if that organisation's standards of care, or responses to this incident, are considered to be inadequate.

Given that RehabCare is in the independent sector, there are three possibilities as regards its status:

- It could be a voluntary organisation that operates as a charity and is therefore subject to the law regarding charities (Charities Acts 1960, 1985 and 1992).
- It could be a voluntary organisation or a private organisation run on a non-profit-making basis, sometimes referred to as an 'intermediate organisation' (Ware, 1989).
- It could be a private organisation run for profit.

Whichever is the case, the organisation itself will be a legal body and able to enter into contracts, but the basis on which it can do this will vary (Ashton and Ward, 1992: Ch. 11). Detailed consideration of this is outside the scope of this book, but it is worth noting that the organisation itself has a duty of care. It may also be held legally accountable for its actions, although for private organisations there is here a very real distinction between limited companies and those which are simply partnerships. Generally speaking, directors are responsible for the operation of a limited company, which has limited liability for its actions (hence the name), while it is the partners who are responsible for the partnership and their liability is unlimited. In extreme cases the organisation or partners, like any individual, could be prosecuted if the lack of care were so severe, or the negligence so gross, that a criminal offence had been committed. However, this is comparatively rare. There has, in fact, been only one conviction for corporate manslaughter: the conviction in the Dorset canoeing tragedy (*R. v. Kite and Others* [1996]). The Zeebrugge harbour disaster also provides a further example of the courts' great reluctance to convict for corporate manslaughter (*R v. P&O European Ferries Ltd* [1990]).

Police

The roles and duties of the police are set out generally in the Police Act 1964 and the Police and Criminal Evidence Act 1984. One of the duties of the police is to prevent crime and to investigate it when it does occur, and an immediate responsibility would clearly arise in this case. In the course of their investigations, the police are entitled to rely on the co-operation of other agencies, and the police similarly have a primary duty to record crime, even if the chances of appre-hending the offender are limited.

The role of the police in assisting victims of crime has recently been considerably developed (Home Office, 1990a, 1990b, 1996; Marshall and Merry, 1990). In many areas referral to victim support schemes is automatic, so this may already have occurred in this case. However, this should not be taken for granted.

Crown Prosecution Service

The Crown Prosecution Service was established in 1987 under the Prosecution of Offences Act 1985 to take over responsibilities formerly held by the police in relation to evaluating evidence and deciding whether an offender should be prosecuted. If a prosecution is mounted, the Crown Prosecution Service will present the evidence to the court and will therefore be particularly interested in the quality of the evidence and the competence of the prospective witnesses. The Crown Prosecution Service has discretion over whether or not to prosecute, and in carrying out this function relies heavily on the Code for Crown Prosecutors (Crown Prosecution Service, 1994a). This code focuses on two tests that determine whether an alleged offender is prosecuted: the evidential test and the public interest test.

The evidential test broadly states that prosecutions will only be mounted where there is a 'realistic' prospect of conviction, taken to mean that courts are more likely than not to convict, which implies a kind of 50/50 rule of thumb. A number of factors, principally those concerning the admissibility of evidence, are listed as relevant in making this decision. This will always include considering whether witness are legally competent, and in order to determine this, potential witnesses' ability to understand and give reliable evidence must be taken into account.

The public interest test is more controversial, and only since 1994 have the criteria for its use been openly stated. Fundamentally, this test considers whether prosecution is worthwhile, which moves decision-making into a much wider arena. A list of relevant factors has been openly declared (Crown Prosecution Service, 1994a, 1994b), ranging from delay, genuine mistakes and mental or physical illness as factors against prosecution, to the use of a weapon, abuse of trust and the vulnerability of the victim, which would argue for prosecution. Perhaps of equal significance in some cases is the Crown Prosecution Service's duty to decide what charges should be brought. In a number of cases this aspect of the Crown Prosecution Service's role has caused disquiet when lesser charges have been preferred to the more serious. Davies *et al.* (1995) cite examples of these, besides discussing the role of the Crown Prosecution Service more generally.

In this particular case the Crown Prosecution Service will probably be concerned with the ability of Pauline and Anne as potential witnesses. If the two men 'helping police with their enquiries' are charged, a report will be sent to the Crown Prosecution Service, who will then take over the conduct of the case. At this stage the evidence that the victims can provide would be carefully assessed, and it is open to the Crown Prosecution Service to liaise with social workers or others who may know the victims well and be able to give an opinion about their potential reliability as witnesses. Indeed carers could take the initiative here, although the final decisions with regard to prosecution rest with the Crown Prosecution Service. In very rare cases a private prosecution has been instigated by victims dissatisfied with the Crown Prosecution Service's decision not to prosecute.

Victim support schemes

Victim support schemes are essentially local schemes that offer to put victims in touch with trained volunteers and also offer a range of advice and guidance. Local programmes are linked to a national co-ordinating body that can provide general information about schemes available in particular areas.

Access to the service varies between different areas of the country, but telephone numbers of the local scheme should be available through the local police, probation service or Citizen's Advice Bureau. It is important to remember that schemes are intended to provide help and support at a time of crisis for anyone who is the victim of a crime. Its counsellor may not have special expertise in dealing with people who have a learning disability, although increasing attention is being paid to this sphere of work by victim support schemes generally.

In 1994 Victim Support offered support to the victims of over 1 million crimes (Victim Support, 1995: 14). This apparently large number includes distributing letters or leaflets with invitations to victims to contact the local support scheme (63.6 per cent) and also includes face-to-face counselling (24.4 per cent). Victim Support assisted with 11,631 claims for compensation as well as supporting 58,593 people attending court as witnesses. The majority of help is offered on a short-term basis, but it is estimated that nearly 10 per cent of victims maintain contact with victim support counsellors for longer than 3 months (Victim Support, 1995: 15–16). Specialist support is offered for people who have experienced violent bereavement and for victims of sexual violence. Support is also offered for people who have to attend court as witnesses, this service now being available in all Crown Courts.

The provision of information about victim support schemes is automatic in some areas, but this needs to be confirmed locally. Carers may of course require help or advice from victim support counsellors for themselves and may need to be encouraged to refer themselves to such schemes. Certainly, people with learning disabilities may need to be assisted with contact with the schemes, which operate on the principle that victims will contact them if they need support or help.

Probation service

It may seem odd to include a discussion of the probation service here, but it is often forgotten that probation officers have a crime prevention role, as do the police. The duty is to participate in arrangements 'concerned with the prevention of crime or with relationships between offenders and their victims or the community at large' (Probation Rules 1984, Rule 37).

Furthermore, there have also been some recent developments that have extended the role of the probation service into some direct work with victims. This reflects an increasing emphasis on consultation with victims as part of the judicial process (Home Office, 1990b, 1996). Probation officers are now required to make contact with victims of certain crimes at specified times (Home Office, 1995). The crimes concerned are those in which the offender was sentenced to 4 years or more; a crime in which the sentence was less than 4 years may sometimes be included if there was a sexual or violent element. The purpose of the contact is:

- to provide information to the victim about the custodial process
- to obtain information from the victim about their concerns or wishes concerning the conditions of release.

The initial contact has to take place within 2 months of sentence being passed. The probation officer must offer to be a point of contact for the victim, but the victim obviously has the right to decline and take no further part in the process. Later on, when the date of release approaches, victims should be told of the month and location of release. Victims have no rights to object to the release itself but can express a view on the conditions of release and have the right to express their concerns in confidence to the probation officer, without these being passed on to the prisoner (Home Office, 1995).

The press

It is fairly common practice for the police to keep journalists informed of crimes occurring in the locality, and much space in local newspapers is given over to crime-reporting. There is no standard set of rules governing the reporting of all crimes, although information regarding the victims of certain crimes will be withheld and the reporting of rape trials is constrained by the Sexual Offences (Amendment) Act 1976, which prohibits the publication of a rape victim's name.

It may well be that disclosure of the victims' names and addresses will cause a lot of anxiety and may even provoke a repetition of the crime, but whether names are published is a matter of journalistic discretion. It would always be possible to request that the victims' names should not be disclosed, and in this case the *Netherthorpe Echo* complied with this request.

Which law is relevant here?

Reassessment of needs

There is no automatic entitlement to additional services through becoming the victim of a crime, but the crime does give rise to a need for a re-examination of services provided and clearly imposes certain extra demands on the caring agencies. Given that Pauline and Anne may have already been assessed in accordance with provisions of the NHS and Community Care Act 1990, there may be a duty to reassess. Need might be widely defined here: it could range from alternative accommodation to short-term counselling. The duty is to make arrangements, to co-ordinate, to act as a broker but not necessarily to provide services directly, as will be seen from closer examination of the provisions of the NHS and Community Care Act 1990. Chapter 2 provides a general discussion of community care assessment, including the reassessment of need.

Quality control and inspection of services

Suppose, for the sake of argument, that further enquiries suggest that questions need to be asked about the quality of supervision and care provided by RehabCare. What provision exist to raise these questions?

The Registered Homes Act 1984 provides for the registration and inspection by local authorities of voluntary and private homes where four or more persons are being cared for in a home. The Registered Homes (Amendment) Act 1991 extends these provisions to homes caring for fewer than four residents. The Act is intended to apply to homes outside the statutory sector that provide both *Authority* and *personal care* to people in need of care by reason of old age, disablement, mental disorder or drug or alcohol problems. The Act must be

206

considered in conjunction with the regulations that deal with matters such as the running of the home, the number of residents and the provisions of services and facilities (that is, telephones, sanitary facilities, heating, safety precautions and medical arrangements) but do not specify what 'adequate' staffing or 'good enough' care is. In extreme cases, where it is thought that the person running the home is 'unfit', the premises are 'unfit' or the home will not be run 'appropriately', registration can be refused. If registration is refused, the proprietor can appeal to the Registered Homes Appeals Tribunal.

The extent to which the Act applies in this case hinges on the extent to which the residents receive Authority and personal care. If the home is a group home in the sense that a group of people simply live there and basically care for themselves, quality assurance in terms of services will rely on general provisions of the NHS and Community Care Act 1990. In essence, this means that if services are bought by the local authority following on from a needs-led assessment, it is for the local authority to enforce standards, presumably with the ultimate threat of withdrawing funding, and in achieving this end, local authority-sponsored residents would have access to the local authority's complaints procedures.

The crime

Before examining the specific areas in which the law relates to the crime itself, it is important to distinguish between the public aspect of the case, which relates to the crime and its investigation, and the private aspect, which concerns how the individual might seek redress. In legal terms this distinction is mirrored by the division between criminal and civil law. It is worth noting the contrast of aims between the *criminal law*, which is preoccupied with controlling and sanctioning the behaviour of those who commit crimes, and the *civil law*, which makes provision for damages or compensation for those who have suffered as a result of another person's action. This contrast will become only too apparent as we proceed with the examination of the case. Before embarking on this part of the chapter, however, it would be useful to recall the major differences between criminal and civil law, and the different kinds of proof required to satisfy the courts in criminal and civil cases. In criminal cases the case must be proved 'beyond reasonable doubt', while in civil cases a lesser degree of proof, the balance of probabilities, is required.

As far as the crime itself is concerned, which law has been broken?

Taking money or property to which one is not entitled is clearly theft; stealing from a house by forcing entry would be burglary. In this particular case the use of violence to push the residents out of the way may give rise to additional potential charges in relation to assault. Although it is tempting to think that the offence of burglary is 'aggravated' by this assault, this would not be correct in this case since the offence of aggravated burglary as such applies to offences of burglary in which a weapon is used.

> A person is guilty of burglary if, having entered any building or part of a building as a trespasser, he steals or attempts to steal anything in the building of that part of it or inflicts or attempts to inflict on any person therein any grievous bodily harm.
>
> (section 9(1)(b), Theft Act 1968)

> A person is guilty of aggravated burglary if he commits any burglary and at the time has with him any firearm, or imitation firearm, any weapon of offence or any explosive.
>
> (section 10, Theft Act 1968)

If the police investigation is conclusive, that is, someone is arrested on suspicion of committing the offence, a number of issues arise. These relate to:

- the need of the police to secure evidence, including that of the victims of the burglary
- the need of the Crown Prosecution Service for reliable evidence should the case come to court
- the potential outcome of the court case insofar as it provides potentially for compensation.

In addition to helping police by providing a statement, it may be that the police ask victims to provide evidence of their physical injuries by being photographed. They might also be asked to assist in identifying the assailant, through identifying photographs or attending a formal identification parade.

Police interviews

In the course of their investigations the police will wish to interview the victims, and in due course the victims may be needed to provide a statement and/or give evidence. Final decisions on whether to proceed with a prosecution rest with the Crown Prosecution Service, but in the meantime it is important for the police to obtain evidence that is as reliable as possible. Reliability in this case will require the evidence to be:

- obtained as soon as possible after the incident
- consistent and clear, given in the knowledge of how and why evidence will be used.

The Police and Criminal Evidence Act 1984 lays down (in section 66) that police action in particular circumstances shall be governed by a code of practice. The Act primarily refers to actions in relation to the suspect, but it may have a very limited application here in relation to the questioning of witnesses. The code of practice makes it clear that an 'appropriate adult' should be present where a suspect is 'a juvenile or a person who is mentally disordered or mentally handicapped' (Home Office, 1991). Although these rules do not directly apply to witnesses being interviewed, it might as a precaution be wise for the police to do this and to interview a witness with the same safeguards. Otherwise, there is a risk that the court will disallow the evidence since the person being interviewed might be considered unable to answer questions competently or reliably.

The role of the appropriate adult in this context is simply to ensure that the person being interviewed understands what is happening and understands the questions being asked. The appropriate adult is not the person's legal advisor; it is usually taken to mean a relative but can also include a social worker or indeed any adult who is prepared to undertake the task. It ought to be someone who can ensure that police questions are understood and can enhance that person's ability to understand what is going on. Some local authority social services departments provide training for staff to undertake this role.

One significant gap in the legal provision for vulnerable adults is the fact that being a witness or victim of crime does not entitle someone to the legal advice and assistance, other than for general purposes, available to anyone under the solicitors' legal aid scheme.

A fuller discussion of the Police and Criminal Evidence Act 1984 will be found in Chapter 9, which deals directly with vulnerable adults who are suspected of committing offences.

Giving evidence in court

At this point the question of witness competence becomes relevant. In order to satisfy the courts of the assailants' guilt, the court will need to be satisfied beyond reasonable doubt that the accused person committed the offence. Evidence of the person assaulted is clearly crucial; that person has to be competent to give such evidence as reliable evidence in a court of law. Note that the term 'competence' has here a particular meaning, namely that the person understands the concept of truth, which would be demonstrated by such matters as the consistency of their account and an accurate recall of events in sequence. This may be a significant issue for people with learning disabilities, and the Crown Prosecution Service has been subjected to some criticism for not pursuing cases on the grounds that vulnerable adults are potentiality unreliable witnesses.

The current position is therefore that no special allowance is made for the difficulties or stress that may affect vulnerable adults' potential for providing reliable evidence. Indeed, the opposite is in a sense the case since there are additional safeguards, or additional warnings, that the court will introduce in order to prevent the accused being convicted on 'unsafe' evidence. It is not surprising therefore that a number of cases never go as far as a criminal trial, since even if the witness manages to withstand the stresses and trauma of giving evidence, it is likely that the court will accord that evidence less weight because of that person's apparent disability. This would apply equally to people with dementia and even to people with a record of past psychiatric hospital admissions.

The Report of the Pigot Committee on Video Evidence, which focused particularly on children as witnesses in cases of abuse, suggested that video evidence should also be a means whereby vulnerable adults could give their evidence in court, but the report's recommendations in relation to adults have not been implemented (Home Office, 1989).

Compensation orders

'Compensation orders' here refers to orders made by the court as a result of a criminal trial. There is an important distinction between these kinds of order and the compensation that an injured person might seek through civil proceedings in, for example, a county court. Entitlement to compensation through civil proceedings is dealt with below.

Compensation orders in criminal cases can obviously only be imposed where there has been a successful prosecution (Criminal Courts Act 1973 as amended by the Criminal Justice Act 1982 and Criminal Justice Act 1991). In addition the award of compensation reflects the court's perceptions of justice, and this is related to the circumstances of the offender and not necessarily those of the victim. The amount of compensation will clearly reflect the damage caused to the victim but will also reflect the offender's ability to pay such an award. Specifically, courts will avoid making orders that require a long time to pay by instalments, and will also avoid leaving discharged prisoners with debts since this is considered to encourage the commission of further offences. The net result of this is that relatively few compensation orders are made by the courts, and awards that are made tend to be relatively low.

Pursuing a civil claim for damages

The whole incident highlights a number of rights that people have with regard to service providers and also with regard to redress (technically, civil action in law). It is comparatively rare to seek redress from the perpetrators of the crime, although more common in some other European countries (Mawby and Walklate, 1994: Ch. 6).

In theory anyone could pursue a civil action independently of, and in addition to, the criminal law processes. However, the telling factor that stops this is the likelihood of actually obtaining any financial compensation from the assailant. After all, what is the point of suing someone who is unlikely to be able to pay a reasonable amount of compensation?

What about other avenues for financial compensation? It would in theory be possible to seek redress if it were considered that any of the agencies involved had been negligent in carrying out its duties. The legal context here is one in which negligence would, however, have to be proved. There would need to be an action that someone took, or failed to take, that led to the injury. In this particular case, there are a number of possibilities:

● It might be suggested that RehabCare failed to provide adequate supervision of the group home: there should have been staff on duty and there were not; there should have been staff immediately available and there were not; there should have been better training

211

or preparation of residents in order to help them when emergencies like these arose.

● It might be suggested that the local authority should not have placed these particular people in such a vulnerable situation; it should not have endorsed the placement with RehabCare, or it should have insisted on higher standards of supervision, or whatever.

Whichever is the case, it is necessary to establish more than just what happened should not have happened, or even that someone did something wrong. The guiding principle is that negligence must be established. Is there a duty of care? According to Lord Wilberforce in a court judgement:

> the question has to be approached in two stages. First one has to ask whether, as between the alleged wrongdoer and the person who has suffered damage, there is a sufficient relationship of proximity or neighbourhood such that, in the reasonable contemplation of the former, carelessness on his part may be likely to cause damage to the latter, in which case a prima facie duty of care arises. Second, if the first question is answered affirmatively, it is necessary to consider whether there are any considerations which ought to negate, or to reduce or limit the scope of the duty or the class of person to whom it is owed or the damages to which a breach of it may arise.
>
> (*Anns v. Merton London Borough Council* [1978])

Criminal injuries compensation

A more positive option would be to try to secure compensation from certain statutory bodies simply on the grounds that someone had been hurt and ought to be compensated. This is broadly the remit of the Criminal Injuries Compensation Authority.

The Criminal Injuries Compensation Scheme was started in 1964, being extended to cover incidents of family violence occurring after October 1979. It is administered by the Criminal Injuries Compensation Authority acting under authority delegated by Parliament. The purpose of the scheme is to provide compensation for people who have been the victims of crime, regardless of whether the offender has been caught and convicted. In this sense the scheme is unique: all other avenues of redress require applicants to be able to identify those responsible for their injury.

The legal provisions concerning the Criminal Injuries Compensation Scheme are to be found in the Criminal Injuries Compensation

Act 1995. However, this is simply an enabling Act allowing the Home Secretary to determine the specific scheme, which includes tariff awards for injuries and eligibility criteria. Reference must therefore be made to the actual Criminal Injuries Compensation Scheme. The current scheme is dated 12 December 1995, with an accompanying guide dated April 1996.

Under the scheme that came into force on 1 April 1996, claims are only acceptable if:

- injuries are attributable to crimes of violence
- the person who claims is themselves physically or mentally injured as a result, but note that claims for mental injury from people who have witnessed a crime of violence are now only acceptable if the claimant witnessed an injury occurring to someone who 'had a close relationship of love and affection' with that other person
- made within 2 years of the incident, although this may be waived in certain cases, especially sexual abuse
- assessed at more than minimum figure, currently £1,000 (awards now being made on a comprehensive tariff system that consists of 25 levels).

There is no specific requirement that someone should have been convicted of an offence, but the applicant is expected to have reported the crime to the police and to have co-operated with their enquiries. The incident must have been reported at the earliest possible opportunity. Only very exceptionally will the Criminal Injuries Compensation Authority make awards where the incident has not been reported, or not reported immediately.

It is not essential to establish who the perpetrator of crime is, but there must be a criminal injury as a consequence of the crime; however, injury can include emotional or psychological damage.

The procedure is by way of application to the Criminal Injuries Compensation Authority. It is possible to make applications on someone else's behalf. Specifically, in relation to adults unable to manage their own affairs:

> If you are applying on behalf of an adult who is legally incapable of managing his/her own affairs, you must be properly authorised to do so. Provided that we consider you to be a suitable person we may appoint you to act as the applicant's representative for the purpose of the Scheme. This will enable you to authorise all our enquiries and to decide on the applicant's behalf whether to accept the award, or ask for a review or to appeal to the Criminal Injuries Compensation Appeals

Panel. Before we take this step we will require medical evidence that the applicant is incapable by reasons of mental disorder as defined in the Mental Health Act 1983 of managing and administering his/her property and affairs.

(Criminal Injuries Compensation Authority, 1996: para. 3.1)

Applications are considered by a claims officer of the Criminal Injuries Compensation Authority who decides whether the applicant meets basic eligibility criteria and then determines the tariff band that applies. The tariff schedule is very detailed and specific, being set out in detail in the various guides to the scheme (Criminal Injuries Compensation Authority, 1996). A medical examination by a doctor nominated by the Authority may be required. If the applicant is not satisfied, he or she can appeal to the Criminal Injuries Compensation Appeals Panel; their decision is final.

Payments can be reduced or even refused if:

- the applicant delayed informing the police
- the applicant has criminal convictions, even if these are not related to the incident concerned. (The extent of the reduction is assessed on a penalty points system related to the sentence awarded by the court and the time that has elapsed between the sentence and the receipt of the application by the Criminal Injuries Compensation Authority.

Payments are in the form of a single lump sum assessed in accordance with the tariffs laid down by the Home Secretary. They can be paid in the form of an annuity in order to provide index-linked, tax-free payments. Interim payments are also possible, but once final payment has been made, it can only be reviewed if the applicant's medical condition deteriorates.

Home Office circular 20/88 advises the police to take the responsibility for informing victims of crime about the Criminal Injuries Compensation Scheme and about the possibility of obtaining a compensation order through the courts if the offender is convicted.

Advocacy/empowerment

Section 50 of the NHS and Community Care Act 1990 requires local authorities to have complaints procedures. This issue was raised in Chapter 2 when considering the rights of redress for people dissatisfied with the outcome of an assessment. In essence these procedures consist of a formal three-stage process (informal, registered and review panel), which local authorities are obliged to establish in accordance with the Complaints Procedure Directions of 1990. This might be appropriate if there were dissatisfaction with the quality of support offered in this case, or perhaps where oversight of the placement itself was considered to be lax.

These rights might well be in addition to rights of access to complaints procedures within the home itself, which would presumably come under RehabCare's management arrangements. In this way it is quite possible for Anne and Pauline to have two avenues of redress: RehabCare's own procedures and the local authority's procedures.

The care assessment process and the principles underlying the NHS and Community Care Act 1990 imply that consideration should be given to providing an advocate. Advocates could be provided through a local advocacy scheme or could possibly be a solicitor or legal adviser, although the issue then arises of who would pay for this service. Procedures laid down in the NHS and Community Care Act 1990 and the Disabled Persons (Services, Consultation and Representation) Act 1986 relate to rights to be heard and involved in the assessment process and do not include resources for paying for the services of the advocate.

Moving beyond complaints procedures, other kinds of legal redress might well necessitate legal advice. One avenue might be to make a formal complaint, and request for compensation, to the Commissioner for Local Administration (the Local Government Ombudsman). The grounds for such a complaint would be 'maladministration' on the part of a local authority, and any compensation (which cannot be enforced) would be assessed on the basis of the degree of suffering caused by the maladministration. This topic was also considered in Chapter 2 under rights of redress. Submission of a case to the Commissioner for Local Administration needs careful preparatory knowledge of local authority systems and procedures, hence the need for a skilled advocate. Suing a provider organisation or a local authority certainly requires qualified legal advice since there are substantial obstacles that may need to be overcome. The requirement to demonstrate lack of care is onerous and requires a knowledge of the rules of evidence and an ability to secure the specialist proof that the court will require.

There are a number of avenues of redress in which Pauline and Anne would be deprived of the help of an advocate. Advocacy is not possible for people who are witnesses in criminal court cases, so no real direct say is possible with regard to whether courts should make compensation orders. Also their vulnerability as competent witnesses

215

is a real hazard in this case; it limits their potential means of redress and may mean that they suffer a humiliating experience in court, which could obviously be very distressing.

Taking a longer-term view, one could ask what steps should be taken to prevent this incident recurring. Should there be some kind of assertiveness training for Anne and Pauline to help them deal with unwanted visits to the home? Should there be some kind of education to make vulnerable adults aware of the occasional dangers posed by unwelcome visitors? Is there a way in which they can call upon immediate help if needed in an emergency? Could the organisations involved do more to forge closer links with the community so that neighbours share responsibility for the community's members? As a prelude to this, could more be done to persuade local residents that vulnerable adults are part of the community rather than a separate group who are somehow exclusively the responsibility of 'the authorities'?

This brings us into a wider discussion of the case, which relates it to changes in policy and practice that can be seen reflected in this case.

Social policy context

Concern for the victims of crime has grown considerably over the past 20 years or so. Indeed the number of studies and reports has mushroomed (for example Shapland, 1985; Walklate, 1989; Home Office, 1990a, 1990b; Williams, 1995). The motivation for this may have been partly political, linked to increasing concern especially from the New Right concerning 'law and order', but it is also true that a number of initiatives to provide practical support and help for victims have been instigated. Chief among these has been the growth of the victim support movement, which began with the formation of the first scheme in Bristol in 1974. This is now nationwide, local schemes being run by a management committee, which includes representatives of the police, social services and probation service. The emphasis is on direct assistance and support to victims of crime; such help is usually provided by trained volunteers (Trust, 1987; Victim Support, 1995). One valid point made by such schemes in relation to the 'law and order' debate is how little attention is paid to the victims' needs, how disempowered victims often feel by the judicial process and how comparatively little money is spent on support for victims of crime. The national Victim Support Association, for example, points out that, of over £10 billion spent on the criminal justice system each year, only 0.1 per cent of government spending is allocated to victim support (Victim Support, 1995: 17).

However, since this concern has been recent, much of it has been general. Little attention has been directed towards specific groups within the community, although a substantial piece of research in relation to children as victims of crime was carried out in Oxfordshire and Bedfordshire in the late 1980s (Morgan and Zedner, 1992). Other research has generally been confined to statistical information. Very limited interest to date has been shown in people with learning disabilities as victims of crime, although recent work on 'invisible victims' is a notable exception (for example, Williams 1995).

It would be interesting to know whether the growth in 'community care' and the move to close long-stay hospitals has resulted in an increase in vulnerability. It is clear from the case study that people with learning disabilities now face dangers in the community that they may never have had to face in the sheltered protected environment of hospitals or large institutions. This is one aspect of recent policy changes to which little research has been devoted but is one which ought to command the attention of both crime prevention and social care agencies. Some attention has been directed to this in studies of invisible victims. Williams (1995: 101–12) suggests that because people with learning disabilities have for a long time been 'out of sight':

- they are often unseen or ignored as victims
- crime against them is unrecognised, especially in crime statistics
- perpetrators, especially when they are professional carers, are unrecognised
- laws concerning abuse of people with learning disabilities are unclear and confusing, with a confused police response
- attempts are made to prevent them becoming recognised as victims through gate-keeping processes which mitigate against successful prosecution of those who commit crime against people with learning disabilities
- sometimes victimised again by the criminal justice process itself through police interrogation or appearances in court as witnesses.

Running alongside the wider issue of social attitudes towards people with learning disabilities, and the consequences of those attitudes, there is the whole general issue of help and support for victims of crime (Mawby and Walklate, 1994). In addition there are a number of specific ways in which the needs of vulnerable adults are not addressed by social work or social care agencies:

- Responsibility for helping people who are the victims of crime is not, as such, part of statutory agencies' duties.

- Consequently, reliance is placed on voluntary schemes that may not exist in all areas and may not have the expertise to respond to people with disabilities.
- Care staff asked to assist police investigations or consulted by the Crown Prosecution Service may have very limited experience of criminal justice work.
- Unwillingness to prosecute the perpetrator of the crime may leave the vulnerable adult feeling that they were somehow partly to blame and would debar them from compensation orders in criminal cases, and it is not clear to what extent or in what ways care staff should help them.
- Empowering people with learning disabilities who are the victims of crime is time-consuming, and there is a temptation to ignore the issue in order to devote time and resources to other identified needs.

This, of course, brings us straight into the issue of resources at a broader level and the priorities accorded to different groups within society. It could certainly be argued that the needs of people with learning disabilities have been overlooked for a long time and that the relatively recent upsurge of interest is belated, but nevertheless welcome.

During the twentieth century, victimology has progressed in its recognition of marginalised groups. Debate now specifically encompasses women, children, domestic victims and black and minority ethnic groups. The principle is the same for all – the 'invisibility' of the victims has been created by the unseen barriers between them and the achievement of justice.

To reduce the victimisation of people with learning disabilities, we must see crimes as crimes, perpetrators as perpetrators and victims as victims, and then notice and question the invisible barriers in policy, practice and our minds that prevent them achieving redress (Williams, 1995: 112).

Conclusion

This case study has raised a number of issues concerning people with learning disabilities as victims of crime. The discussion has, of necessity, been wide ranging since a crime often triggers a need for a response at a number of different levels. It is important to be aware of these potential needs since it is too easy to overlook, or play down, the impact of a crime on vulnerable adults because of their disabilities.

While the scenario presented here concerned two people with learning disabilities, much of what has been said applies equally to older people, people with mental health problems and people with physical disabilities. Their legal rights are the same. What will vary is the vulnerable person's ability to pursue their own rights and the extent to which they will need assistance with this. What will not vary, unfortunately, are the difficulties that confront vulnerable adults and their carers when it comes to vulnerable adults securing their rights as victims. There are a number of reasons for this, which have been outlined in the chapter. There are also a number of practice issues that have been explored and are worth considering if effective help is to be given and vulnerable adults are to be empowered. Ultimately, the extent to which vulnerable adults are accorded special recognition as victims of crime depends on social priorities and a realisation of what those special needs are. As a means to this end, the rise in interest in the whole field of victimology, and specifically in vulnerable adults as victims of crime, is welcome.

Further reading

Mawby, R. and Walklate, S. (1994) *Critical Victimology*, Sage, London.
Smith, J. and Hogan, B. (1996) *Criminal Law*, 8th edn, Butterworths, London.
Williams, C. (1995) *Invisible Victims*, Jessica Kingsley, London.

9

Promoting Rights

Introduction

This chapter includes a brief review of the wider issues highlighted in the various case studies discussed in this book. Rather than describing and analysing the current legal provision, however, the debate moves on to consider what reforms are needed.

In what respects is current provision inadequate? What issues have the case studies highlighted? How should the legislative framework be reformed? What approach should be adopted in order to meet the needs of vulnerable adults?

Susan wants to know what help the social services department can give her mother, who has just been registered as partially sighted. However, she discovers that:

- there is still confusion about who is entitled to an assessment and what exactly a local authority has to do as a consequence of carrying out an assessment
- in assessing needs, the local authority appears to be able to take into account their own resources and potential ability to meet need
- questions remain about how objective an assessment actually is.

The manager of an independent home has a resident with a hearing and speech impediment who wants to go home. In responding to this, the social worker discovers that:

- it is not clear when and how advocates are appointed
- there is ambiguity concerning what advocates can actually do
- the law regarding attention to people's ethnic and cultural needs is weak.

cont'd

Raymond has been in hospital for 9 months recovering from a very serious road accident. He needs accommodation and practical support for the rest of his life. There are a number of ways of arranging this, but none is entirely satisfactory. Specifically:

- there is a risk of disagreement between the social services department and the health authority about who should be doing what
- there is a need for an avenue of help with property matters that is not as 'all or nothing' as the Court of Protection
- the whole issue of delegating responsibility is a potential minefield, and principles that regulate property decisions are not consistent with those which relate to personal health and social care.

John and Sylvia live in a centre for people with learning and physical disabilities. They have decided they want to get married. They discover:

- a number of issues concerning marrying and living together that they were unlikely ever to have considered
- that social workers are unsure how to respond, partly because of the lack of specific provision for people with disabilities
- that no special provisions appear to be made to secure rights to accommodation.

Betty Smith believes her neighbour is being physically abused by her carer.

Twelvetrees management have to respond to an allegation of sexual abuse of a vulnerable adult.

Beechwood House are suspicious that one of their residents is being exploited by a relative.

They all discover that:

- there is no statutory duty to investigate allegations of the abuse of vulnerable adults as such
- there are no clear national procedures set out for responding to abuse and no specific legal context for doing so
- consequently, the local authority has to rely on its duty to identify and assess needs in order to provide services that might, coincidentally, offer a degree of protection.

A GP is concerned about someone who appears to be very confused and unable to look after herself. In this case:

- there is a mix of very clear statute laws and some vaguer common law principles and precedents
- legislation concentrates on mental health issues, in particular the need for the public to be protected
- decisions taken at the assessment stage can predetermine progress thereafter, and abuse of the rights of older people is all too easy.

cont'd

221

> **Pauline and Anne**, who live in a group home, are the victims of a crime committed in broad daylight. The fact that they have learning disabilities disadvantages them because:
>
> - it severely restricts their rights of redress against the assailant
> - it may mean that their competence as witnesses in court is challenged
> - it is not clear who should help them and what should happen next.

And we can now add:

> The system for helping adults who are vulnerable adults is badly in need of reform because:
>
> - it is a mish-mash of provisions with no obvious path through them
> - no special recognition is given to vulnerability as such
> - the law itself badly needs codifying, and in some cases updating, with the respective responsibilities of the different public authorities clearly set out.

Proposals for reform

Clements (1996) has described the current state of legislation regarding vulnerable adults as reminiscent of the child care law as it was before the Children Act 1989. He is wrong: it is worse. At least the word 'children' provided some clue to where to look for relevant legislation, albeit that that legislation did desperately need consolidating and codifying.

Vulnerability as such is not a concept that occurs in law and is not an intrinsic part of legislative thinking. Consequently, provision is haphazard and unsystematic. But what if a system were introduced modelled on post-1989 child care provision? Would this be an improvement? What other possibilities are there?

A Children Act for vulnerable adults?

More than once in this book mention has been made of the proposals by the Law Commission (1993a) to further the rights of incapacitated and vulnerable adults. In Chapter 6 we outlined the Commission's distinction between incapacity and vulnerability, and also summarised their proposals for importing Children Act procedures and principles. Chief among these was the notion of emergency protection orders where there was suspected serious abuse, which complemented the key role anticipated for social services departments in investigating abuse. The institution of case conferences and advocacy and representation (a guardian ad litem for adults?) would clearly run alongside these, although these did not actually translate into firm proposals from the Commission.

Eastman (1994) and others have taken issue with this approach, arguing that the importation of this model, while superficially attractive, is fundamentally misguided. The reasons relate not to the imperfections of the procedures suggested, but more to the underlying principles. The process of abuse investigation has a quasi-judicial feel to it that cuts across current thinking on empowerment and the provision of services. It risks evolving into an 'abuser search', with the implication that abusers are to be blamed and punished. While abuse may occasionally be malicious and deliberate, more often than not it is the result of intolerable strain. Therefore the approach ought to centre on service provision that reduces potential stress and anxiety for carers. For this reason a more attractive feature of the Children Act 1989 might be Part III of that Act, with its emphasis on identifying need and providing services, although it would still be a mistake to think that child care legislation is directly interchangeable with legislation relating to vulnerable adults.

What blocks reform?

The attempts that have been made by the Law Commission (1991, 1993a, 1993b, 1993c) to conduct a wholesale review, although subject to some criticisms, have generally been considered useful and productive, yet until recently relatively little had been heard by way of response from policy-makers. What reasons can be put forward to explain this?

First, there is the obvious question of defining vulnerability since vulnerable adults do not form a homogeneous group, easily identified in the way in which children can be by their age.

Second, there is no obvious arena in which issues of civil liberties can be decided since there is no court system or procedure to respond to vulnerable adults as such. While it is true that the High Court has certain residual common law powers, devised and developed over many years, these have tended to centre on property rights rather than rights to protect an individual as a person.

Third, while it seems obvious to nominate social services departments as the responsible bodies for intervening where vulnerable adults are abused, there is clearly a conflict between protection and people's rights to self-determination, and between service provision and freedom of choice. These are not easily reconciled. The constant controversy created by duties to protect children is surely evidence of this.

Finally, there will always be a reluctance to intervene unless there is a clear purpose in doing so. In child care social work, a range of resources usually exists for offering help and support to families in difficulty, with the back-up provision of substitute care if need be. Resources for vulnerable adults are selected as services to meet needs and do not readily adapt to the element of compulsion implied in a system of protection. In a similar vein, resources will be geared to meeting certain kinds of need, with the result that facilities that vulnerable adults might need may not be available. The question then becomes, intervention for what purpose?

Alternative models

While it is not the intention of this book to present a comparative analysis of different policy approaches to vulnerable adults (see Cooper and Vernon, 1996, which includes a section on disability law in different countries), it is nevertheless worth considering a couple of alternative models.

First, the Americans with Disabilities Act 1990 presents a rights-based model that is very different from the British approach. Its difference lies in its formulation and emphasis rather than its outcome.

The Americans with Disabilities Act 1990 was promoted as a measure dealing with human rights rather than one calling for the selective deployment of resources for the special needs of a 'deserving' minority. As such, it was difficult for politicians to oppose in its passage through Congress. As a civil rights Act, it does not have exemptions but does includes specific provisions in four areas: employment, public services, private sector services and telecommunications. The emphasis throughout is on prohibiting discrimination, but whereas in UK legislation the onus is on the 'victim' to prove the discrimination, in US legislation it is the other way round. For example, employers have to show that their employment practices provide for the 'reasonable accommodation' of disabilities, here meaning in terms of facilities and job structuring (hours of work, training and so on). With regard to service providers, denial of participation, unequal participation, unjustified segregation and unnecessary screening practices are all proscribed; if challenged, the organisation has to show that it did not engage in these.

The second model is more of a consolidated legislation approach that focuses on the needs of vulnerable adults and tries to address these systematically. The Australian state of Victoria, for example, passed four Acts in 1986–87 that were together seen as a package addressing the needs of people with disabilities; these were the Guardianship and Administration Board Act 1986, the Mental Health Act 1986, the Intellectually Disabled Persons' Services Act 1986 and the State Trust Corporation of Victoria Act 1987. The first and last of these provide for a Public Advocate who 'has a function to act like an ombudsman for people with disabilities' (Lawson, 1992: 2), which includes the promotion of services, advocacy programmes and public education. In addition the Acts provide for a Guardianship and Administration Board that has the power to make 'lifestyle or personal decisions', financial decisions, special protection (investigation of abuse) or consents for major medical procedures. Interestingly, the legislation operates on declared principles that include a requirement to make the least restrictive order and a presumption of competence. It also adopts a comprehensive definition of disability that does not link incompetence in managing one's personal affairs to specific disabilities. Broadening choice is a declared aim, as is the recognition that service delivery and protection of rights are incompatible, that is, that guardians cannot be service providers.

Conclusion

The need for a comprehensive review of law and policy in relation to vulnerable adults has been an implicit theme running right through this book. The publication of the Lord Chancellor's consultation paper (Lord Chancellor's Department, 1997) in December 1997 came as a welcome breath of fresh air yet it remains to be seen what will actually be translated in law and practice. There is no doubt that wholesale legal reform is needed, and needed urgently.

We have identified some proposals for reform and alternative models, but in the meantime, given that dramatic legal changes do not appear to be imminent, what can practitioners do?:

1. Make themselves more aware of how the law applies to vulnerable adults.
2. Raise awareness of the limitations of the law and its inconsistencies at every conceivable opportunity.
3. Raise the profile of work with vulnerable adults generally.
4. Use whatever limited means the law currently allows to empower rather than disempower the people they deal with.
5. Encourage others to do likewise and particularly challenge the myth that the law is irrelevant.
6. Encourage vulnerable adults themselves to articulate their desire to participate in society and to have laws that both protect their vulnerability and enhance their rights as citizens.
7. Push for the removal of discriminatory aspects of the law.
8. Explain that vulnerable adults desperately need a better framework of laws, or rather that they need an actual framework of laws to promote their rights and to facilitate their ability to participate in a society that has committed itself to community care.
9. Convince politicians and policy-makers that reform of the law is long overdue and is urgent and vital.
10. Convince anyone who has the slightest concern for other people that vulnerable adults deserve and need a better deal.

Further reading

Cooper, J. and Vernon, S. (1996) *Disability and the Law*, Jessica Kingsley, London.

Law Commission (1993a) *Mentally Incapacitated and Other Vulnerable Adults: Public Law Protection*, Consultation Paper 130, HMSO, London.

Law Commission (1993b) *Mentally Incapacitated Adults and Decision-Making: A New Jurisdiction*, Consultation Paper 128, HMSO, London.

Bibliography

Ashton, G. (1995) *Elderly People and the Law*, Butterworths, London.

Ashton, G. and Ward, A. (1992) *Mental Handicap and the Law*, Sweet & Maxwell, London.

Barham, P. (1992) *Closing the Asylum*, Penguin, London.

Barnes, M. and Maple, N. (1992) *Women and Mental Health*, Venture Press, Birmingham.

Bennett, G. (1993) *Elder Abuse: Concepts, Theories and Intervention Therapy in Practice*, Chapman & Hall, London.

Bird, R. (1997) *Domestic Violence and Protection from Harassment: Family Law*, Jordan, Bristol.

Brayne, H. and Martin, G. (1997) *Law for Social Workers*, 5th edn, Blackstone, London.

Cameron, E., Badger, F. and Evers, H. (1996) Ethnicity and community care management. In Phillips, J. and Penhale, B. (eds) *Reviewing Care Management for Older People,* Ch. 10, Jessica Kingsley, London.

Chapman, A. and Marshall, M. (1996) *Dementia: New Skills for Social Workers*, Jessica Kingsley, London.

Clapham, D. and Franklin, B. (1995) *The Housing Management Contribution to Community Care*, Centre for Housing Research and Urban Studies, ?place?.

Clements, L. (1996) *Community Care and the Law*, Legal Action Group, London.

Cooper, J. and Vernon, S. (1996) *Disability and the Law*, Jessica Kingsley, London.

Coulshed, V. (1991) *Social Work Practice: An Introduction*, Macmillan, Basingstoke.

Cretney, S. (1986) *Enduring Power of Attorney Act 1985*, Sweet & Maxwell, London.

Criminal Injuries Compensation Authority (1996) *A Guide to the Criminal Injuries Compensation Scheme*, HMSO, London.

Cross, R., Jones, P. and Card, R. (1995) *Introduction to Criminal Law*, 13th edn, Butterworths, London.

Crown Prosecution Service (1994a) *Code for Crown Prosecutors*, HMSO, London.

Crown Prosecution Service (1994b) *Annual Report* (1993–4), HMSO, London.

Dalrymple, J. and Burke, B. (1995) *Anti-oppressive Practice: Social Care and the Law*, Open University, Buckingham.

Davies, M., Croall, H. and Tyrer, J. (1995) *Criminal Justice: An Introduction to the Criminal Justice System in England and Wales*, Longman, London.

Department of Health (1989) *Community Care: Caring for People in the Next Decade and Beyond*, HMSO, London.

Department of Health (1990a) *Care Management and Assessment: Managers' Guide*, HMSO, London.

Department of Health (1990b) *Community Care in the Next Decade and Beyond: Policy Guidance*, HMSO, London.

Department of Health (1990c) *Mental Health Act 1983 Code of Practice*, HMSO, London.

Department of Health (1991) *Care Management and Assessment: Practitioners' Guide*, HMSO, London.

Department of Health (1992) *Confronting Elder Abuse*, HMSO, London.

Department of Health (1993) *No Longer Afraid: The Safeguard of Older People in Domestic Settings*, HMSO, London.

Department of Health (1994a) *Hospital Discharge Workbook*, Department of Health, HMSO, London.

Department of Health (1994b) *Implementing Caring for People*, Department of Health, HMSO, London.

Eastman, M. (1984) *Old Age Abuse*, Age Concern, Surrey.

Eastman, M. (ed.) (1994) *Old Age Abuse: A New Perspective*, Chapman & Hall, London.

Fernando, S. (1988) *Race, Culture and Psychiatry*, Routledge London.

Fontana, D. (1989) *Managing Stress*, Routledge/BPS, London.

Ginsburg, N. (1992) *Divisions of Welfare*, Sage, London.

Goffman, E. (1961) *Asylums*, Penguin, London.

Gostin, L. (1983) *Court of Protection*, MIND, London.

Griffiths Report (1988) *Community Care: An Agenda for Action*, HMSO, London.

Griffiths, A. and Roberts, G. (1995) *The Law and Elderly People*, Routledge, London.

Hantrais, L. (1995) *Social Policy in the European Union*, Macmillan, Basingstoke.

Hill, M. and Bramley, G. (1985) *Analysing Social Policy*, Blackwell, Oxford.

Home Office (1989) *Pigot Report of the Advisory Group on Video Evidence*, HMSO, London.
Home Office (1990a) *Crime, Justice and Protecting the Public*, HMSO, London.
Home Office (1990b) *Victim's Charter: A Statement of the Needs and Rights of Victims of Crime*, HMSO, London.
Home Office (1991) *Police and Criminal Evidence Act 1984 section 66 Code of Practice*, 2nd edn, HMSO, London.
Home Office (1995) *Probation Service Contact with Victims*. Probation Circular no. 61/(1995), Home Office, London.
Home Office (1996) *Victim's Charter: A Statement of Services Standards for Victims of Crime*, Home Office, London.
House of Commons, Scottish Law Commission (1997) *Report on Vulnerable Adults* (HC258), HMSO, London.
Jack, R. (1994) Gender issues in elder abuse by formal carers. In Eastman, M. (ed.) *Old Age Abuse: A New Perspective*, Chapman & Hall, London.
Jones, A., Kroll, B., Pitts, J. *et al.* (1992) *The Probation Handbook*, Longman, London.
Jones, R. (1996) *Mental Health Act Manual*, 5th edn, Butterworths, London.
Keane, A. (1996) *The Modern Law of Evidence*, 4th edn, Butterworths, London.
Kosh, M. and Williams, B. (1995) *The Probation Service and Victims of Crime: A Pilot Study*, Keele University Press, Keele.
Law Commission (1991) *Mentally Incapacitated Adults and Decision-making: An Overview*, Consultation Paper 119, HMSO, London.
Law Commission (1993a) *Mentally Incapacitated and Other Vulnerable Adults: Public Law Protection*, Consultation Paper 130, HMSO, London.
Law Commission (1993b) *Mentally Incapacitated Adults and Decision-making: A New Jurisdiction*, Consultation Paper 128, HMSO, London.
Law Commission (1993c) *Mentally Incapacitated Adults and Decision-making: Medical Treatment and Research*, Consultation Paper 129, HMSO, London.
Lawson, T. (1992) *Guardianship: New Opportunities for People with Disabilities*, Office of the Public Advocate and Guardianship and Administration Board, Victoria, Australia.
Letts, P. (1990) *Managing Other People's Money*, Age Concern, Surrey.
London Borough of Greenwich (1993) *Recognising and Responding to the Abuse of Adults with Learning Disabilities*, London Borough of Greenwich Social Services Department, London.
Lord Chancellor's Department (1997) *Making Decisions on Behalf of Mentally Incapacitated Adults*, HMSO, London.

Lovelock, R. and Powell, J. (1995) *Shared Territory: Assessing the Social Support Needs of Visually Impaired People*, Community Care/Joseph Rowntree Foundation, York.

McCreadie, C. (1994) The nature of abuse. In Eastman, M. (ed.) *Old Age Abuse: A New Perspective*, Chapman & Hall, London.

McCreadie, C. and Tinker, A. (1993) Abuse of elderly people in the domestic setting: a UK perspective, *Age and Ageing* **22**(1): 65–9.

McDonald, A. and Taylor, M. (1995) *The Law and Elderly People*, Sweet & Maxwell, London.

Mandelstam, M. and Schwehr, B. (1995) *Community Care Practice and the Law*, Jessica Kingsley, London.

Marshall, M. (1990) *Social Work with Old People*, Macmillan, Basingstoke.

Marshall, T. and Merry, S. (1990) *Crime and Accountability: Victim Offender Mediation in Practice*, HMSO, London.

Mawby, R. and Walklate, S. (1994) *Critical Victimology*, Sage, London.

Means, R. (1996) Handling other people's money. In *Care Plan*, pp. 24–7, Positive Publications, ?place?.

Means, R. and Smith, R. (1994) *Community Care: Policy and Practice*, Macmillan, Basingstoke.

Mental Health Act Commission (1993) *Annual Report 1991–3*, HMSO, London.

Meredith, B. (1995) *The Community Care Handbook*, Age Concern, Surrey.

Merry, S. (1990) *Crime and Accountability: Victim Offender Mediation in Practice*, HMSO, London.

Morgan, J. and Zedner, L. (1992) *Child Victims*, Clarendon Press, Oxford.

National Audit Office (1994) *Looking After the Financial Affairs of People with Mental Incapacity*, HMSO, London.

Newburn, T. (1993) *The Long Term Needs of Victims: A Review of the Literature*, Research and Planning Unit Paper 80, Home Office, London.

Newdick, C. (1996) Patients or residents: long-term care in the welfare state, *Medical Law Review* **4**: 144–70.

O'Donovan, K. and Szyszczak, E. (1988) *Equality and Sex Discrimination Law*, Blackwell, Oxford.

Ogg, J. and Bennett, G. (1992) Elder abuse in Britain, *British Medical Journal* **305**(6860): 998–9.

Payne, M. (1995) *Social Work and Community Care*, Macmillan, Basingstoke.

Penhale, B. (1994) Assessment and intervention: issues in old age. In Eastman, M. (ed.) *Old Age Abuse: A New Perspective*, Chapman & Hall, London.

Phillips, J. and Penhale, B. (1996) *Reviewing Care Management for Older People*, Jessica Kingsley, London.

Phillipson, C. and Walker, A. (1986) *Ageing and Social Policy*, Gower, Aldershot.

Pritchard, J. (1995) *The Abuse of Older People*, 2nd edn, Jessica Kingsley, London.

Pritchard, J. (1996) *Working with Elder Abuse: A Training Manual for Home Care, Residential and Day Care Staff*, Jessica Kingsley, London.

Probation Service (1996) *Training Materials for Contact with Victims*, Home Office, Probation Training Unit, London.

Public Trust Office (1996a) *Making an Application*, Public Trust Office, London.

Public Trust Office (1996b) *Duties of a Receiver*, Public Trust Office, London.

Public Trust Office (1996c) *Fees*, Public Trust Office, London.

Public Trust Office (1996d) *Handbook for Receivers*, Public Trust Office, London.

Public Trust Office (1996e) *Information for Nursing Homes, Hospitals and Other Carers*, Public Trust Office, London.

Roberts, G. and Griffiths, A. (1995) *The Law and Elderly People*, Routledge, London.

Rowntree Foundation (1994) *Adaptations for Disability*, Housing Research Paper 123, Joseph Rowntree Foundation, York.

Rowntree Foundation (1995a) *Housing Needs of People with Physical Disability*, Housing Research Paper 136, Joseph Rowntree Foundation, York.

Rowntree Foundation (1995b) *Housing Management, Community Care and Compulsory Competitive Tendering*, Housing Research Paper 135, Joseph Rowntree Foundation, York.

Rowntree Foundation (1995c) *The Effect of Community Care on Housing for Disabled People*, Housing Research Paper 155, Joseph Rowntree Foundation, York.

Samuels, A. (1987) Prosecution and the public interest, *Justice of the Peace*, 6 June.

Scull, A. (1982) *Museums of Madness*, Penguin, London.

Seed, P. and Kaye, G. (1994) *Handbook for Assessing and Managing Care in the Community*, Jessica Kingsley, London.

Shapland, J. (1985) *Victims in the Criminal Justice System*, Gower, Aldershot.

Skellington, R. (1992) *Race in Britain Today*, Sage, London.

Smale, G. and Tuson, G. (1993) *Empowerment, Assessment, Care Management and the Skilled Social Worker*, HMSO, London.

Smith, J. and Hogan, B. (1996) *Criminal Law*, 8th edn, Butterworths, London.

Taylor, B. and Devine, T. (1993) *Assessing Needs and Planning Care in Social Work*, Arena, Aldershot.

Trevillion, S. (1992) *Caring in the Community: A Networking Approach to Community Partnership*, Longman, London.

Trust, D. (1987) *Help for Victims of Crime and Violence*, Thorsons, Wellingborough.

Vernon, S. (1993) *Social Work and the Law*, Butterworths, London.

Victim Support (1995) *Victim Support Annual Report*, Victim Support National Office, London.

Walker, R. and Walker, M. (1997) *The English Legal System*, 8th edn, Butterworths, London.

Walklate, S. (1989) *Victimology: The Victim and the Criminal Justice Process*, Unwin Hyman, London.

Ware, A. (1989) *Between Profit and State: Intermediate Organisations in Britain and the US*, Polity Press, Cambridge.

Whitehorn, N. (1995) *Court of Protection Handbook*, 10th edn, Financial Times/Pearson, London.

Williams, C. (1995) *Invisible Victims*, Jessica Kingsley, London.

Wolfensberger, W, (1972) *The Principle of Normalisation in Human Services*, National Institute on Mental Retardation, Toronto.

Index